THE ATHLETE CENTERED COACH

Bill Patton

RYDER!
CONGRATS
ON GRADUATION
WINNER!

In loving memory of Dennis Fogg

1957 - 2018

Carry On My Wayward Son, See You In Heaven

athlete (ăth'lēt,)▶

n. A person possessing the natural or acquired traits, such as strength, agility, and endurance, that are
necessary for physical exercise or sports, especially those performed in competitive contexts.

centered (sĕn'tərd)▶

adj.   Being at or placed in the center.
adj.   Self-confident, goal-oriented, and well-balanced: "He's a centered guy. He's always seemed to know
what he wanted, and gone after it in a concrete way" (Vanity Fair).

Bill Patton has been coaching sports and, more importantly, changing young lives for the better for more than 30 years. The Athlete Centered Coach is a must-read for anyone coaching youth sports at any level to help ensure that their young athletes have a rewarding experience and one that they will remember for all the right reasons for the rest of their life.

~ Greg Bach,
Sr. Director of Communications
National Alliance for Youth Sports
Author of Secrets of Successful Coaching

The Athlete Centered Coach by Bill Patton is a monumental effort which is sure to help bring an upgrade to the software development of coaches. Want to be a complete coach? If so, read this book!

~ Frank Giampaolo,
Best Selling Author
International Mental/Emotional Coach
The Tennis Parent's Bible

Preface

The bulk of athletes around the world are dissatisfied with the conditions of their training. This is a grave tragedy, when sports ought to be a source of joy and recreation, even when played at a high level. In recent years, we have been hearing examples like the U.S. Women's National Soccer Team, and the relatively poor conditions of their facilities and amenities, when compared to those of the less successful men's program. That is a travesty due to the incredible success and popularity they have enjoyed for many years. Why is that? The largest chunk of the problem is that organizations, coaches and even parent's do not take an athlete centered approach. Athletes many times can be bullies, and exhibit maladaptive behaviors that will not serve them well in life, period. How do coaches allow athletes to act in a manner that is damaging to the community? Governing bodies, coaches, programs and even some parents do not take a holistic approach to the whole lifetime of their little or emerging athlete. Short term results orientation and ego-driven focus are ruining the experience, and in many cases the longer term health and well-being of the player. The purpose of this book is to solve this problem by degrees, to increasingly empower coaches and sport stakeholders to change the worldwide culture of sport. The aim is to make a major contribution to the literature of athlete centered coaching, and promote the idea until it is the norm.

We the athlete centered coaches begin by asking all stakeholders to first consider themselves to be collaborators first, and agents of change second. Collectively, we also call on everyone in the sports community to band together as much as possible to create the greatest possible sports culture of athlete empowerment, fair play, character development, love of the sport, giving back to the games we say that we love. The solution to this vast problem is the engagement of more and more Tier 2 coaches. Tier 1 being recreational, developmental, fundamental, and even excellence driven technical coaches. When great Tier 1 coaches become Tier 2 coaches, everything changes.

The two main characteristics of Tier 2 coaches is that they start with 'The Zone', and their players being to access that more and more, and maybe more importantly they are holistic coaches who see sport as a part of life, and one that requires balance, health, and all manner of attitudes and activities that bring quality of life. You will see those two themes prevail throughout this book.

Tier 2, or athlete centered coaches are true collaborators and influencers in their sport. They become true collaborators with all other suitable stakeholders, coaches especially are advised to take a close examination or re-examination of their own coaching philosophy. This work takes a long look at developing a coach's philosophy, because without one, a coach is a rudderless vessel in the fast changing ocean of information, relationships, and techniques. The coach's philosophy serves as a deep source of stability and direction to keep the coach from being swept away by currents. How can a coach help co-author a player's story, if they have not written their own story? Additionally, when coaches have a firm hand, guiding athletes in the most precise direction they can steer, they will give more confidence to those who may go on a voyage with them.

Furthermore, the more deeply the coach understands his or her own biases and predispositions, the more authentically they present themselves to their audience. People are drawn to authenticity, even sometimes when they might disagree with another, the definite understanding about who someone is and what they stand for in any given arena provides clarity, and a mutually beneficial relationship can be established with this trust.

This book is mainly written by myself, but a great debt is owed to Styrling Strother who put many hours into   conversations, proofreading, providing direction to the content, and executive decision making as to the vision and scope of the output. A big thank you also to Scott Ford a founding member of the Sports, Energy and Consciousness Group - SEC Group for granting me contributing member status, and for the them that will provide a thread through this work. In the second edition a true acknowledgements page will be created, including those of you who provide constructive feedback from the first edition. There will be a speedy turn around from one edition to the next. Don't blink.

Foreword

In the summer of 2013, I walked through the gate to a backyard party in Northern California where I was introduced by my friend David Crain to a coach named Bill Patton. After a "Hey, nice to meet you!" I sat down at a round table and one of the first questions from Bill to me was, "So Styrling, you're a tennis coach, what do you think about cheating in junior tennis today?" Now, this question might have taken some coaches off guard, but not me. Bill was not aware that had actually been thinking through solutions recently and dealing with my players on this very issue. As a good ole' southern boy with lots of fire in his belly, I addressed Bill's question with passion and conviction. I said that it was a problem for sure, however, the solution was not to get more line judges or chair umpires, it was more players standing up, calling the score and confront their opponent at the net, not from the baseline, and explain that they were each going to respect one another by not trying to rip each other off and make unfair calls.

I also went on to explain to Bill that coaches were partly responsible for the increase in player cheating because we have failed to teach players how to properly handle unintentional or even deliberate cheating with good manners and proper etiquette. Even some coaches teach their players how to cheat to win points and that's not a coach who believes in athlete centered coaching. After talking with Bill a few more hours, I could tell that there was a distinct reason why he asked me this question and wanted my opinion. It was as if he was searching for a solution to something he was dealing with at that moment in his life. What I didn't know at the time was that Bill was thinking about a career change away from coaching. I turned to Bill and said that I believed there is an "East Coast meets West Coast" connection here between us and we should get together again and collaborate as coaches to help tennis athletes become their best. He later told me how doubtful he was of that taking place, because of his iminent retirement. Instead, my new friend began work on his first book The Art of Coachng High School Tennis, and I was an early supporter of his efforts, and even a bit of a fan. Not only did he not quit coaching, but he has become far more influential in coaching circles.

Now it's six years later, Bill and I have become good friends through traveling together and writing many articles on athlete-centered coaching, as well as our own tennis books, inspiring parents, players, and coaches to rise up and meet the challenges of becoming their best on and off the court. We both have grown together in a spirit of true collaboration as we both subscribe to the idea of the athlete-centered approach. It's not about the fame of a coach and the pride of a parent, although those can come as a result of a player doing well on the court. What is extremely important is that the athlete is challenged every day to mature and grow up with the confidence, wisdom, and knowledge of how to properly respect other competitors throughout the winning and losing in competitive play. Athlete Centered Coaching is an incredible resource for any parent, player, or coach who desires to provide an atmosphere that activates and nurtures excellence in athletic development. I know how much we have both benefited from thinking on this vital topic, and invite you to join us on the journey.

Styrling Strother

PART ONE

THE WHY AND THE MINDSET

Success is peace of mind,
which is a direct result of self-satisfaction,
in knowing you did your best,
to become the best you are capable of becoming.

~ John Wooden, Legend of Coaching

Introduction

One of my favorite sports movies of all time is 'Miracle', the story of the 1980 U.S. Men's Gold Medal Hockey Team. While obviously it's a slightly fictionalized account to tell the story, the fact that Herb Brooks was intimately involved in it's creation lends some authenticity. The movie is a real tear jerker for me. I cry without much control, tears streaming down my face for the scene where after a disengaged performance with poor intensity, Coach Brooks, stating plainly, 'You don't want to work during the game, then we will work after the game.' has his team do sprints until they vomit in the now dark arena while onlookers seem aghast at this mad man. The sentiment that makes me cry is, 'He really loves those guys'. I would love to know whether or not Mike Eruzione really said, 'My name is Mike Eruzione and I play for the United States of America.' However even if he didn't say exactly like that, the story telling is superb. This whole thing is about creating stories! The athlete's tale is partly scripted by coaches, but their own hand must set the words in motion.

The goal of athlete centered coaching is for a coach to play a role in the lifelong sequence of the person who will grow and gain a myriad of life skills through the pursuit of excellence. Coaches who see a role in helping an athlete get to whatever their next level and often assist in making that a reality find considerable satisfaction in coaching. Wherever we find ourselves on the developmental ladder of a player's timeline, each link that we can make a positive one, creating improvement and mitigating adversity launches the player upward. Everyone's journey is different and we cannot know until the story plays out, whether a short term failure ends in success, or an achievement precedes a fall. All we can do is the best we can do from moment to moment, using as many resources of wisdom as we can find, collaborating with players, parents, coaches, programs, associations and all the differing social aspects of our sports.

If there is one theme I want you to see in this work it's about time, space and being fully present, completely engaged one second at a time. I had written the original manuscript for this book, completing it in early 2018, when a great 90 minute talk with Scott Ford, a founding member of the SEC Group, gave me an idea to string that theme as much as possible through every chapter. It was a blessing and a curse, and I found it necessary to take three full months off from writing. When you get to the end of writing your longest book to date, coming to the realization that the book will need to be completely rewritten, that is not a happy feeling. I took some time away, created some think time, and now here it is.

In the modern age of hybrid publishing, it's actually very easy to update a manuscript. So, I am trying an experiment, which you will be a part. I desire your input into the second edition. Anyone who has purchased this book in eBook form will be given the new edition, if they request it via email. In the second edition there will also be some guest chapters written, and if you are interested in writing a guest chapter, please submit a topic to me, and I will gladly consider it. While this book has gone through a bit of editing, there could be an error here or there, do not hesitate to contact me, and I can fix these things, and I am always available if you have an questions about what you are reading. You can be a part of this story, just as I hope to be a part of yours and your athletes. While we might not ever create a story that is made into an inspiring movie, the screenplays to replay in our player's lives can be many times more influential for them.

Enjoy,

Bill Patton 04/17/2019

CHAPTER ONE

Logic

**Fame you'll be famous, as famous as can be,
with everyone watching you win on TV,
except when they don't,
because sometimes they won't...**

~Dr. Seuss, Oh, The Places You'll Go!

This book is about making you more of a winner, but what is the game? In many regards, you must already be a winner of some sort, since you have the desire to read and become more; and the game, It's the game of life. The sport of the coaching life, as part of your entire way of living. Conventional wisdom in sports revolves around outcomes and the subjective evaluation of how good the outcome was compared to how it should have been, might have been, could have been. Comparing people and teams to others to see who is better is a common theme, as people love to try to debate best player of all time, best team of all time, and it's a fun thing to do, even if it borders on impossible and insane. Comparisons, but not often do people talk about path, processes, growth of the individual. Outcomes that meet our approval are good and we like to confer the status of winner or loser, even if we don't really like to say it that way.

Faulty Logic Based on Subjective Judgements

In many nations around the world there is a faulty logic revolving around sport that goes like this: Sports are a competition. Competition has winners and losers. If you are a winner that is good. If you are a loser that is bad. Winners are to be admired and emulated, while losers should try to be more like winners. Winners are better people than losers. Maybe you think I went a bit too far with that last statement, but I assure you that there is an undercurrent in many people's subconscious way of thinking that says exactly that including my own. Our evaluations of people is based on their track record, so until Dan Jansen won a gold medal, he was a loser in the eyes of many, even though he was many times a national champion, a world champion, because he fell going for gold. When he did win gold, to some he finally became a winner, but to some he was still a loser because he didn't do as well as he should have. Dan Jansen is an example of someone I know very little about as a person, but taking this one example of a famous failing in public, it's not a stretch to imagine the thinking of people in the sporting world as they observe all the differing outcomes of athletes.

Losing to Winning = Redemption?

People use the word 'redemption' often in reporting how someone made up for a past failure. Frankly, that's ridiculous. It's also ridiculous to hold someone's past failings ever in front of them, rather than celebrating their current success, or the process that made them what they are, and the path they are on moving toward greater accomplishments in the future. Tiger Wood's has now become the ultimate meme of this very thing, as many will obsess on the lowest part of his life, and now celebrate his redemption by winning The Masters after an 11 year drought of major wins.

I had a running joke with a friend who was a sports writer for the local newspaper as he covered my teams. Often he used this word, redemption. You can't change the past, but the past is certainly part of what formed you into the person you are today. Part of the reason people carry their past along and seemingly miss out on a terrific present is this notion of attempting to make up for past mistakes. Only one can really produce redemption for all, but that's another story.

Looking at the Future Through a Telescope

We also love to project into the far future, so that we can be the ones who predicted that this one would be a pro. It doesn't matter that we burden players with the curse of the word 'talent', or a truckload of expectations of how good they could be if only they applied themselves. When parents or coaches load up these unrealistic goals onto players for their own glory, they also seem to absolve themselves of responsibility if the ultimate goal does not come to fruition.

Staying centered in the present, and enjoying those moments one by one without looking too hard at the future, and allowing our young athletes to leave their pasts behind, that's liberating. Doing the work of getting better is far more enjoyable moment by moment.

So many things can go wrong. My great friends and roommates and I who were all coaches loved to discuss all the factors that could get in the way of a young talented athlete from becoming world class, even though they have all the physical, mental and emotional tools to make it happen. From lack of parental support, to malnutrition, to lack of access to facilities and coaching, injuries and so many other factors that can become major roadblocks to success. Even when people feel like they are doing a lot to further an athlete along, many times the form that takes actually works against them. One common theme among great athletes is that at some point in their development they dealt with a major form of adversity that they had to overcome. So, in our vast personal wisdom of trying to smooth the path of the talented, in some ways we do them a disservice.

The Work Only Gets Done Now

While we can't predict what will happen in the future, and we might not be the solution to anyone's past problem(s), we can pay attention moment by moment to the processes at play as we help instill a growth mindset teaching all the skills necessary to become the best possible athlete for now and the future.

Transformed Logic

Our logic can be transformed to state:
Sports are a form of a game.
Games require skill acquisition to play.
Learning to play is fun.
Playing at a higher level is more fun.

Most Important Thought: Action Item(s):

CHAPTER TWO
Start with the Zone

Do what you can, with what you've got, where you are.

~Theodore Roosevelt

There is a revolution going on in coaching. It has been moving at a glacial pace, but now is beginning to pick up steam as many new young coaches look for better connected ways to reach athletes. Many veteran coaches have trained in the classical sense of developing players fundamentals, helping them problem solve their way through problems of competition, and given their players mental strategies for better performance, but now are taking things a step further. Many believe that sometimes when everything lines up, a player can play in the zone. Many coaches and mental game experts including sport psychologists believe that there are no set strategies for entering the zone. But now, there is a small but growing cadre of coaches, players and thought leaders in sport who are discovering over the last 40 years reliable gateways to the zone. Playing in the zone is one thing, living in the zone is a completely different thing, which takes a certain level of mastery, and is a never ending pursuit to become more and more a master of our personal zones.

The Zone

What is 'The Zone'? The best answer is that it's what allows us to have our best performances the ones that flow automatically and to near perfection. There are no finite answers, but the earmarks of some of the characteristics of being in the zone are: feeling fully centered, calm, having high positive energy, free to act, a sense of automatic decision making, attaining seemingly enhanced vision of the performance, space, or of the ball, and many other manifestations of a heightened performance state.

In the same decade, two different approaches to reaching the zone were more fully understood, and while one became well known and widespread, the other languished in relative obscurity. Tim Gallwey's

The Inner Game of Tennis, which is read by many coaches in various sports, including former Super Bowl champion football coach Pete Carroll and all his players serves as a guide to what has become known as the Inner Game, a more mindful approach. The other lesser known, but possibly more influential and specific entry point was discovered by Scott Ford and others, and it can be found in *Integral Consciousness and Sport*.

A Rhythm and a Place

As we get more deeply into the zone, there are some other questions we can ask. When is the Zone? Where is the Zone? To compare the two, one has more to do with experiencing our sports through markers of the senses of vision and timing, the famous exercise of saying 'bounce' when a ball bounces, and 'hit', when you make contact, having full attention on a certain place, like a release point of a throw. (My experience shows that this technique helps more than 85% of all players, but not all) In later chapters I will get into my theory about why this is not universally helpful. Now, consider the integral approach, which in the short term of my coaching experience has helped nearly 100% of my players, and I say nearly, because what I see are the results, but I am not sure if any of my players feel less than 100% successful. Mr. Ford's accidental discovery, was two-fold. He was playing around with a different way to pay attention to the ball. If he brought his awareness mainly to one plane in his field of vision, he easily entered a zone state. Staying in the zone state required a better sense of being in the here and now. Both approaches bring about a sense of being fully present with the task at hand, and a dimming of the outside factors that could distract away from the ball. Ford also realized that every experience of seeing the ball is that of seeing the past, while moving is in the present. The place where contact with the ball will be had is a future place. Being fully present all along the way really aids in performance. Many errors can be eliminated when we let go of trying too hard to bring the future a bit earlier, or dwelling on the past.

Time/Space Continuum

While it might sound like science fiction, what we need to enter the zone as a coach or player is a more developed sense of our interaction with the time/space continuum. Essentially, in simplest terms learning to be fully present moment to moment. This is, of course, easier said than done, but really only a matter of developing new habits and in a short period of time, players can approach these 100% positive performances. For my part, I have been on a mission of mindfulness since 2010, and it all began with simply slowing myself down, but now after going through many permutations of slowing down and being mindful of the different thoughts and attitudes that I hold, I was finally ready to move into being fully present moment to moment. As I reflect back on my youth, I see that much of what adults were telling me was that I had been stuck in the past, trying too hard to bring the future, or lost in a daydream of another time. I had a unique gift for wishing to be elsewhere. But now with the help of Scott and other influential coaches, I know my portal to being fully present. I now use my improved presence with my players, in my own performances, and with other coaches to do a better job.

Let's dig a little deeper into presence. Being fully present marries two types of experiences of time in our minds. Manmade time is an imperfect creation that has built in mechanisms to make up for its flaws. Universal time outside of ticking clocks is more perfect, and we can dwell in it. What is the difference between flowing present and the absolute present and do they coexist? Go back to the top of this page. When you read those words, they were in your absolute present, but now they are in the flowing past. Now come back to these words, your flowing present is also connected with your absolute present. If you are also thinking of other things, then you are not fully present with this material. The first word of the sentence came before the others, but if you were fully present for that reading, then your flowing present and your absolute present were connected at that moment. As soon as another thought comes about something related, the past or future, then you are not fully present with this text, but you may choose to be fully present with what was conjured in your mind. The choice is yours, maybe you want to take a time to reflect on the other thing you are thinking about and be fully present with that thought. Be fully present with whichever idea is most helpful to you.

Serious Problems Solved By Presence

Let's make a dramatic shift toward the real problem of not being fully present. There are tremendous problems in sport as we know.

Each of your reading this has a unique opportunity to be part of the global sports solution.

Many of the errors on the field, and problems in training or off the field stem from being stuck in the past, or reaching, in a vain attempt to bring the future more quickly. This is why teams promote violent players, players take performance enhancing drugs, and kids learn to cheat to bring success earlier than the time in which it's truly deserved. When adversity is met, it's very common for players to get stuck in that adversity, failing to find a way around, and potentially carrying that adversity forward. Getting stuck may also look like using a game style that worked with the athlete was 12 years old, but now no longer works because by the time that player reaches full maturity, so have the other players. Like Aesop's fable of The Tortoise and the Hare, those that slowly and steadily developed a complete game learned to neutralize that certain style. Or they methodically built up the physical plant of their bodies to overcome adversity. Then that player stuck in the past finds it more difficult to adapt moving forward. I urge you to come to a place where holistically you can be healthier, a better example and a guide to athletes of all ages to come to the healthiest place in sports: The Present.

Most Important Idea:

Action Items:

CHAPTER THREE
Omni Athletes

There is no doubt that for many, substance abuse co-occurs with mental health issues. A 2004 Harvard University study described patterns of depression and alcohol abuse among young adults in college, and confirmed that 'a substantial fraction of college youth are experiencing poor mental health – at any given time approximately 5 percent – and that these youth are at high risk for alcohol abuse, with depressed young women at highest risk.'

~ NCAA Guide Mind, Body and Sport

I love the phrase created by the Sports Energy Consciousness Group or SEC Group - Omni Athlete. It seems like the highest ideal to which athletes can aspire, and we are finding many more athletes of all of levels of sport who aspire to be more than just a performer. I want to break this down into two pieces, the athlete as a whole human being with many combined facets of training, performance, periodization, recovery, and vacation time. Living a balanced lifestyle with great mental hygiene, rest, nutrition, pre-habilitation and re-habilitation and all the other balancers that allow for not only peak performance but long term health and wholeness as a person. Captured in one essence, the pursuit of the highest levels of sports performance may call for some difficult choices in how time is spent, but it ought not to create a negative quality of life. In addition, while simultaneously training for the ultimate with nearly single minded focus, using some time to prepare for the inevitable transition away from being an athlete into some other meaningful work is crucial to the quality of life.

The Cost of a Lack of Balance

I see a man who lives on the street near my home. He wears a football uniform from a Divison I program nearby, and it sure looks authentic and like it fits. How many former athletes are broke or living on the street because they were nowhere close to approaching becoming an Omni athlete. Going 'all-in' for the scholarship or the minute chance of a pro career left them with no coping skills for life. Many get the scholarship to play the sport, while the opportunity at an education seems secondary, or less. Coaches can create a bridge to using sports as a training ground for all other successes. Players can choose to buy into that part of the training or not. If the bridge is built, the player still must be the one who crosses, although those directing the program can call them to the other side. Do we always call them to the other side?

Sport as a Gateway Drug

Some sports become gateway drugs to other types of drugs. There is some interesting data in one study, athletes are about half as likely as their college peers to use marijuana occasionally, or frequently, and 100% less likely to use cocaine. Even so, the risks for an athletes career are immense with so much more attention and punishment given for illegal drugs. But what often is not studied is the prevalence of performance enhancing drugs. I hear casual conversations among former college athletes that players throughout college and high school are using HGH, steroids and other substances, because they have to complete this before they are tested.

The New Athlete Entrepreneur

While I don't want to delve too deeply into the issue of athletes as entrepreneurs, brands unto themselves, preparing those who will ascend to the highest levels in the game is a consideration that can have an impact on all other aspects of their career. Also, in a highly charged political landscape, it is possible to be a maverick and a trail blazer, or commit career suicide with one ill advised public statement. Wise coaches can position themselves as wise confidants in these matters. Knowing the risks and costs of certain types of activism is something a player ought not to blindly step into without wise guides.

The school where I coach has a strong social media policy, and social media behavior that reflects poorly on the school can be punishable by suspension or even expulsion and it has happened before.

I borrowing this phrase from the SEC Group, and want to actively promote it as a standard way to think about the ultimate athletic experience. The mind body connected athlete, will mindfully approach these things, and the influence of a coach with the growth mindset will also help.

Most Important Thought: Action Item(s):

CHAPTER FOUR

Performance = Potential - Interference

But who said that I am to be measured by how well I do things? In fact, who said that I should be measured at all? Who indeed? What is required to disengage oneself from this trap is a clear knowledge that the value of a human being cannot be measured by performance —or by any other arbitrary measurement.

~ W. Timothy Gallwey

One of the greatest contributions to the understanding of inner sports come from W. Timothy Gallway who created the formula:

Performance = Potential - Interference

If potential is the talent and capability of a performer, then interference is the only thing in the way of optimal performance.

When I was coaching youth soccer at the recreational level, we had a wide range of talent on our team, from a boy who would go on to play in the MLS, and on the U.S. Men's Soccer Team, to boy's who could barely run. Our most talented players did not stay in recreational soccer for long. The others did, and the one boy who had some developmental difficulties needed a role to play. So we taught our extremely talented players the discipline of playing within a team, and we taught our less talented players how to do their very best. The one slowest kid, had a very specific assignment in the midfield to read the play, not give ground, and move to where he saw the play developing. He did not have a very wide patch of grass to defend, and we surrounded him with faster players who could give support to the edges of his zone. We were not going to succeed in making this child a dramatically better athlete, but we did succeed in freeing him from the responsibility of covering a much wider area of the pitch, that would have had him overwhelmed.

Identify Potentials

We had no idea that the one boy would later become a professional athlete. But we did free him up to play more of the field, and we were not jealous for a moment when he moved up to a more challenging level of soccer. In identifying potentials, it's important to always seek the best for each player. As we did with the non-athlete, we still stretched him to play the widest possible area he could to minimize the burden on his teammates. We also enforced a standard that other better players ought not to go out of their zone to cherry pick balls that could be played by that player, thus putting them out of position, and diminishing his experience.

Coaches as Interference

I was teaching at a middle school, and was asked to sit on a committee that would oversee athletics. The 8th grade basketball coach, an amazing wrestling coach and myself, the high school tennis coach were in a meeting. Between the wrestling coach and myself we were in complete agreement that middle school sports should be much more about giving everyone an opportunity to play, rather than going all out to win championships, because developmentally we don't know who will develop later physically. Of course, you want to win, but balancing playing time as much as possible was vital to the our shared mission. High school sports also can retain a bit of this sharing, but a greater emphasis on excellence at that level, is to be expected because there can be a lot on the line in the future of these young people as athletes.

There was a major conflict in one of our meetings as we discussed an incident with the undefeated 8th grade basketball team, as the 6th best and lower level players who were barely getting on the floor, no matter the score. At least one girl who was a decent player reported that she felt intimidated to go into the game because she felt so much pressure. The message she got from the coach was ' You better not to lose the game for the undefeated team'. This coach had created a culture of fear that was predicated on the top 5 players being head and shoulders better than anyone on the bench. Subbing a top player was seen as a risk of losing. When we simply began the discussion about this, in a fairly non-threatening way, Coach B became quite agitated to the point where he started to shout and he left the meeting hurling insults. Clearly Coach B is not an athlete centered coach. It's obvious that he had little interest in his whole teams development, or their future as possible high school athletes, because his focus was only on the immediate glory of having an undefeated season.

Identify Interferences in Players

Everyone has a finite amount of potential, but that potential actually has much more room for growth than we allow it to do so fully. It's also pretty universal that everyone has some kind of interference. Reducing the amount of interference in a coach's work and/or in the athlete's life or routines in their sport. The interference could be social, mental, physical or even spiritual. Helping players identify their own interference is delicate work, and not to be taken lightly. The rest of this book delves into many different types of interference and some of the complex issues associated.

Coaching is easy when the athlete trusts you implicitly and the interference is simple to identify. Undeveloped trust and greater complexity to the problem should be a red flag warning us that we will have to lay some groundwork prior to really digging in to obstacles in players performance. The coach doing their own inner work to identify their own interference, not only makes the one who would guide less blind, but also a better model of how to remove the blockages. Almost every chapter has an inner work component for the coach to consider how to turn there focus back to the athlete.

Most Important Thought: Action Item(s):

CHAPTER FIVE

Building Your Unique Coaching Philosophy

If everyone is thinking alike, then somebody isn't thinking.

~ General George S. Patton

Everyone's career as a coach evolves over time, but many coaches stick with what they think they know. The coaches who continue working diligently to pick up new skills little by little until they become masters. At the beginning of my career I had more grandiose visions of what I could achieve as a coach, if every just did what I said. I was immediate results and outcome oriented. I had something to prove to myself and the outside world. I wanted to be recognized for being a great coach with my fixed mindset in place, I wanted people to think that I had 'it', a gift, I was a natural. But there are not many naturals in this business, and moving past having a finite view of talent, I continued to take advantage of every continuing education opportunity I could find. When I would go to conferences, if the presenter needed a volunteer to go on court as a guinea pig, I as the guy who raised his hand right away. What a great way to make that lesson even more valuable. I retain very little of the core principles from 30 years ago, but the same level of competitiveness. Over time, gradually, moment by moment like the effects of a waterfall on a rock, my coaching has been shaped into a more patient approach. My philosophy is much more transformed by being an educator first, and an achiever second, putting the person first and the athlete second. Sure, I am still all about winning and learning to win, but the way I go about it is very different than they way I began.

Don't Be a Clone

It seems silly to say it, but I am not trying to make a clone here in this work. I expect you the reader and coach to be different from me and my approach, instead I want to hear your voice, so that I can learn something new from you. One of the best reviews I have received on any of my books said, '**While I don't agree with the author on everything**…', and that is as it should be, because I don't want to lead a cult, and the rest of the review was complimentary, capturing the essence of this book being more a conversation starter, a think piece rather than THE authoritative source of all coaching knowledge. There was probably a time when I wished people would agree with everything I say. I also know that the collaboration between all of us who are like-minded will be an influence on you, and by extension, the industry of coaching. When all the like-minded coaches who believe in true collaboration come together, the potential is there to transform the entire sporting world.

Refining Our Coaching Principles

It's a funny thing to hold strongly to principles, while at the same time allowing them to be challenged, tested, and refined. We all have to start somewhere. We see some coaches who hold fast to a dogmatic approach, that is deeply intrenched in old-school coaching techniques, for whatever reason. On the other end of the spectrum, there are coaches whose philosophy is not rooted in anything, and they are subject to the whims of players and parents or the latest coaching fad. Those coaches have a hard time standing up for a principle with their team. I want to encourage you to examine and re-examine your coaching philosophy. This is a great thing to do ahead of a period of being very busy as with any new phase of programs. Another great time to reflect on our philosophy is before or right after a season. If you want or need to change the direction of your program. Albert Einstein said, 'Insanity is doing the same thing over again, expecting different results.' In order to get a different product, then our philosophy should dictate a different course of action.

Gradual Transitions

If we look at the absolute now like a mighty evergreen tree standing on a landscape, we see something majestic standing resolute against the ravages of the weather, but what we don't see are the minute changes happening moment by moment as it grows, blossoms, the leaves fall, and goes through this cycle year after year until it slowly dies. The major work of changing our coaching philosophies will look a lot like that tree.

In order to develop a top notch coaching philosophy, having a handful of key principles is essential. Much of the power comes through simplicity. In discussion with other coaches about what they believe or don't believe in, sometimes you find detractors, and it's ironic to me that the detractors are not usually the ones who have strong opposing views, they are usually the ones who don't seem to believe in much of anything. My pet theory is that they rail against those who stand on principle, because something inside them is triggered by the contrast between a principled coach and themselves. I have had interactions in coaching forums where I face criticism, but when I question them about where the problem is in my coaching philosophy, they fail to be specific. When I ask them for a solid alternative, I have yet to get an answer that is something that resonates with me. You will meet people like this who will question what you do in a critical way, but when pressed, they won't have sensible alternatives, but if they do, then listen to them. The part of the equation that I find difficult to reconcile is how disrespectful some of these people can be even in their presentation. So, as a matter of developing a stronger sense of self-respect, develop a philosophy that has an element of respect for others as well. It takes work, and sadly some coaches do not want to take the time to do that work.

Substance Over Self Satisfaction

Strangely enough, I see coaches who don't seem to value anything other than what will boost their own ego. They aren't necessarily thinking about what is best for their players, the league, helping other coaches, and/or the health of their sport. It's as if they have to prove something to others. Their whole philosophy seems centered around creating an image, short term results that can be seen, recruiting players they have not developed so that they can bask in purchased glory. You, being one of the conscientious coaches can find better motives making all of your efforts to improve directed to the players, the community and the health of your sport and the greater sports community. To further expand on this topic, I am going to go on a lengthy analysis of a poem that embodies much of the character traits of great coaches. My hope is that you will take some careful time with each chapter, and latch onto one concept to work with creating a little bit of time to reflect.

Most Important Thought: Action Item(s):

CHAPTER SIX

"If" As a Framework for Leadership

The first responsibility of a leader is to define reality.
The last is to say thank you.
In between, the leader is a servant.

~ Max DePree

One of the classic poems of all time, also functions as a great framework for personal growth in the area of leadership. As coaches we are necessarily leaders, and the better we do with our leadership, the more we can inspire athletes to move toward the same levels of maturity. We must model the behaviors we want to see in our players. At their best, sports act as a vehicle for many of the important character issues we experience in life. The poem is 'If' by Rudyard Kipling*, and it poses numerous conditions that, if you or I meet each one, then he would estimate that we have become fully mature, and may lay hold to many blessings. Of course, it's not hard by extension to say that where he says Man, we can easily include Woman too!

Grace Under Pressure

Many people are familiar with two lines from a poem that are the last things players see before entering center court Wimbledon:
'If you can meet with Triumph and Disaster, And treat those two impostors just the same.' (Personified, big T and big D)
When you read the whole poem, then those cryptic lines begin to make much more sense as part of the bigger picture of character development over the long term.

If

If you can keep your head when all about you
Are losing theirs and blaming it on you,
If you can trust yourself when all men doubt you,
But make allowance for their doubting too;

If you can wait and not be tired by waiting,
Or being lied about, don't deal in lies,
Or being hated, don't give way to hating,
And yet don't look too good, nor talk too wise:
~ Rudyard Kipling

It's important for us to stand on strong principles that we can rely on, so that when things are difficult, we know in what we can trust. If the principles we believe in as coaches are strong enough to weather the storm of players', parents', fellow coaches, and administrators' doubts, then surely it will be tried and true. One principle that is foundational in my program is that, 'We begin with the end in mind.' From the 7 habits of highly effective people. All of our preparation is for a strong finish of the season. This, of course, will be tested, when we lose an early season match that might be winnable, it may have been a winnable match if we were not training so hard, if we were more short term focused. Players and parents then question, 'Won't that loss affect our seeding in the playoffs?' My answer to that is, 'I would rather be a better team that is underrated, than to be an incompletely trained team and be overrated.' Of course in some sports like football with so few competitions, there are no games you can allow to slip. In sports with longer seasons where the coach can plan enough contests to have a record that will get the team into the playoffs, one loss is not pivotal.

At the school where I was questioned on this, we won the following match-ups as the lower seed. In my boys were seeded #9 then defeated #8 routinely and #1 in a major upset on the road where all of our conditioning paid off enormously in long matches. Our well trained 2008 girls were seeded #10, eking out emotional upsets against the #7 seed and the #2 seed. In 2009 my boys entered as a #3 seed, partly fueled by upsets from the year before, they surged to a sectional championship beating the #2 and #1 seeds **in the same day**, with a huge come back win in **97 degree heat** in the finals. That's good proof! Last year my last place team that seemed to be improving very slowly made a quantum leap in the last two weeks of the season, coming very close to beating an overconfident #1 team, following that up with individual victories over that team in tournament play. No matter what your plan is, expect some questioning, and check for validity. Even after explaining to all the necessary parties, there can still be seeds of skepticism. Such is life.

* Some people see Kipling as a controversial figure. I set that aside and look only to this work and the words it contains taking the meaning that is valuable. I recommend that you thoroughly research the man, and you may find concerns put to rest.

Important Thoughts: Action Item(s):

CHAPTER SEVEN

If You Can Think...

If you can dream—and not make dreams your master;
If you can think—and not make thoughts your aim;
If you can meet with Triumph and Disaster
And treat those two impostors just the same;
If you can bear to hear the truth you've spoken
Twisted by knaves to make a trap for fools,
Or watch the things you gave your life to, broken,
And stoop and build 'em up with worn-out tools:

~ K

How do we keep things in perspective? What is the meaning of winning and losing? Do we become enslaved by our goals? When trust is broken and things fall apart, do we simply pick up our tools and begin again? This would be a prime opportunity to re-examine what we do as coaches. Is there something about our philosophy that broke down? Have we had a moment that we were not prepared to handle? I have had many of those, although they come less and less often. At this writing I am dealing with one of the more severe threats to team chemistry in my career. But, now I have a much stronger and patient approach to dealing with players who disrupt the delicate mix of the team. Perhaps there is a disconnect between the people we were sent to serve, and the philosophy we use to serve them. Maybe you have discovered, just as I have in the past, that your philosophy is a not a good fit at the institution where you thought you wanted to serve. If you can't effect change on the culture of the larger organization, then it might be time to take your round peg and stop trying to get it in a square hole.

Square Pegs, Round Holes

No matter how good you are, or how well-developed your program is, you or I will be subject to some extent to the leadership of those who are captains in the program. Great I have coached for one year at a couple different schools where the culture of the school and my approach were a gross mismatch. I have athletic directors essentially lie to me about what the real values of the school really are, and then when I was hired, and serving found out that the answers that came in interviews did not reflect the real atmosphere of the school. So, I had the very uncomfortable job of establishing my program in a place where it ran counter culture and buy in from my players was really tough, since only a few kids on the team really understood or agreed with my values. Some might say that you adapt your philosophy to the environment, but I find those to be non-negotiable. On the other hand the way the program is delivered can often be catered to the people you serve and that's a good thing. But there is no way I am going to expect less than 100% commitment and effort, ever! It's possible to have a one and done experience, and so be it.

Faith is Required

Everyone is fallible, and players sometimes have character issues that cannot immediately be solved by encountering a coach with a great system. Even Jesus said he could not do miracles in certain places, because no one in that area believed in him. I recently had a three year stint at a school that I finally decided was not a good fit for me. There simply weren't enough players who valued what I offered, so rather than prolong the inevitable, I stepped away, and am now focusing more energy on other endeavors that are better received. A different coach is in that place now, and he is a better fit with that group, and seems to be making strides in the right direction. Strangely enough, I believe that it was the astonishing success that we had in my first year at that school that lead to so many problems moving forward, because of a major problem with 'comfort zone'. The interesting thing about the timing of my departure was that simultaneously my private students began wanting more of my time. Finding a place that holds the same values or at least very similar can great additional synergy that will help to seamlessly build your program within the culture of that place. Being counter-culture can be fun, but also a lot of extra work.

Meshing with Team Leadership

What should have been the leadership of the team I left, was destroyed by a lack of commitment to academics, selfish attitudes, and a lack of perspective in the value of competition. This also calls to mind that it's better to have process-oriented goals where measuring improvement is the standard, rather than solely having outcome-oriented goals. Some outcome oriented goals are fine, but when most or all of the teams goals are based on wins, losses and championships, that can have us feeling like a failures even after massive improvement. You can have all the tools to make athletes better, all the technical, tactical and mental game skills to build athletes, but if they are not buying in on the basic foundational commitments, then there really is not a good fit. Even with a really good group of conscientious athletes it can take time to develop trust in the program you are putting in place. Any new coach engenders a fear of the unknown in the players who have to make that transition. Ultimately, the ideals we hold to are going to be tested, and possibly ridiculed, so it's important for us to know how strong they are. We might have to fight a battle of a certain plank of our program. Every thing we try to achieve is a risk to some degree, and we won't always succeed. Some of the legendary coaches of all time have been in programs or schools where they were not in the best place, but when they found that place, then it was magic. Sometimes though, we succeed in a way that is different from what we first intended. There are many coaches that I admire who don't have a lot of outward success in the outcomes of their players, but they do improve, learn life skills and come away with a lifelong appreciation for the sport and the role the coach played in their lives.

CHAPTER EIGHT

If You Can Force Your Heart...

If you can make one heap of all your winnings
And risk it on one turn of pitch-and-toss,
And lose, and start again at your beginnings
And never breathe a word about your loss;
If you can force your heart and nerve and sinew
To serve your turn long after they are gone,
And so hold on when there is nothing in you
Except the Will which says to them: "Hold on!"

~ K

It's a game. The game is a drama. The outcome is not predictable. What what seems like it could be the pivotal moment for one team, the other team can seize on an opportunity, swinging the contest the other way. In a tennis match on match point will you hit an ace, a double fault, or the wildest unconventional shot that no one would ever coach? I have seen players walk off with an ace, a player who double faulted on match point for a sectional championship, and one who hit a forehand sharp angle half volley drop shot at a 10 degree angle to the net while holding a backhand grip. Think about it. The other team holding match point was so stunned they lost the next three games and the match.

Mental Perspective and Quick Recovery

How do we prepare our players for what can be wild swings in seeming fate? I say seeming, because the mental preparation to have the ability to take a stunning moment, and become unstunned, clear minded and ready for the next play is a hallmark of the ultimate in mental training. In the case where one player makes a very strange or 'lucky' play, I want my players to have already a well developed ability to let it go, preparing for the next play. There are moments that are actually very funny during competition. I want my players to enjoy those for about three seconds, laughing, then get right back to business. Not only recovering from the momentary set backs, but the entertaining moments that take our minds away from the task at hand and in the bigger picture learning to string every little up and down into a consistently high level of play.

Developing Perspective

Developing a philosophy for how to deal with winning and losing, fine-tuning it so that it completely meets the needs of wisdom along the athletes path can have a dramatic positive impact on players. Those that learn to win and lose with grace, humility, and poise are also the same ones that many times rise to the highest level of what their talent will allow. Ultimately, we want to celebrate sportsmanship and great competition, whichever end of the scoreboard we find ourselves facing. It was still just a game, even though it was one that we cared about deeply.

Important Thought:　　　Action Item(s):

CHAPTER NINE

If You Can Talk with Crowds...

If you can talk with crowds and keep your virtue,
Or walk with Kings—nor lose the common touch,
If neither foes nor loving friends can hurt you,
If all men count with you, but none too much;
If you can fill the unforgiving minute
With sixty seconds' worth of distance run,
Yours is the Earth and everything that's in it,
And—which is more—you'll be a Man, my son.

~K

Finally, what are the social motives behind competition? Do we teach players to be humble champions and how to lose well? Do we assign too much meaning to winning and losing? Or are we teaching the moment to moment joy of working on improvement? Do our relationships ride on the outcomes, or on the journey together? Do we show equal respect to every person that we encounter in the journey. Sadly, we tend to elevate the star player, we coddle for the sake of capturing reflected glory. Can we reach a place where we don't necessarily assign more respect and dignity to people who are stars, verses the ones who keep the lights on? Not too many people would come to the stadium if the trash were not picked up in the aisles after every game. In California there is a significant shortage of game officials in youth sports leagues, because many don't want to spend their free time collecting abuse from parents. Those officials are people too, and if you are the coach, I would expect you to get your parents under control.

Affirm Character Beyond Station in Life

Training players with principles that affirm who they are as people, bringing out their strengths, and helping them to recognize and mitigate their weaknesses takes time. Having the opportunities to mix with important people, and lift up the less fortunate are both available in sport. I'm reminded of a viral video of Reinaldo, who was disguised as a homeless man in the a town square, people walking here and there. He was playing with a soccer ball, and he was doing some amazing tricks, but no one recognized him, so they ignored his amazing skill. Reinaldo approached small children to see if they would just kick one ball with him. He kept this up for a long time before anyone would play for a moment, and when they finally did, he removed his disguise revealing his identity, at which time people wanted to swarm him. They just didn't know that they were on the wrong end of a social experiment.

When the amount that you receive from sport is nearly equal to what you give back, then the whole sport is enriched. How can we have a philosophy that has giving back in it? Sometimes, the most simple thing you can give is your respect, to everyone you encounter. One magic moment of recognizing someone can open up opportunities.

Your Authentic Self

This above all: to thine own self be true,
And it must follow, as the night the day,
Thou canst not then be false to any man.
Farewell, my blessing season this in thee!

~ Polonius, Hamlet's father

You are reading this because you have a growth mindset. If you didn't, then why bother? This entry is about analyzing your next best step in developing your coaching philosophy. Not my philosophy, not another coach's philosophy, your philosophy is the one that really matters. And really it starts with you. A coach needs to be an authority to some degree, and that authority is greatly enhanced when it continues to come from the more and more authentic you. You will find that your authentic best, will be greeted well by everyone else who also is trying to bring their best forward. You won't always understand one another or agree, but when we bring great reverence and respect to the vital roles each person in the grand scheme plays, then things move better and faster in the best direction.

CHAPTER TEN

Examining Coaching Principles

The river is now. This moment. This breath between us. The space
between your heartbeats. The moment before you blink. The instant
a thought flashes through your mind. It is everything that is around
us. Life. Energy. Flowing, endlessly flowing, carrying you from
then...to now...to tomorrow.
Listen: you can hear the music of it. Of the passage of time.

~ Lisa Mangum

Great coaches establish their coaching philosophies built upon
timeless pillars of principles. Players then can rely on a seemingly
absolute present developed by a mentor who is not changeable
moment to moment. My coaching philosophy bedrock was inspired
by Jim Loehr's 'Realistic Goals' from the Science of Coaching Tennis.
Jim is one of the most influential sport psychologists ever. He
explained that winning on the day, not getting nervous, and playing
perfectly are not always realistic goals. We must always be prepared to
compete against better players who may leave us little chance for a win
today. Some level of nervousness is good and necessary in order to
have a good performance, as those sensations may simply be the flow
of adrenaline, so the message 'don't be nervous', really isn't
appropriate. Additionally, there are so few flawless performances in
the history of sport, letting go of that ideal is healthy for the athlete.
Instead, we want to help players flow with realistic goals that can be
incorporated into any program. I can't encourage you enough to make
these your own, and adapt them into your program in a way which
aligns with your values, and those of your community, team, families
and players. Over time, I have taken the realistic goals of Dr. Loehr and
developed my own template, which I will share in the next few
chapters.

Overview of Four Pillars

When we learn to give all that is needed moment to moment, and nothing that isn't desired in the flow of time, then we maximize what can be accomplished with little wasted effort.

Trying harder, having more fun, being smarter, and improving faster are almost always guaranteed to help athletes become as successful as they can be. However, there are few finite answers! Let's look at four characteristics of process oriented improvement through the lens of the flow state, the absolute present when it meets the flowing present.

Of course, we need to plan our time, investing moments into placing the most important tasks of a season into the schedule. More importantly how well do we flow with the outcomes of our plan? Making decisions moment by moment in a flow state to give more time to a major objective, while possibly skipping a minor objective, if things are not going well can make all the difference in the outcomes of players and teams. When we stop, look and listen, decide THEN act, we can make better decisions on the fly and reduce confusion. When we fully engage with the observation of what is really happening, or what we think we are seeing, we gain some insight we need for the next steps in the plan. But then when we take our observations to our players, for them to give their perspective, we can dialogue and discover what is really happening through their experience. As we continually flow through this process over again, we refine our moves as we go.

Analyzing the Timeline

When major objectives are accomplished ahead of schedule, being ready to go to the next challenge level, or new task can add a nuance to your game. Taking advantage of all the time we have, while not forcing more activities than can be mastered may be the difference between winning and losing. However, if we aren't fully engaged in the present moment, acting decisively, those opportunities for advancement can be missed. No matter what happens you and I as coaches need to decide how long to dwell with any certain activity for mastery, challenge, advancement, progression or regression.

Identifying the different stages of an athlete's development and their ability to do things rapidly or methodically helps with the choice to progress or regress. The age and maturity of athletes influences their ability to deal with changes in time and space, and the demands on their ability to concentrate. Amazingly gift athletes may pick up a new skill in just a few short reps, so moving forward to sharpening it, and putting it into a competitive environment only serves to create more efficiency and less boredom. Very young athletes may need a faster pace between activities to meet them at their shorter attention span. As the years go by, more demanding activities, and lengths of time are used. Excellent coaches begin to stretch and challenge their players to concentrate for longer periods of time, even when in the short term it may be slightly unmanageable for the player. You can foster their self-discipline to manage that. Pay attention to the effects on your group, of the amount of time given to each activity.

Players Analyze Too

Feedback from the players and parents can also provide a basis for change. It's almost always wise to listen carefully to parent and player feedback, many times it's even more important to fully explain the objectives, and the reasons why for the method of training being used, along with the length of time. I like to ask my athletes when they seem to be struggling, if they want to continue at this challenge level, or are they feeling frustrated. If a task seems to be drudgery, I might ask them if they are bored. Depending on what seems right, we might finish that task immediately, or give it five more minutes.

So, be patient, take your time and really be fully present in the moment that you are making the decision to make a change. One great safeguard is that in the initial moment the default decision should be not to change anything. After some consideration, there is more time to think through making a measured change in activity. In the building trades there is a great phrase, 'measure twice, cut once'. Which is very effective in eliminating mistakes, because you can't uncut a 2x4. Immature athletes and pushy parents sometimes can be very impatient when it comes to getting what they want in the training environment. So, we must not get ahead of ourselves. When coaches are pushing too hard to bring the future into the present, or are stuck in the past and trying to make up for lost time, then it comes across in their coaching, infecting the culture and the moment. That type of coaching attitude creates an opening for second guessing by outsiders. Be fully present with your coaching! Keep your principles in the forefront of your mind to guide each step.

Important Thought: Action Item(s):

CHAPTER ELEVEN
100% Effort

**We're not asking you to be perfect on every play. What we're asking
of you and what you should be
asking of each other is to give a perfect effort from snap to whistle.**

~Bob Ladouceur

1. Giving 100% Effort Moment to Moment

Perfect effort, I had not heard this anywhere else. Effort level is
maybe the most manageable aspect of playing or coaching sports, but
it requires that we pay attention to it. Elite athletes can detect even the
most subtle drop off of intensity, and immediately intervene to correct
it. While everyone else will need to learn how to manage their effort
level to create it's presence in nearly absolute terms. It's universally
true that everyone will experience a slight dip in their effort level.
Managing intensity levels can be the highest priority for coaches and
athletes. Balancing out the equation, we also need to be aware of
excessive tension. In hockey they call it 'squeezing the stick too hard'.
Rainer Martens in his ground breaking research on competitive anxiety
found that there is a different between our mental anxiety and our
physical manifestations of it. Giving 100% effort is best when there is
an optimal level of tension and relaxation for the demands of the sport.
Basketball players might need to be more relaxed than most athletes,
and wrestlers perhaps the most tense, but when they become too
relaxed, or too tense, then 100% effort is compromised.

When coaching a team new to me, I notice that my players have not
often been exposed to anyone who really manages the amount of battle
they bring to every moment of practice and performance. High school
and college coaches can really major in this, while elite level coaches
many only need to dabble in this principle. Elite athletes are expected
to have figured that out by that stage in their careers. Recreational and
developmental sports mentors with very young athletes will do their
players a huge favor by giving the gift of high effort orientation to their
players, regardless of the attitude they bring to wins and losses. At the
high school level, the largest dividing factor among high school

athletes may be which teams give the greatest effort in practice, games, and mental preparation for competition. The De La Salle High School Football Team, subject of the movie, *When the Game Stood Tall*, made 'perfect effort' one of their most important mottos. It's a constant theme with that team, and having read the book the subject of effort level came up again and again.

Coaches Model Effort for Players

The coach has to give great effort, the players have to approach 100% effort, and when someone begins to give less, someone has to notice and say something. That responsibility almost always falls on the coach. Great captains can also spur the team along. I have coached at 7 different schools, been a part of many different sporting programs, and one aspect always seems the same. The player's perception of what 100% looks and feels like, differs from my perception. Perception is the key word, because when what you see differs dramatically from what they see and feel, it can take a bit of time to open their eyes to that. You take a strong risk of losing the team, in their hearts and minds, if this shift toward 100% effort takes too harsh a turn. Sometimes, players are quite shocked to hear that you or I think that they are not giving their very best effort. It's upsetting to be confronted with that. Taking the time to have some empathy with our athletes, especially when we are the one who is new to a program can go a long way toward helping facilitate the increase in effort level. Nonetheless, we strive to develop greater effort level, because it's more fun to win than lose, and when you give your best effort, you have your best chance at winning. I like to ask my players rhetorical questions like, 'If you take two nearly equal players and one gives 100% effort and the other 95% effort, who will win?' They will give the right answer, and then I affirm that by saying, 'yes, just about every time'. The player/team giving the better effort will win the vast majority of those match ups. Players who give 100% effort also make greater gains in every aspect of practice, whether it's the physical, mental, emotional investment of energy that they make throughout the time.

In an effort to create better quality over quantity of training, noticing the first moment that any of of the players is not giving 100% effort can be the crucial moment. Take notice of that moment. Identifying when NONE of the players on your team understands and/or effectively gives 100% effort is another crucial moment. Be fully empathetic in that moment too. When none of them are aware of what it means, then it takes extreme patience to begin to groom that in them. Sadly, coaches go the other way with a scorched earth approach, screaming and yelling, when really they can find the players who are giving the best effort, ask for more, then have the other players begin to see the difference between their effort and the top player on the team. There may be a moment when someone accidently goes all out, and you can praise that! So, whether you are maintaining very high standards with a team that has already been groomed well for excellence, or your team is at the beginning of the journey to leave their comfort zone and move toward 100% effort, you have to know where you are on that continuum. Inexperienced coaches may find themselves going from one extreme to the other, while more experienced coaches take the pulse of their team and know which end of the equation to begin working. I find more often than not, that first I must teach the reality of giving 100% effort moment to moment, then shifting to a mindset of maintaining that level.

100% Effort Culture

Establishing a team identity of high effort level is not as easy as it looks. On most teams, it only really takes one player taking it easy to infect the whole team with reduced effort levels. Each player has an influence on each adjacent player. So capitalize on the psychological phenomenon called 'Contagion of Emotion', where people who are brought into close proximity to each other, start to feel the same. Creating a fun atmosphere, where players really like to play the game, and play to win can also be a particular challenge. This is especially true when parents are either overly engaged with pressuring their child, or not interested in fully engaging to encourage them in sports. A holistic minded coach, looking at their short amount of time on the child's timeline, does their best when they help educate parents to have developmentally appropriate attitudes about the current season of life of their child. I wrote *Play Sports Right: Your Way* for this reason, so that parents and young athletes could discuss how their sporting life is going to proceed. Children are not adults, which seems like an obvious statement, but many adults who work with kids seem to have a fantasy that they will raise their child to adulthood sooner than the others, thus accelerating their little one into the future faster. But, kids can be prone to moments of profound weakness and foolishness, and without starting a new conversation, there are many examples of parents and children who in attempting to grow up faster, many times ruin themselves. Simply giving 100% effort and not trying to do unnatural things to boost that is part of the safeguards of the high effort culture.

Getting 100% From a Season

How do we help players and parents to make better decisions in the here and now? How do we give them strategies to recover from mistakes? How do we protect the team experience, and help our players become stronger people showing more wisdom on the playing field for now and into the future? These questions will be answered as we move forward.

Engaging the process of improvement, affirming players who improve and celebrating achievements can be the most motivating thing we ever do in any educational setting. Our players yearn for praise and acknowledgement, but at the right time and in the best way. Recently, I held a final team dinner to celebrate a team that went 0-16 on the season. I have decided that this program will not have individual awards moving forward, instead I speak about each player for a couple minutes, sharing some of the nuances of the positives that they bring to the team, while trying to find something that expresses their unique personality, the part of them that could not be replaced. In fact, I try to do this off the cuff, rather than writing it out, the net effect being that there is more of an interaction with the player, rather than reading notes, and the sincerity is right there. The fact that I had taken the time to engage each player enough throughout the season to come up with these snapshot profiles of them allows me to honor them appropriately. To me, that's more of a 100% effort than making 3x5 cards, or not really saying anything unique about each player.

The 110% Myth

It's not possible to give 110% effort. If 100% is all you have, how can you give more. In fact, this phrase is such a high pressure idea, that many players will become tense, trying to give more than they have. All that stress creates a lot of wasted energy, and that means they might only really be giving 90%. In my experience many young athletes have a perception of their best effort which is below the actual 100% they they can give. I see this repeatedly. The Borg Scale of perceived effort is something you should know about, and your players can self assess. When the player is able to internally monitor their own effort level, then a major building block in their development has been achieved. But we have to get away from perpetuating non-sense myths.

My Take Away: Action Item(s)

CHAPTER TWELVE
Enjoyment

The Universe is very, very big. It also loves a paradox. For example,
it has some extremely strict rules. Rule number one: Nothing lasts
forever. Not you or your family or your house or your planet or the
sun. It is an absolute rule. Therefore when someone says that their
love will never die,
it means that their love is not real, for everything that is real dies.

Rule number two: Everything lasts forever.

~ Craig Ferguson, Between the Bridge and the River

Sports are essentially, games. Play them! Make positive memories
that last forever. Enjoyment comes along moment to moment, so does a
lack thereof. Along the way we have choices to enjoy the passage of
time, try to pull the future forward, carry the past forward, or avoid
dealing with the present moment, along with other possibilities.
Having a sense of gratitude for being alive now, and having the
privilege to play a game any game, at the present moment unlocks
some of the barriers to high performance. Like the line from The
Rookie, where one character answers his own question, 'Hey River,
you know what we get to do today? We get to play baseball.' 'Enjoy
the Competition', is a powerful phrase and each word is loaded. When
it comes to fun, how do we know when it's happening?   Players
having fun and/or experiencing a flow state many times report a
feeling of being fully involved in the moment at hand, and not
thinking about the future, nor dwelling too strongly on the past.

The Continuum between Male and Female in Competition

'Enjoy', generally speaking, is what gives boy's the most trouble in
competition, mainly because in general, they often assign more
meaning to the outcome, and they are generally more driven to win
than girls. They think winning makes you a winner, and losing makes
you a loser. A great coach recently said, 'In order to feel good about

themselves, boy's need to perform well, and girls need to feel good about themselves to perform well.' Of course, when we make general statements, there are exceptions, so I am not going to argue too deeply about that, so be aware of the exceptions, and my goal is for everyone to find a good place in the middle.

Again, in general, competition is the word that many girls struggle with, because they more likely to value relationships more than the outcome, and want to be seen as cooperative and helpful. So, enjoying a fine game of tennis is not very difficult for most female players but, really competing hard to win the match with a high degree of determination, could risk the relationship with the girl on the other side. Taking the time to underline the value of sport, as not only a way to compete, but also a way to have fun with both boy's and girl's teams provides a helpful healthy balance. You may find that your teams respond better to higher levels of play when they bring enjoyment to it. Teaching all players to realize how much they have to be thankful for by running around and playing, provides perspective about a sports competition's place in a balanced lifestyle. So few of our athletes will go pro, and really not many at all will even play Division I in college, so the mission for the 99% is to help foster a life long love of sport. Teaching about the strength of character and maturity that comes from effectively dealing with competition, while maintaining good relationships, is a priceless lesson moving forward in those players' lives.

Practice Fun

In practice situations, this means coaches must incorporate something that the players find fun almost every day; something about practice needs to be enjoyable. On a daily basis with practice I work hard to plan a large group drill game to finish the last fifteen to twenty minutes of practice every day. It's always a game that mixes fun with the potential for teachable moments and a variety of skills necessary to do well. So, it's not a waste of time. If you are a coach who thinks adding an element of fun to practice is a waste of time, I dare you to try it for two full weeks, and see how your team changes. If you don't know how to do it, ask your players for suggestions.

As a yearly effort I try to schedule the maximum number of competitions that are appropriate for the level of my team. The higher the number of competitions help them they can learn to really play, and I find players appreciate having more competition and less practice time.

Look for Feedback Within and Without

We can gauge our own internal enjoyment of what's happening on the team. Are you having fun, are your fellow coaches? Do the parents who come by seem to enjoy whats happening? If you aren't having fun, then most likely you are not making it fun for others. Of course, you might not be having fun because of some kind of breakdown in your team's behavior, attitudes, performance or some other factor. I can say, when my team is having a major issue that blocks their ability to play together or play well, then I am not having fun. An injury stops the fun immediately, so we have to be realistic. Every once in a while some drills that we perform with our teams are going to be a bit monotonous, or grueling, and if they can have fun with that then more power to them, but we want to avoid overloading our practices with drudgework.

Look beyond your own feelings of enjoyment. Just because you are having fun, does not mean everyone is having fun. It's a great idea to periodically ask players if they are enjoying themselves. The act of asking that question also makes a statement, in the form of actions speaking louder than words, that you care about the quality of their experience. Taking a moment to talk with each player as time allows, to find out what the experience is like through their eyes gives you the feedback you need. Be ready to really listen, even if the answer is not one hundred percent yes, it can be one of the most important moments on your team. Getting to the bottom of what is not fun for one, or a handful of players can mean the difference between a bad, good or great season. Of course, the message is that not everything is going to be fun for everyone is vital to developing the maturity of teamwork.

On the other hand avoid over-reaching to appease a sad sack player who never seems to enjoy anything, or the over-achiever, who is never satisfied that enough work is being done. We can't expect ourselves to immediately solve deep seated issues, but we can make an attempt at steering our players into a more positive direction. I was recently chatting with a high school soccer player who mentioned that her team is not doing well, but that's not what bothers her. She is bothered by the lack of unity on the team and how some players seem to yell at others for not performing the way they want them to play. I encouraged her to try to get her teammates to frame their interactions in the most positive way they can, to help make the whole experience more fun. I won't ever know if she was successful, but I trust she will make an effort.

Overly Serious - Fun - Silly/Goofy

Sometimes my players interpret the fact that I want them to have fun, by thinking that being silly or goofy, or disrespectful in competition is O.K. Other times they think it means that I don't care if they won or lost. We sort those out pretty quickly. I show them with my hands something like a heat gauge in the car, overly serious is too hot, silly and goofy is too cold, and fun is right in the middle. Teams with losing track records tend to be more goofy as a defense mechanism to protect them from the pain of so much losing. Elite teams that are in a competitive situation with a team that they can beat easily, sometimes drift into a goofy and disrespectful way of playing in competition, trying trick shots, prolonging the pain for their opponent. In those moments, I want my players to make quick work of it, so we can all move on to the next thing. Against weaker teams, using bench players more, and practicing a skill that needs to be developed is an opportunity to bring some challenge level to the situation. Regardless, disrespecting the opposition is not fun for anyone. Spending enough time to develop the enjoyment of competition many times will help your players and teams to perform better in key situations, reducing pressure.

In order to help my players with this, I try to put things in perspective for them. I might remind that that there is a kid somewhere in a hospital bed who would love to come out here and lose today. I will also present some major social problem, and let them know that winning today does not solve that problem. Having some appreciation for what a privilege it is to compete on the day, helps players to be more grateful, keeping the event in its proper place. Protecting the integrity of our sports by keeping an eye on fair play and fighting hard to protect that is another way we make the competition more enjoyable. I can't think of a single person who has more fun with referees call a game slanted toward the other team, or a player is wantonly cheating, not one person. Remember kids say they play sports to have fun, so if you or me do not provide a fun atmosphere, we are losing athletes.

My Take Away: Action Item(s):

CHAPTER THIRTEEN

Strength and Wisdom

If I had six hours to cut down a tree, I would spend four hours sharpening my axe.

~ Abraham Lincoln

The final two pillars have to do with the sharpening of our players in ways that go beyond simple techniques or strategies, but in the mental game, the physical contest, and a process orientation. Do they take the lessons away from the match up?

Show Yourself Strong and Wise

People make 11 decisions in 7 seconds, or is it 7 decisions in 11 seconds based on their first image of laying eyes on you. A couple of important ones are: Do they look trustworthy? Are they friendly? Are they a strong competitor? How we present ourselves initially and throughout the competition says a lot about where we are in the development of great character. Showing strength, is part of presenting good body language. Using a confident walk, keeping your head up, directing eye contact with the opponent, and confident speech sends the message that you are in the game until the end. Being wise is seen in great demeanor, being diplomatic with the opposition and officials, exhibiting great sportsmanship, setting an example of composure for all around, and maintaining high standards of behavior. A wise player does not allow the opponent to affect them mentally, emotionally, or to continue to make bad calls without some kind of intervention. The wise player may choose to ignore some aspects of the opponent's behavior, but will never allow bad calls to continue unabated or distract them from the next play. The most important play is always the next one. I work with my players on how to deflect and not absorb the negativity that the opposition brings to the occasion. If the player is visually distracting, or intimidating we don't look at them between plays. We avoid dwelling on their negativity. We have things that we say to ourselves and our teammates that prevent them from getting inside our heads. We keep your visual focus on the task at hand. If the way they speak or things they say are annoying, let it go in one ear and out the other. Of course, you might have to answer them, but many times your game will do all the talking. There may come a time when a player must alert a coach or official to unsportsmanlike behavior of the opponent for the sake of the competition, performance of the team, and/or the safety of the competition. One of the worst things I have heard in youth sports, was when a few players on one team found out that an opponent's father had died, and another father had left the family behind. They used that to abuse their opponents. That is a special brand of low integrity, and I only hope that they receive the full measure of justice coming to them for their unkind way of playing the game.

Inner Talk and Feelings of Inadequacy

One of the hurdles for many young athletes is overcoming their own feelings of inadequacy or lack of confidence. Building players up in confidence can help facilitate their ability to be assertive. Eventually the confidence that wells up on the inside begins to express itself on the outside. Sometimes role play, or object lessons are the way to develop the inner assurance to respond well in the present moment. Tough situations requires great responses from players, who take on the challenge. Take time to imagine common scenarios that trip up your athletes, like a trash talking opponent, and run through the scenario, so that your players will be trained to respond properly in the moment. This can actually be a fun thing to do in practice. A lecture on the topic might not be as instructive as players acting out best counter moves to the manipulations of bad sports. Stooping to the level of the other player is never a part of those solutions, especially when it means using the same behaviors or worse. Fighting fire with fire is rarely the solution, with very few exceptions.

Confident Fighter Image

Showing strength and wisdom mainly has to do with sportsmanship, body language, attitudes toward others, and the determination to see things through to the end. I want my players to project an image of being a confident fighter who will play hard every single play until the very end of the game, no matter the score. Being a team player is a major part of the wisdom of sports participation, since many of the life skills for future success in many of these young people's future endeavors are found on the sports field. So, players who don't blame teammates, and whose messages are that 'We can play better', 'We can do this' are the ones who bring unity. When we as coaches build into our programs a daily life skill component, we can maximize the teachable moments. We can get a lot done in a short period of time and periodically, a moment happens that changes the course of a player's life forever. The vast majority of course corrections I have been able to provide have been positive ones, but certainly there were intentional and unintentional negative outcomes that lead to adversity for the player or former player. I am not perfect, and have had to apologize to players and families at times for a failure to be a positive role model. Having the strength of character to admit failure and ask forgiveness may be the most important lesson a coach can ever teach. Showing strength is NOT a form of convincing people that we are infallible or invincible.

Fitness Aspect of Showing Strength

If we get a little more detailed about being strong, it has to do with taking care of the conditioning to prepare for competition, but also the body language aspect of sports, and yes both do go together. General George S. Patton said, 'Fatigue makes cowards of us all'. Fighting against fatigue comes with great conditioning. When your body is stronger and more fit appropriately for the actions you perform, then of course it's easier to keep your head up, shoulders back and maintain great posture, poise and composure. I want my players to be able to look opponent's in the eye when appropriate and avert their gaze when it can cool things down. The decision to consistently project strength takes time, but can be learned in degrees even by a player with terrible body language. These types of themes will be found throughout the rest of the book.

One Moment Can Change Everything: Be Wise

One particular player I was coaching was a junior in high school, and she was displaying somewhat inappropriate behavior, nothing horrible, but more annoying than actionable. Even so, I called her mother to talk about this young lady and the gray area behavior she was displaying. I got her permission to do anything within reason to reign her in a bit. There was a time that she sat in my chair just before I was about to sit in it, and in a somewhat flirtatious and insubordinate way. I asked her to get up, and when she did not immediately do so, I flipped the aluminum lawn chair backwards on the very soft and full lawn, tossing her out of the chair. Then I informed her that she can complain to her mom, but I already got permission to do as I saw fit. I called the mom immediately to tell her what I had done and why. The girls never attempted anything like that again. I had her reigned in, and our player coach relationship improved. Later that year outside at the tennis courts where the team plays, she came to ask me a favor related to senior year activities. When I said yes, she attempted to give me a full frontal hug, which I denied, and practically used some martial arts skills to avoid. The very next moment my team captain came around the corner. Most certainly, if I had allowed the one young lady to hug me, then there would understandably be a problem. Again, I called the mom to let her know about this, and that any type of flirtation needed to stop immediately. This young lady became a clutch performer and she played a major role in winning a championship. It was unwise for her to flirt with the coach, and/or show him disrespect.

A few years later, I got a call from the mother that the daughter had been in a nearly fatal car accident and was lucky to be alive. That young lady felt her life flashing before her, taking stock of the things that matter in life. When the mom called me, she mentioned that her daughter recalled to her my efforts and she now understood what I was trying to do, and that she was appreciative of reaching out to the parent. The lesson of staying on this side of propriety was learned in a tragic way. When we take the time to teach the life lessons of sports, our players might learn that at a time when they need them most.

My Take Away: Action Item(s):

CHAPTER FOURTEEN

Learning and Process

Improvement gives you your best chance at victory in the future.

~ Anonymous

Learning and Improving

A working definition for learning is 'A relatively permanent change in behavior'. This of course presumes that less than permanent changes of behavior preceded it. Improving would indicate that those changes in behavior are positive and productive. When, each day, some incremental improvement takes place, then quite a bit can be accomplished during a season. Acknowledging improvements that show the fits and starts toward final learning is important to players. Young coaches including myself make the mistake of being too hard on inexperienced players and assume a stance of all or nothing. Too high a level of perfectionism can be a serious threat to a player's improvement, because its so hard for them to gain a footing of confidence in the face of continual criticism. This is where taking time to reflect, and fully grasp the lessons, comes into play. I like to have my players share out one, two or three things they learned on the day. In larger groups, I might have five people share one item each. This makes slightly more tangible that something was better today. In smaller groups, I might have each one repeat back one thing they learned on the day. Working one on one, I ask for up to three details of improvement on the day.

Learning Progressions: Incompetence to Competence

There is a progression in learning that goes through stages where learners discover what they don't know, begin to learn something new, put it into practice and finally are able to perform it without much thought in the same way your car seems to drive you home sometimes. It all starts with unconscious incompetence, exploration followed by conscious incompetence, then some teaching and conscious competence, and finally unconscious competence. When we are unconsciously competent, then we don't know that we don't know something. When we are presented with fresh material or asked a question to which we don't know the answer, then we run headlong into conscious incompetence. So, we go from not knowing that we don't know, to being aware that we don't know something, maybe for the first time. With instruction we move toward having some competence as long as with some mindfulness we can do what we have been taught. This can be a very mechanical time of learning. With practice and familiarity, we are soon able to execute unconsciously, the action becomes automatic, we don't have to think about it any more.

When players report back, not only do they learn better because of the hear themselves speaking, but they also become teachers, and their way of phrasing it might just be the key to unlocking another player's understanding. This type of deep practice is helpful because the teacher learns as much as the student, and when they can explain to others, they then also become more fluent within themselves. Operating this way also safeguards you from students who might say 'We didn't learn anything today', on the ride home from practice.

Self Confidence from Physical Skills

A.S.I.C.S. Is a Roman acronym for A Sound Mind in a Healthy Body. If all our learning moves in that direction, that beyond the level of athletic potential our students have, we look to help create more healthy people. There are countless studies that show a connection between physical health, outdoor activities, engaging with people in cooperation that have a positive impact on mental health it behooves us to pay attention to the improvement of every player. It's only natural to give a bit more time and attention to the very best players who might win the game for us, or the worst players who need to learn how not to lose the game. Everyone in between can be reached and my ultimate goal is to spread my attention as equally as I can throughout my lineup, getting to know each player and their strengths and weaknesses. I want to help every player to achieve the very best they can in sports and in life. So, maximizing the learning and improvement for everyone is my highest ideal.

My Take Away: Action Item(s):

CHAPTER FIFTEEN

Check Ourselves: Self-Talk

Evidence is conclusive that your self-talk has a direct bearing on your performance.

~ Zig Ziglar

Now that we built some pillars upon which to lay the rest of the structure, the rest of the game is talking ourselves into being the person that executes them. We first have to 'act' before it becomes comfortable. We have to 'fake it until we make it'.

The Default Position is Negative

Even though people claim to hold themselves in high regard, the thoughts that spontaneously occur to them—their "mental chatter," so to speak—is mostly (up to 70%) negative, a phenomenon that could be referred to as negativity dominance, says Raj Raghunathan Ph.D. In an article in Psychology Today. Self-talk, being the inner conversation we have in our heads. It can also be deeply ingrained subconscious patterns of thought. It's much easier for us to think negatively, speak negatively, act and project our negativity onto others. Coaches, by our very nature should be more positive, but it's not an automatic response. The athlete centered coach need not be negative or positive, but simply an objective observer of what's happening. People often call me a 'zen' coach, which I understand, but I don't feel like that hits the target with me. Sure, I went through a bit of an eastern thought phase in training to play and coach, but now I'm much more interested in the research about how our brains work. Lo and behold, many of the eastern modes of thought hold up under the scrutiny of good research. Objective observation is another way of saying that you are listening to the whole situation, really letting it soak in with your eyes and ears, and even within your spiritual self, the values of your program that you laid out earlier. Of course, positivity is a much better alternative and negativity is to be trained away as much as possible. We have to accept some of the bad with the good.

Depth of Observation

This genuine seeing, feeling and otherwise sensing the athletic environment along with the states of the players, helps us to take a step back to detect the nuances of our teams. We might see how players interact to help each other. We work to understand how a player deals with a challenge, whether by taking a learning attitude, or one of frustration. We can look at any any task, breaking it down by asking some very grounded questions: Where are you? Where do you want to go? Is that the best place to go from here? What is in the way? Can the roadblocks be realistically removed, scaled, or beaten in the time allowed? Is there an alternative or a lesser, greater, or alternative destination? What is the action plan? What is the first step? This way players can begin to discover for themselves the strategies that work, and when they do, they take greater ownership of the experience.

The Reflective Coach

Time spent in reflection of how a practice or a match went, is time well spent. Taking a few minutes to play back the interactions, the performances, the changes in people and competition on the day, gives us material with which to move forward. What the lessons of each day? In which ways did we succeed, and in which areas do we need to improve? Taken objectively, simply as what happened, and what do I want to have happen next time? Which incremental improvement will I bring to my players or team in the next coaching moment.

Framing the discussion of what we see as a coach in directives, or counseling would be a mistake. I like to ask a question. 'Yesterday, I thought I saw ____ and it seemed like you _____, and your opponent _____. What do you think? How did it look from your end?' The Positive Coaching Alliance has a great slogan, 'Ask, Don't Tell. Keep Emotional Batteries Full'

We then would discuss any necessary adjustments to our plan, or whether the performance means we can accelerate, or if perhaps it was just an anomaly. When all of a sudden your player has an out of their mind performance, it can be risky to assume that it's their new baseline, but it may be a risk worth taking. Hard to say.

My Take Away: Action Item(s)

CHAPTER SIXTEEN

Shock Authenticity Affirmation

Developing/Adjusting the Plan

We help a player develop a plan of attack to achieve a goal. Goals presume competence. The goals in themselves can be considered to be positive because there is an underlying assumption that a player can achieve it. Under the surface, there can be some deep seated negative behaviors, thoughts, and other factors that can sabotage moving toward the goal. This is where our objectivity comes back in helping us to stop, think, and take inventory of those thoughts both positive and negative, to identify which are true, which are false, empowering and which are hindering the cause.

Have you seen a doctor who, when he meets a patient, having a very superficial discussion and observation of the patient's health heads over to the paddles to shock their heart? Imagine if they did that to every patient. It would only take a matter of days before that doctor would be out of business, and more than likely under arrest. This is hyperbole, but there is some similarity to what coaches do, in that they try to shock their athletes into performance too often, before even taking the players temperature. There are legitimate moments when a coach needs to turn the tables on players, to shock them in order to gain their full attention. Those moments are few and far between, and might not happen every season. You will read my stories about giving a shock to a player or a team, and I have done that only a handful of times in 30 years of coaching. So, put the paddles down!

Sometimes we fancy ourselves as the great TV physician, Dr. House, who treats for everything, until the liver, kidneys and other vital organs are ready to give out, before we figure out what's wrong, and magically end all treatments that are not solving the problem. What a horrible fantasy. Stories like that spring from a deep seated negativity, and that character surely bore that burden.

Synthesizing into Authentic Messages

A far better way to influence your charges on a daily basis is to live the message you are sending. Being positive can take the form of having pithy sayings, but I would caution you to choose those wisely. This kind of positivity only goes so far. One of my favorite life coaches in the world says, 'Affirmations are like frosting on excrement.' They have no real effect unless backed by action. If we get old school for a moment, we would say, 'You better walk your talk.' Test your sayings out to see if they resonate with your players. If you model, then walk them, openly struggle with them, then there is a much better chance you will come from a place of authenticity. If they don't seem to resonate, ask players what they know about the meaning of what you are saying. I have had some of the most amazing talks with players when they asked questions about what confused them about my sayings. We then were able to refine the meaning.

If I ever give a brief lecture on any given topic, I usually go on a bit longer than my player's attention span, but when I see that they are checking out on me, I stop. At that point I ask, 'what was one thing that resonated with you from what I just said', we discuss that a minute or two more and then it's done, we move on to the next activity. If they have nothing to say, then I must not have provided any value, or maybe they just need a little think time, I might ask them again later during another break. I never let my players or teams off the hook from taking at least one item away from a 5 minute talk.

Checking for Understanding

Occasionally they don't understand what I'm saying, so they don't find a meaning that makes any sense to the context of their experience. Or maybe a few of the more mature players understand, and they can parrot back in 'kid speak', which then makes use of the zone of proximal development.

Don't be afraid of long pauses in silence. When I begin asking questions of a new team, I am almost always greeted by silence, because they aren't used to being asked open ended questions. I am coaching a new team, and it's the same old thing, I ask questions, I'm greeted with silence, then after waiting, I finally get a herky jerk answer, and finally over time my team gets used to the questioning and they learn to trust that I am not going to humiliate them if they give a 'wrong' answer.

Helping our players understand where they are in the time/space continuum of being 'present' can be among the most powerful lessons they can ever learn. You have probably heard this very corny saying, which I use at least once per season, 'The past is history, the future is a mystery, and today is a gift, and that's why it's called the present.' I like this one a lot because it keeps me focused on the only time I will ever have, now, today, this moment. It also helps my players to focus on what they can affect and let go the things that have happened, or what they might worry about. Then we stop and take an objective look at what can be accomplished today, which moves us toward our goal. Identifying when our players are ahead of things, feeling pressure, trying to bring the future more quickly than it naturally comes, can help us to calm them down. Noticing when someone is carrying negativity from the past, provides an opportunity to help them learn to let go, moving toward a better future. When you get a full team of fully present individuals working on the same task, great power to improve will come from that.

Real Affirmations for Real People

When we give positive compliments to our players, it's fine to give them a casual praise for something superficial like their appearance, although you have to be careful how you frame that one. It's far more effective, appropriate, and meaningful when positive statements are given for values brought forward in the player. Noticing effort level, attitude, achievement of a new skill, and the like can make all the difference, especially in an area where an athlete has struggled in the past. Paying attention to the very first awkward impulse toward improvement can be the most influential moment you will ever have with your athlete, because it can be the thing that gives them confidence to move forward. Again, it's very easy to be negative, and our minds naturally gravitate to what is wrong. We want massive improvements too quickly, and we often compare against perfection too often. We look for problems to solve, things to fix, issues about which we can complain. Since the average person has three negative thoughts for every one good thought, it stands to reason that we can work to mitigate the negatives, and try to speak mainly the positives. Boxers as athletes and mental game players are well-noted for having made efforts to have the tidiest of mental games. One such champion boxer said, (Ray 'Boom Boom' Mancini), 'I can't afford to have a single negative thought because if I had one negative thought, I will end up on my back.'

Personal Message

In writing this book, many many times I have had negative thoughts that would discourage me from writing, and I have had to turn those around, because I have the one person in mind who wants this information. You!

My Take Away: Action Item(s)

CHAPTER SEVENTEEN
Sports, Energy, Consciousness

He has told you, O man, what is good; and what does the Lord require of you but to do justice, and to love kindness, and to walk humbly with your God?

~ Micah 6:8 ESV Bible

Facilitating and allowing athletes to engage the spiritual side of sports. Nearly all of my top performers have had a deep ethic, something that grounds them. Some have religious affiliations, and God is their inspiration, guide and the one who sets their parameters. For others they ascribe to another force, known or unknown, maybe a feeling of being drawn toward destiny, or just a set of principles by which they live. For others it may be a humanistic development of their own ethic, goals and dreams. It's a tremendous honor to be allowed into that conversation. I have almost never initiated any kind of spiritual discussion to attempt to make my player accept something, however I have expressed my own experience, and where I derive the spiritual power and the ethic to coach my very best. I'm not going to outline that here, but I will say if you have an ethic, then truly live it, empower your athletes to live theirs. I'm happy to discuss this with you one on one.

Seeking a Higher Level

Encouraging athletes to be seekers in this regard is a great thing. Many of the rituals and superstitions that athletes abide by are a reflection of this outlet in their lives. Making it something that is unassailable is also important. When an opponent finds that we have a spiritual weakness, and that if our tiny idol is easily disturbed that it can wreck our mental game, they are sure to pick on it. Having played a lot of pick up sports in the inner city, I can tell you that I know what it's like to be probed for relative chinks in my armor. I know that players in many sports have found that button that says, 'You aren't good enough', and pressed that one. It got an immediate reaction, and it was something that I needed to manage, or go into a tailspin.

Weakness in Our Armor

No matter how closely we hold to our above ethic, we will all fall short of what we aspire to do. Some opponents will pick up on that. One of the more evil things I have heard of, is youth athletes delving into the personal lives of their opponents, and needling them about things like their parents divorce, or the death of a family member. How will you as a coach react if that happens? Coaches who allow such behavior certainly are not reading this. We have to be prepared for some very uncivil actions by our opponents. How will we respond according to our ethic, while making it quite clear that we don't accept the behavior of the others.

Worst of the Worst

One example of this comes from the days before social media or cell phones. In the days before a championship showdown between my team and the team that held a 19 year reign on the league, members of the opposition pulled pranks, and harassed my players. My team captain came home to find garbage dumped all over his front porch. That night he got a phone call saying, 'You better lose tomorrow, we know where you live'. My team captain did not tell me about that prior to the match. So I was a little taken aback when in the pre-game, I asked the captains if they had any final words. My main captain said, 'Yeah! Play like they are trying to kill your mom'. I was a bit shocked. I waited until after the match to find out what that was all about. At our end of season meeting, I brought this up to the full group of coaches and our league commissioner. The opposing coach probably had no idea his players were doing that, but the way he ran his program he may have been happily ignorant as long as they won.

In my own competitive experiences growing up in Oakland, California, I have been threatened with physical harm if I performed well and our team won. There was a moment when our coach in the middle of a road competition, ordered us to pick up our belongings, as soon as the buzzer sounded, as quickly as possible, heading straight to the bus without stopping. This type of sports culture must end. We must all band together to end it. We can do that by elevating the ethics of everyone around us.

CHAPTER EIGHTEEN

Understanding What is Happening

It takes a village to raise a child.

~ Igbo and Yaruba Proverb

In this real life situation, I am the private skills development coach, who works with a player who wants to have a great experience on her high school team.

Team Play

Anya is in the middle of her high school season, so I don't expect to see her much until that she is done. A major reason for that is that one of my key philosophies is that I try to make sure my private lesson students feel free to give their all to their team. That philosophy came prior to the athlete-centered approach. I believe in team play!

Realistic Environment

On a certain Saturday, our normal small group training was cancelled because of illness and lack of availability of the others in the group. So, I offered Anya a private lesson slot, an offer which she did not often take because she mainly wants to play other players her age and not a broken-down guy in his 50s. I can completely understand that. I mainly want my players to play in the most realistic setting to the level at which they play. But Saturday was an exception, and Anya chose the private lesson.

Communication and Decision Making

In a text, I asked her ahead of time what she wanted to work on in her game. Our relationship is now at a place where I know what her intentions are; when she wants a private lesson, there is usually a certain skill she wants to develop. Saturday, it was all about her hitting backhands deep to the other players backhand. This was a wise decision on her part. In a later chapter I will get into the importance of the student developing into a decision maker who can drive the lesson. Hitting a deep backhand back deep is not the sexiest shot to learn, but a very important cog in beating another player and not being beaten. It would be like asking for an extra helping of vegetables at the dinner table, even when dessert is available.

Understand and Confirm

When she arrived, we warmed up and I probed a bit more to try to really understand what she meant when she said deep backhands. She confirmed that she wants to be able to take deep backhand shots to her and return them deep to the backhand of the opponent. We didn't have to talk long about the whys and wherefores because we have gone down that road before. That's another piece of my coaching philosophy, 'Trust a player's prior knowledge'. In the early going of a coaching relationship, the need to communicate is intense, and as things go along, then fewer and fewer words are necessary. As you can see, my previously developed and refined coaching philosophy has already had a major effect on the player's work and we had not really done anything yet on court. And then, we got to work!

Defining the Task

We warmed up a few backhands, then started working on defining and then hitting the target area. If the player does not know how to define a deep shot, how can they hit it? My definition for deep is anything in the second half of the big rectangle. So we tried this for 10 minutes. Along the continuum of challenge to mastery, we have to find a realistic challenge level so that players can overcome that obstacle and gain confidence, when they fail repeatedly then we need to regress to a lower level to build confidence. The further along athletes get, the greater challenges they can face, and they may also have a higher frustration tolerance as well. I trust the genius of the player. Sometimes, they simply perform exactly like they want to, and I say, 'Yes, do it like that.' Then we talked through some key indicators of how that happened and moved onto a higher level of challenge.

The Performance

Anya was hitting almost everything five to ten feet short of the target and spraying occasional shots wide. Teasingly, I asked her, 'Do you see the target?' She indicated that she did. You might be surprised, but many times that question can trigger something in the player to perform better, see better, focus better. I am not sure of the function, but it sometimes pushes the right button. Not this Saturday. She continued to spray. Over a few more reps, I noticed that not only was she stopping her racquet in its path, but also had varying swing paths that were not along the 'figure 8' swing shape. So I asked her to feel if she was stopping her racquet and to keep it in motion even if very slowly in preparation for an incoming ball. Her accuracy improved. She was trying so hard to aim, that she took away her own smoothness of shot. When she went back to performing naturally her shots were more accurate.

The Asking

Anya could now hit a few balls in the target area. I asked her, 'What else do you need to get more balls in the target area?'. Many times students have the answer. Something I picked up from the Positive Coaching Alliance is **'Ask, don't tell'**. So I ask her what she thinks she needs to do, this empowers her to take ownership. When players answers run out, their curiosity kicks into gear. Anya did not know what to do, so I brought her to the net for a quick talk. I showed her the ball and asked her where she thought she should meet the ball for a deep crosscourt backhand. She pointed to the exact back of the ball, so I redirected her. I said, if you hit it there, it's going in the middle of the court and short. Why not hit it lower on the ball and a little more to the left? She said ok.

The Transition

Within a few minutes, she was hitting the target area more regularly, but didn't seem to be able to hit two in a row. She would hit the target, miss the next shot, and I would ask, "Don't you like to hit the target?" in a bit of a fun sarcastic, probing tone. This happened a few times, but then something very interesting happened.

The Moment

Anya hit the target area, then hit the next ball 20 feet away, low to the forehand. I gave her some grief and she did better in the short term. Then she hit the target area and another ball low to the forehand. I stopped everything and asked, 'Stop. What's going on here? What are you doing? Why are you hitting so far away from the target on alternate shots?'. There was a long pause, she did not know the answer, and I did not immediately know the answer either. But it hit me, 'Are you hitting shot combinations? Are you 'winning the point'?'

It was an aha moment, because Anya was so well-trained on hitting Deep Cross Court / Short Angle combinations from our previous work, that she automatically follows up a deep shot to the backhand with a short, low-angled forehand shot for the opponent. In fact, there was nothing wrong with her performance of the deep backhand shot, she was performing on a more evolved level, outside the demands of the drill. If we had allowed it to, it could have been a source of frustration, bad feelings, assigning meaning beyond what was really happening. We could have defined her performance as failure. Instead, we both realized that it was success and at a much higher level than I was trying to achieve.

Where many coaches might simply drill and kill and demand that Anya hit the target area, I was able to affirm her previous training, and then say 'ok, now shut that program off for a few minutes. We are simply working on this one shot.' She said 'OK' and she then hit a few shots in a row into the target area. So, it was an athlete-centered moment, but only because I myself had done the work of developing my principles that allowed it to happen in a way that would also function to empower, affirm, and also redirect the player to the task at hand. If I had not been prepared to make that shift to attempt to see it from Anya's subconscious training, it would have been bad. At no time did Anya take over the lesson completely and I was not subject to her whims. Instead, she created the agenda for the day, and then I managed it using principles that work.

Three Days Later

I was honored when she asked me to write her a letter of recommendation. This is one of the highest compliments you can receive as a coach because that means the player trusts you to convey them in a positive light and that you know who they are to a better degree than the other adults around them. In light of they way Anya and I operate in a spirit of collaboration, I am happy to name her in this work.

My Take Away: Action Item(s):

CHAPTER NINETEEN
Common Fears of Athletes

Courage is resistance to fear, mastery of fear, not absence of fear.

~ Mark Twain

Everything we really want is usually on the other side of fear. It's a universal struggle, everyone has them, but we each also have our own different mix. Some people are more fearful overall than others. Sport has a way of helping people to overcome fears, and I am not sure why dealing with fears in the physical realm can help so much in the mental, emotional and physical realms. Sometimes these fears can be debilitating, leading to mental illness which untreated can have tragic outcomes. In recent years, some outstanding athletes have come forward to identify their own mental health issues. Michael Phelps is perhaps the highest profile athlete to do so.

Fear of the Unknown - doing something with which we are not familiar. This can be almost a daily occurence in practice.

Fear of Success - going beyond the comfort zone of what normal success looks like. It's similar to fear of the unknown. Deep down some people feel like they don't deserve to succeed.

Fear of Failure - the embarassment of trying to do something different and not succeeding, especially in a public venue. It's just going to affirm what I already know, so why prove it again.

Fear of Arrogance - some people have had a deep humility imprinted on them, or they naturally repelled by gaining attention. Some people will avoid engaging in activities that will bring attention, and may defer to other athletes, even when they are superior in general or on the day. To avoid appearing arrogant, they do everything they can to avoid the limelight.

Fear of Inadequacy - It's common for people to believe that they are not good enough, and they try to fake it. But then, they also try not to put themselves in situations where their inadequacy will be exposed.

Fear of Not Enough Time - When you see people who are always in a rush to get something done, or they fill every moment of their lives with activity then they may fear that their is not enough time. In sports that have no clock, like tennis or baseball, they might rush a play rather than taking an ideal amount of time to make the play.

Fear of Responsibility - the root of this fear often comes from the adults who say, 'you are so talented, if only you applied yourself', 'see I told you, you should do it that way all the time'. What the athlete comes to see as guarenteed, is that the parent or another adult is going to chide them no matter what. If they succeed, then they will have greater responsibility to succeed even better next time out.

Fear of Being Evaluated - these are your excuse makers. It was never their fault, there was a reason why it happened a certain way. The events were   never a true reflection of who they are, because they aren't ready to accept an honest analysis of who they are and what the state of their game is.

Fear of Missing Out - similar to fear of not enough time, this fear is growing in the U.S. Among families. These people seem to be in a race to have as many experiences as possible, but they lose sight of the quality of the experience. So, they have more or less a planned mediocrity. The athlete will maintain great grades, while being in the school play, on the leadership team, and play their sport, but they will ask for days off from practice, and they will miss leadership meetings, and they will get ill, which leads to being behind in school.

It has been said that the opposite of fear is love. So in essence, athlete centered coaches are going to love their athletes enough to reassure them through their fears. We can identify fears, acknowledge them and address them. When we show our athletes that we understand what they are up against in their minds, we may also be able to gain some capital to reassure them. We can start to show them more about what is on the other side of their fear. If you have been coaching for a while, you have already done this. You now have athletes that you can point to who crossed over to the other side.

Learning to play without fear, or knowing the exact antidote to fear in the moment is liberating. I know my chief fears when I play, and when they pop up in my mind, I know what my internal dialogue needs to be in order to move past the pangs of being afraid. Sometimes just enough fear can be a powerful motivator to avoid a poor performance. Helping players balance that can be an amazing experience for everyone and is among the top life skills a coach can teach. One common theme that is an antidote for fear is to stay in the moment, don't get too far ahead, don't bring the past forward, just do what you can do right now to the best of your ability. We will delve into this much more deeply in the next chapter, a guest chapter by Linda LeClair.

CHAPTER TWENTY

Dealing With Fear

**Dissolve your fear and free your energy to flow
into playing the game you love,
and living the life you desire!**

~ Linda LeClaire

What is Fear? How does fear keep you from achieving your goals? How can you dissolve fear? How can you coach from love energy instead of fear energy? How can you help your players to play from love energy instead of fear energy?

Fear is the biggest deterrent to playing your best. It holds you back. It blocks your energy! It keeps you from achieving the success you desire.

Fear is a natural and appropriate response to a danger from the outside world. Fear is the origin of the 'fight or flight' signal to your body when you are in danger. This signal triggers the body to send all its resources to your limbs in order to respond to the danger. All other systems are shut down. This is good if you actually are in danger from an outside source. However, most of the time, the danger you are in, is coming from inside of you. You can't find a solution to the danger because there is no danger. It is a danger that you have created with your mind. You perceive a situation as dangerous. In reality, there is no danger. Unfortunately, the perception of danger has the same effect on your system as an actual danger does. Your system shuts down and goes into fight or flight mode. This is not effective in competition. One blocks your energy, the other scatters your energy. You no longer can see a clear strategy for victory. Your body is looking for an escape from the danger. It isn't looking for a solution to a tennis match. So what do you do? How can you avoid this trap?

Managing Energy in Harmony

As an Energy Coach, I teach coaches and athletes how to work in harmony with their energy to produce the results they desire. I teach them Energy Techniques that they can then use to create this harmony and coherence for higher level performance. We know, thanks to Quantum Physics, that our bodies are energy and information. It is your job to fuel the correct information into your body. Information is fuel for your Energy System.

You can read in more detail about this topic in my two earlier books: The Confidence Factor (2009) and in Yes, God Speaks to Women, Too: A Message of Health, Healing and Hope, (1998)

I want to start this conversation about dissolving fear by first explaining two basic facts about your energy.

1. Your energy can be stuck, scattered or flowing freely and in balance. How do you want your energy to be? I hope you answered, flowing freely and in balance!

2. Your energy vibrates at different frequencies. When it is vibrating at the higher frequencies I call this frequency Love Energy. When your energy is vibrating at the lower frequencies I call this frequency Fear Energy.

Operate Out of Love Energy

When you come from Love Energy, your energy is flowing freely and in balance. When you come from Fear Energy, your energy is either stuck or scattered.

Love Energy comes in many forms. Some examples of Love Energy are: Confidence, Belief, Patience, Trust, Flexibility, Determination, Openness, Growth, Calm, Passion, Excitement, and Hope. Just repeating these words with feeling can produce a shift in your energy to a higher frequency!

Leave Fear Energy

Fear Energy comes in many forms. Some examples of Fear Energy are Doubt, Impatience, Victim Mentality, Stubbornness, Arrogance, Greed, Frustration, Anger, and Lack of Belief. Just repeating these words with feeling can produce a shift in your energy to a lower frequency!

Love Energy in your body appears as energy that is flowing freely and in balance. When you are in Love Energy, your focus is in the present moment! Fear Energy in your body appears as stuck or scattered energy. When you are in Fear Energy your focus is not in the present moment. It is in the past or the future. Doubt, stubbornness, and lack of belief are usually examples of stuck energy. Anger, impatience, and frustration are usually examples of scattered energy.

Moving in Better Energy Flow

Once you understand that you are Energy and Information and that it is your job to keep your energy flowing freely and in balance your life becomes much easier. You feel more in control. You realize that you are in charge of the life you are creating for yourself! You begin creating consciously your wishes, dreams and aspirations.

What does this mean for you as a Coach? First of all, this makes a huge difference in how you communicate with your players. Knowing that fear is your energy either stuck or scattered means that all you have to do to get out of the fear is to unblock your energy or gather your energy. You don't have to get into why you are in fear. But, you do have to recognize that you are in fear energy. For example, if you are in doubt, your energy will be blocked. Let's look at doubt and see how it affects your energy.

Physical Indicators of Fear

How does doubt look and feel in your body?
Some of the effects of doubt/fear:

1. Your feet aren't moving like they normally do.
2. Your eyes aren't seeing the ball clearly.
3. Your head isn't staying down at the point of contact long enough.
4. You aren't following through on your shots.
5. You aren't committed to your shot.
6. You are indecisive.
7. There is hesitation in your shots and footwork.
8. Your thoughts are doubt thoughts.
9. You don't know what to do .
10. You think that you aren't good enough.
11. Your focus is not in the present moment.
12. You don't feel joy.

It's easy to see from reading this list that your energy is blocked. You are not performing at your highest level.

You could work on 'why am I doubting myself?' But, is this a good thing to do during a match? No! That takes you out of the match. You want to make the correction immediately, during the match! You can make that shift!

Know the Origins of Fear Energy

First of all, how do you get into Fear Energy? The main reason you get into Fear Energy is in your thoughts! You start thinking thoughts that create doubt (or some other form of fear) which in turn blocks your energy. Doubt is meant to block your energy. But, doubt in the middle of competition is not the energy you want. You want confidence because confidence is the 'can do' energy. 'Can Do' energy has been empirically proven to help athletes have greater strength, more coordination, clearer thinking and greater overall competence. Confidence keeps your energy flowing freely and in balance. Confidence is the Energy you need to perform at your highest level.

You are in charge of your thoughts. Thoughts are energy! As Gandhi said, 'Your thoughts become your words. Your words become your actions. Your actions become your habits, your habits become your values. Your values become your destiny.' If you choose doubt thoughts, you will doubt and your energy will be blocked keeping you from achieving your wishes, desires and aspirations.

Make a Decision for Better Thinking

Choose thoughts that empower you! Choose thoughts that ignite confidence.

Athletes go into fear energy because they choose to focus their attention on thoughts that either block or scatter their energy. You are not at the mercy of your thoughts. You are the one who is in charge of your thoughts. You chose the thoughts that created doubt in your energy.

Once you connect the dots between your thoughts and your energy you can start immediately to choose more wisely!

Helping Players Make the Shift

How can you as a Coach help your players to stay in Love Energy?

This is probably the most important thing you can do to help your players achieve the success they desire. Fear blocks your players from learning as well as from performing as they know how.

Keep your focus on what they are doing right. Add to what they are doing instead of criticizing what they are doing wrong. Teach instead of criticizing them. Teach them what to do, not what not to do! Whatever you teach them will be imprinted in their minds. If you teach them what not to do, that is what will be imprinted. Whatever is imprinted in their minds is what comes out in competition. Teach what you want them to do!

Sustaining Great Energy

Help your players stay in Love Energy:

You can encourage your team and athletes to activate Love Energy by the way you talk to them. Use the following phrases or similar ones:

- I like the way you hustle for every ball!
- It's great how you focus and listen to instructions!
- I like your positive attitude – your love of the game shows!
- Good body language!
- Take a deep belly breath – Remind them of this often!
- Breathe deep and go to your next best move!
- Use your eyes – Keep your eyes on the ball at the point of contact a couple seconds longer.
- Strong Eyes - Strong eyes are eyes that are exuding energy. It affects the player's body language. It affects the player's attitude. It affects the player's shots. Strong eyes are eyes that are in the present moment.
- You can do it – Tell yourself that you can do it!
- You love competition-show it!
- You belong here!
- You're on a mission – remember that!
- You're on your path!
- Tell your feet to move quicker!

• Keep your head down a couple seconds longer at the point of contact.
  • See the ball in the opponent's frame.
  • I love watching you compete!

Avoid references to athlete's looks! Instead help them to focus on what they can control. For example:

- Their effort
- Their work habits
- Their attitude
- Their confidence
- Their patience
- Their determination

Top Twenty Checklist for Effective Coaching

Effective Coaches in all sports remember to:

1. Start each day with a clear intention-you need a clear intention as much as your players do.

2. Use athlete's names when talking to them. Make sure nicknames are positive.

3. Define rules clearly. Clear rules create a feeling of safety in the environment.

4. Show respect for students and coaches. Show respect in how you talk to them. Avoid sarcasm at all costs. The worse they are playing the more respect they need. You may not be able to respect their performance but you can always respect them as human beings.

5. Park your ego at the door. This isn't always easy but an absolute must!

6. Keep instructions simple! Demonstrate everything! Take nothing for granted! Use positive body language.

7. Keep your problems away from the playing field.

8. Always discuss issues with your students in private.

9. Pay attention to the little things. If you think something is common sense, make sure you are teaching it!

10. Be non-judgmental, observe without judging.

11. Never embarrass a student or use ridicule.

12. Assume nothing!

13. Be present! Stay off your phone during training and matches.

14. Ignite the energy of joy in your training sessions.

15. The more fun they have competing, the better they will compete. Create an environment where fun is welcomed! Tennis is a game! It is meant to be fun!

16. Smile, laugh, express joy and enthusiasm for coaching, for the game, and especially for the player!

17. Be prepared with back up lessons. Be flexible!

18. Let your players know you care about them as human beings!

19. Model the energy you want them to express. Confidence, Belief, Patience etc.

20. Be the kind of coach you would have wanted as a Player.

Why Is It Important To Be In The Present Moment?

Remember, when you are in love energy, you are in the present moment. When you are in fear energy, you are in the past or future. Why is this important? Because when you are in the present moment, it is your conscious mind that is in control. It is your conscious mind that creates your wishes, dreams and aspirations! When you are in fear energy (from a danger you have created within yourself), you are no longer in the present moment.

When you are no longer in the present moment, your subconscious mind takes charge. For example, you are driving down the road and your mind starts to wonder, thinking about what you are going to do once you arrive at your destination. All of a sudden you realize you are at your destination. You don't remember anything from the last couple miles because your mind was in the future. How did you manage to physically drive the car while your conscious mind was on your destination, not the car nor the road in front of you? You were able to drive because your subconscious mind took over. The subconscious mind stores all of our memories and programs. The "driving program" from your subconscious mind directed your body.

Why is this important? It is important because your subconscious mind also stores all of your beliefs. Why is that important? It stores all of your beliefs, both empowering beliefs and limiting beliefs! Because they are subconscious, you don't know what limiting beliefs you have that are blocking you from the success you want. In fact, over 75% of your beliefs are limiting beliefs! If your subconscious mind has taken over, that means that whatever beliefs you have about what you are doing are activated. Your beliefs determine your actions. The function of the mind is to create coherence between beliefs and 'reality.' If you have the limiting belief, 'I'm afraid I'm not good enough', how do you think your body is going to respond? It is going to respond in sync with the fear that 'I'm not good enough!' As long as you stay in fear, you will respond as if you actually are not good enough. Dissolving these limiting beliefs and creating new empowering beliefs is part of the work I do as an Energy Coach with my clients.

Application to Athlete Centered Coaching

As an Athlete Centered Coach, you may have wondered why an athlete performs so well in practice and then doesn't perform in competition at the same high level. In practice, often the athlete is in the present moment, in love energy, thus coming from the wishes, dreams and aspirations of the conscious mind. In competition, if the athletes goes into fear energy, the programs of the subconscious mind are activated. If there is a limiting belief, it will take charge. As an Athlete Centered Coach, how you communicate and where you focus your attention either helps or hinders your players to stay focused in the present moment! That is why the above mentioned suggestions are powerful. They help to keep your athletes in the present moment! If you are in fear energy, your players will pick up on that energy. If you are in love energy, your players will pick up on that energy! Do you coach from fear or from love energy?

Dissolve your fear and free your energy to flow into playing the game you love, and living the life you desire!

My Take Away: Action Item(s):

PART TWO

MINDSET OF DEVELOPMENT

Coaches have to watch for what they don't want to see
and listen to what they don't want to hear.

~ John Madden, Super Bowl Champion Coach

CHAPTER TWENTY-ONE
Model Growth Mentality

If I have seen further than others, it is by standing upon the shoulders of giants.

~ Isaac Newton

One aspect of interacting with some of the world's greatest coaches is what incredibly generous people they are. Generosity and gratitude are amazing qualities among this elite group. Of course, there are no guarantees, but my like minded coaching friends find that the most accomplished coaches have a strong desire to share with others. It behooves coaches who want to enter this realm to really dedicate themselves to becoming lifelong learners.

Walk Your Talk

Players pick up on this growth mentality in the coach and the role modeling that takes place by the simple observation of those being modeled to, and many times on a subconscious level. A powerful part in what sets the tone for a team program is when the coach proves themselves to be a lifelong learner. Players see that, they might not acknowledge it, but they will take notice. Players often respond better to a coach who is eager for new information, and wants to learn about his players. Many players love the sense of being discovered and known well enough by the coach that they respond in kind. That's why I want your feedback about this work, and if I have missed something, I would gladly acknowledge you and your contribution.

My friend Styrling and I have had the honor of sitting at the feet of some of the best tennis coaches in the United States and around the world. Robert Lansdorp, Dennis Van Der Meer, Vic Braden, Bob Brett, Craig O'Shannessy, Frank Giampaolo, Ken DeHart, Don Henson and Martin Baroch to name a few. I never hesitate to learn from anyone who learned directly from Tom Stow, perhaps one of the greatest teachers of tennis that ever lived. It's exciting and humbling to learn from these great guys.

Old School Curmudgeon Growth Mentality

Robert Lansdorp does not fall completely inside the 'collaborative' coach category, but more like a task master, and anyone who wants to learn from him should be ready to sit at his feet and receive a sarcastic tongue lashing, all in good and salty humor.   Robert is not without some very rough edges, so be advised. The amazing thing about Robert is that he does not know what it is about him, that makes him able to coach so well, that he has had five players go to #1, many others in the top 10, and countless other professional and Division I college players. He has not taken any classes, or received any formal training to coach. He just in his own words 'Felt like I knew what to do with anyone who came to me. And, NO they don't all come out the same.' I feel incredibly honored and honestly a little frightened to be helping in the writing and editing much of Robert's early material. What he writes is so challenging, because there are no real true deep mysteries about what he's saying, but the challenge to the reader is so strong and his voice is so firm, that it really causes me to consider my own work. In a section that addresses what coaches expect from players, Robert goes very deeply into the player's responsibility for learning. Players not only need to make a commitment to practicing and playing enough to do well on court, but also make a commitment to learning all that they can.

Three Teachers

Mr. Lansdorp wants players to realize that they have three different teachers. Their first teacher is their coach. It then behooves coaches to be the best teachers that they can be, even so, Robert places the responsibility on the student to do the learning. Second, Robert urges his players to learn from their opponents either in a win or a loss. Even when you have won, your opponent successfully found ways to win points against you, so learn from that. Finally, players should learn from themselves, taking time to reflect on their relative strengths and weaknesses, mindfully playing from a position of strength and learning to erase their weaknesses.

Robert's comments were an affirmation to me about the player as a decision-maker. Our players need to own their own game. Because I want players who will be able to play without hesitation, I want them to learn a style that is their game, so they get to make the decisions about how they will play. Of course, I offer guidance and help with the necessary skill sets for the player to succeed.

Take Robert's Advice, learn from your coaches, learn from your opponents, and learn by reflection on the lessons. Use your imagination to think on the things that are to come and who you will have to become in order to perform the way you want to perform.

Important Thought: Action Item(s):

CHAPTER TWENTY-TWO
Players as Decision Makers

Why waste time proving over and over how great you are, when you could be getting better? Why hide deficiencies instead of overcoming them? Why look for friends or partners who will just shore up your self-esteem instead of ones who will also challenge you to grow? And why seek out the tried and true, instead of experiences that will stretch you? The passion for stretching yourself and sticking to it, even (or especially) when it's not going well, is the hallmark of the growth mindset. This is the mindset that allows people to thrive during some of the most challenging times in their lives.

~ Carol Dweck

The coaching relationship and the collaboration with parents is different in a private coaching one on one situation. There is much more need for more interaction and mutual decision making. The player necessarily is the focal point of the three sided relationship.

Setting the Tone One on One

I set the tone on day one. For few years now, I have a new routine that I use when I meet a player for the first time. I tell the player that there are three different kinds of people: parents, coaches, and players. Then I ask them, 'which one is the decision-maker?' They almost always guess that it's the coach or parent. Very few young players immediately arrive at the conclusion, that they are the decision-maker. After I have said no to both of this options, when they realize by process of elimination that it's not their parents, and the decision maker is not the coach, it's amazing to see the change on their face as they come to the realization that they have been empowered to decide. If you don't take any other action item from this book, I strongly recommend that you present this question to your players and empower them to make decisions. Of course, the younger they are the simpler decisions they will make, as they get older, the more complex the decisions will become.

The next question I ask my new player is, 'who is the expert consultant?, and with very little hesitation they identify that as the coach, I am their expert consultant, 'that's you!'. What should seem to be process of elimination is surprisingly not so when we come to the question of 'Who gives final approval?'. A small portion of youngsters will hope that final approval is mine or theirs, but most understand that it's their parents who hold that most important role, because, 'If they don't like what is happening there, then it's over'. When I have to remind them that it is their parents that give final approval, they sometimes give a look of resignation.

The Qualifying Questions

At the end of the lesson, the litmus test for this new player/parent/coach relationship comes when I share with the parents the outcome of the conversation between myself and the player. 'We decided that the child is the decision-maker, and that I am the expert consultant.' I can see on the parents' faces at that time either obvious tacit approval, mild concern, or an angry offended look. Most parents say, of course the kid is the decision maker, and of course you are the expert, that's why we are paying you. Some parents are concerned about their child being a decision maker, because they might not have a great track record, and then by extension they are concerned about my judgement in naming their child to that role. The parents who want to hold all three roles of decision maker, expert and final approver of the coaching relationship won't bring their little automaton to another lesson, and that's what makes me happy about my qualifying process. Those parents are going to be the biggest headache to deal with, then I don't have as much energy to work with the other collaborative families.

The Curmudgeon Style Qualifier

Unlike you and I, Robert Lansdorp, one of the greatest tennis coaches of all time, and also a very tough curmudgeon of a coach, reports that the parents who bring their children to him are nearly 100% supportive (of those who stay, which is NOT 100%). He goes out of his way to make sure the very first lesson is a scary situation, so that no one will come to him who will waste his time or their own time. Most likely the level of control he has over the environment has a lot to do with that. He shared with me his strategy. He conspires with the player on court who is present when the next lesson arrives. He tells the player on court, 'As soon as that kid gets out of the car, I am going to yell at you, but don't worry I'm not really mad, but just go along with it.' So the next lesson sees that and it sets a tone for no wasted time in the lesson. Now, I am not advocating for that kind of treatment, but when your lessons are over $300/hr and you have a track record for developing 5 number one players in the world, and hundreds, if not thousands of division 1 college players, you can get away with that. I could never make that work for me. Why is that athlete centered? Because it starts with the premise that the student from the very beginning has to choose to be all-in. Many players leave crying and never come back, but they do go on to coaches who are more kind on the outside. To me, Robert is just a big lovable teddy bear who puts on this act, and if you spend any time getting to know him, you realize he loves kids and is fiercely loyal to their future.

Achieving Balance

For the rest of us, ideally parents wield their final approval with enough authority that they can readily accept their child as the decision-maker, when appropriate, and the coach as expert consultant with the necessary communication. Coaches should communicate with parents about the challenges, capacities, and progress of the student. The whole relationship hinges on appropriately honest communication. Not every thought or opinion needs to be shared, but every single one that has a direct bearing on the training or outcomes should be shared at the best possible time.

Important Thought: Action Item(s):

CHAPTER TWENTY-THREE

One on One Within a Team

There is no 'I' and team, but there is a Me, if you try to TAME the TEAM and turn it into MEAT.

~ Unknown

Now to translate this same strategy to a team setting, I want my players to know that they are the decision-makers in how to play their game. I am there to guide them, helping them discover their best style to achieve their best outcomes. In the high school team setting, it's generally less likely that parents will become heavily involved in their kid's tennis, however coaches should be ready to give answers to parents in regard to the methods of the program at any time. Some schools however allow a culture where parents often second guess the coaching staff. Coaches should always be reminded that parents continue to give final approval in the activities of their young people, even through high school. Managing a situation like this can be challenging, but taking the time to educate parents and players on the value of empowering the players and coaches can slowly create a new culture. At some point the coach may have to put their foot down and enforce a tough line that no one can cross, in order to effect the necessary cultural change.

Establishing Trust Parameters

I had a freshman player, who was a high ranked junior tennis player in the USTA, and he had a private coach. His coach is a friend of mine, someone I admire, and could easily talk with at almost any time. This freeman it seemed, did not want to take my feedback during practice, or any coaching during his matches. This became a problem because he was not playing as well as he could. First, he was missing out on vital coaching. Second, the conflict created by him trying to shut me out did not help his play, so the whole thing became a distraction.

One night I called his house to talk with his parents and the young man, after an episode of stubborn behavior. I let him know that I know his coach and can talk with him, that he is the decision maker, and that

I offer suggestions to help him win. It is fully his decision on whether to accept the advice. 'There are things I can see because I am standing still, that you can't see, and there are things on court that you see and feel, that I can't feel, so we work together to solve problems.'

The Result

Things then got better between Evan and I. However, in a sectional playoff match, he decided to ignore my advice and he lost his match as direct result; I am very confident about that. I teased him about that. By the end of the next season, he began to trust me more and more, as I proved that I had come to understand his game, and what he might want to do in a match. A few times during the season, we worked together in matches in which his opponent had started strongly, or he had started poorly, finding ways for him to win in matches that looked like they could not be won. Later that season in the Sectional Championship match it all came to a head. This was our Super Bowl. He won his first set routinely, but then lost the second when his opponent began to come to the net on almost everything. The change in tactics had him confused and upset, it wasn't looking good for the third set. This player then sought me out! Good thing I knew a few different ways to counterattack, so I gave him options, and he made great choices, and won the match. While his match did not finish the victory, it was the pivotal moment that decided it for our team. Because we had built up trust, based on his decision to trust me, he used tactics that he had not been familiar with prior to that moment. That takes a lot for a teenager to execute tactics that are so brand new.

Coach Model the Learning You Want to See

As you can see here, coaches can model an attitude of learning, just as I had to learn about this freshman, to help their players to do the same, which opens the doors to some very exciting outcomes. Of course, this won't always mean a title, but many times it will mean dramatic improvements for the player and team, which is the name of the game. So, make the most of each moment to inch toward these improved relationships. It can take a long time to develop, can't be rushed, but seems to come much sooner with taking good care of each opportunity that arises. Every little decision makes the relationship better or worse, there is no in between.

Coaches in various sports have differing levels of control of how information flows to players and parents. For many coaches the less than 100% accurate information coming from outside of the program can be a pervasive problem. So many people, parents, administrators, players and bystanders want to feel like and expert, they might not realize how out of time their comments can be. Sometimes the simplest suggestion can create quite a bit of damage to a team. When players are hearing ideas and opinions from parents who think they know better than coaches, this puts players in a bind of who to trust. Where on the timeline are these parents? Are they living out their own past, trying to relive their lives through that of their children? Are they so focused on making everything go faster, that they forget that the coach is in charge of directing the process? How do we as coaches find a balance between player and parent proactivity and staying true to the message of what our program offers? How well do we collaborate with players and parents when new information becomes available? As a general rule, more information is best, but as coaches it's wise for us to put a limit on new information. With new information, many times confusion is created for players, and that confusion needs to be reconciled prior to pivotal performances.

On the timeline of development for players to take full ownership of their sports experience the time is always NOW. The time for coaches to act as empowered consultants is always NOW. Parents communicating with coaches, and providing unconditional love, support and approval, the time is always NOW. The sooner the process begins of allowing players to make decisions, and have their decision making tested, fail, corrected and refined the more prepared they will be in the future when more difficult decisions come. The greatest coaches immediately set this tone of player empowerment from the beginning.

Important Thought: Action Item(s):

CHAPTER TWENTY-FOUR
Giving the Sport 100%

The art of leadership is saying no, not yes. It is very easy to say yes.

~ Tony Blair

Having definite goals is an important part of leadership and team building. Defining a goal means not only saying what something is, but also what it is not. When we pursue a goal, during that time we are excluding all competing goals. Therefore, when we have a defined plan for the day, then our first instinct should be to say no to anything that diverts away from the plan. Denying other activities that take us off task, ends the initial threat to the plan for the day. Keep in mind what you want to achieve, that saying no to the wrong or ill-timed things help us to say yes to the right things and the right time. This is easier said than done, and it requires quite a bit of mindfulness to keep it together. This is where the rubber meets the road in our minds, and we need to be the road for our players.

Making Synaptic Connections

Let's remember who we are dealing with in our coaching. For the most part, we are coaching players whose brains have not fully developed yet. Teenagers have a fully developed threat detection system in their brains, but not a fully developed regulatory system to moderate the responses. As the adults, we help them form more synaptic connections so that they can use their cerebral cortex better to make good decisions. One of the most common social ills in developed nations is 'the fear of missing out', some shorten it into FOMO, but what exactly is the threat, it's not even real, because you may simply delay gratification by doing something later. Another major theoretical underpinning comes from social psychology, where studies show that well-defined limits of behavior can help create greater mental and emotional security for youngsters. If you have coached at all, then you know that they will test you! Where there are no limits, players will sometimes create their own. When the rules, standards and/or consequences are changeable, or obviously unfair, players find it difficult to cope and the team becomes a more stressful situation.

When we create our coaching philosophy, each pillar must be non-negotiable for this very reason, so that we aren't just defending an opinion, but a timeless principle that is expressed through our coaching style.

In saying no, we create well-defined limits. However, we can always say yes later, after a period of thought and planning. Saying yes ought not to be because of coercion from selfish parties. For the coach to really stand as a leader, and a conduit through whom athletes learn the life lessons of sports, ability to make a commitment is one of them. Which things and people should we say no to? How should we say no? When and how loud should we say it? How often will we need to repeat it?

Say No To Distractions

Saying no to undisciplined behavior is an important part of keeping players on task. Even the very best kids that we encounter on our high school teams can open the door to some chaos. Some adult professional athletes are known for a lack of self control, maybe they needed one particular coach to help them solve that problem.

It's generally true that less experienced coaches might think that there is something to gain in letting go of control. At the most innocent, a player that we respect and admire may make a request that would change the plan for the day. It may seem like such a nice thing to do. They may express their enjoyment for a certain drill or game, and ask, 'Can we do _____ today?' It seems so easy and natural to trust and listen to one of your best citizens, but in reality, what often happens is that it sets a precedent for being open to changing the plan. Give an inch, and they take a mile. The inner conflict we may feel runs counter to the 'people pleasing' part of our inner self when we say 'no' to such a kind-hearted request. The player or a group of players may even say, 'You are mean!'. However, it opens the door to another player, who is less disciplined, who has not such a good idea to have theirs accepted as well. When you don't comply, then they have a claim in their own mind as to 'favoritism'. I tell my players, 'You know the answer is going to be NO for today, but go ahead and ask your question, then I will take it under advisement for another day.' Very, very rarely I may change the day's plan, but only if what the player offers is true genius and far exceeds what I had on the agenda. The number of times that has happened in over 30 years has to be less than 5 times. A very important part of saying no is to first listen. Players want to know that their voice will be heard, but there is little or no leeway for today's plan to be changed.

So No To Undisciplined Play

It's best also to say no to the behaviors that can ruin a plan. Lazy movement between activities, a lack of following directions, and distracting or off-task behavior can ruin the practice environment. Saying 'no' to undisciplined practice is actually saying 'yes' to a more fun practice because once the day's objectives are achieved, then each practice ends with a large group game. Sometimes saying no can be a game. At one school, I had 26 players on 6 courts with two banks of three courts. I mainly operated from the three courts where varsity players were practicing, and the JV players where on the other three, which had a pretty tough egress over to the three courts I was on. Early on when I wanted to bring everyone together, it would take a few minutes. I said no to that by counting down from 45 seconds expecting everyone to be on court before I got to zero. If they didn't make it, there were some light consequences. We might do some 'fast feet', because 'we need to be more quick'. So simply by setting a standard, on the one side is yes, and the other side is no. Examples of other behaviors that need to end are: arriving late to practice, not giving best efforts, creating distractions or getting distracted by outside circumstances like school friends walking by and starting a conversation. Countless times I have had conversations with players to say, 'No, that's not O.K. Like missing makable shots, not giving full effort because the player is not excited by the challenge presented, and hitting inappropriate shots, or acting in an inappropriate way with teammates.

At least once or twice a season I have had a certain player in mind in developing a special practice to meet that player's need. If other players also shared that need to some degree, all the better, but my focus was really on one player. When you identify the a player who represents a weak link on the team, (never tell them that), when you can bolster their technical, tactical or physical strength, then the whole team is helped. Special attention to one or a small group of players can change the complexion of the season. It seems like almost every season that I create one of these special practices, the player in my spotlight are not present that day. Had I known that they would miss, I may have created a completely different plan to work on another skill in another pivotal player. Which brings up another point: communication is vitally important. Things come up, players get sick, family emergencies, that annoying dental appointment that can't be any other time, etc. We have to be understanding at times, but not when it comes to fulfilling responsibilities to the team.

Bringing Team Discipline To Individual Sports

Developing the commitment and discipline to coming to practice every day is a much more difficult thing in individual sports because tennis players, golfers, track athletes don't see themselves as being vital to the way a practice continues, like a center on a football team, point guard in basketball, or catcher in baseball whose presence comparatively is vital to the team. What we need to teach is how our practice structures depend on certain numbers of players paired in certain ways. One missing player can be a major disruption to our plan, and create a need to completely rework it on the fly. Their presence is required, and the time devoted to the task pays off for them, and the team. Teaching the kids that it's not ok to miss, and that they should say no to other activities so they can say yes to full commitment to the team, will serve them well in their future lives as leaders. Perhaps all of the above seems obvious, but it must be examined closely.

Important Thought: Action Item(s):

CHAPTER TWENTY-FIVE
Capture Thoughts

Prayer is the soul's sincere desire. Your desire is your prayer. It comes out of your deepest needs and it reveals the things you want in life.

~ Joseph Murphy, The Power of Your Subconscious Mind

Our minds are an endless stream of consciousness, so it's necessary at times to stop and think, to really latch onto a thought, pull it out, and look at it. I would catch myself thinking negatively and wonder why. When doing so, I would have a decision to make in terms of what to do with that thought. I can banish it, change it, find the inner bias inside for it, turn it around and make it a positive. If I choose to stuff it or ignore it, then I find it pops up again later. When people try very hard to stuff thoughts, where do they go? I am not certain, but my working theory is that they go deeper into the subconscious mind. When we have these negative thoughts about our players, then we often will speak or act in a way that reflects those thoughts.

Think Time Inspiration and The Beat Down

Have you noticed that some of your best thoughts come at the strangest and most inconvenient times? You might get a great thought while in a meeting, in the shower, while on a hike, or at another time when you don't really have time to think about it fully. The next consecutive thought has the largest bearing on whether we capture it or not.

After a great idea or thought comes to mind countless times my next thought was:

* I don't have time to think about that right now
* That will never work
* I tried that before and failed
* An obstacle that seems unsurmountable
* A person that I would have to see, that I don't want to see
* Feelings of shame or inadequacy

* I will have to grow in a way I don't want
* That's out of my comfort zone
* People will think poorly of me
* I have never done it that way
* It's not conventional
* I will meet with resistance

Stopping to simply write down the positive thing to move toward is a major step toward that outcome. Putting aside the myriad reasons why something can't be done, stopping to think about where I am, what are the impediments to progress?

The Reality of Thoughts About Our Players

Since we are not going to have 100% players that we like a lot and enjoy, managing the thoughts we have about them helps us to do the most professional job possible. It's only natural to gravitate to the more friendly, likable, more attractive and talented players. It can require more mindfulness to be sure to give equal time to the introverted, troubled, and/or less attractive players. Difficult players pose a challenge to us, and they can actually be the reason we become better. We also then model mature attitudes, as they will have a role model for dealing with people who are tough for them deal with. Many times, athletes appreciate the work that a coach put in to help them go beyond their supposed limitations, although they might not fully understand until later in life. I have run into many former students and players who thanked me for what I did years ago, even though at the time, it might not have been pleasant for either of us. In the same way, I have expressed my gratitude to those who challenged me in a serious way to become a better, more effective person. I get these kinds of inputs into my life on a weekly basis and sometimes much more frequently.

Daily/Weekly Praise

My students are sometimes really amazed when every few weeks I drop some very effusive praise on them, and then go back to the somewhat sarcastic observational techniques I often employ. Finding little positives on almost a daily basis is an important I must qualify here that I never use sarcasm meant to put my players down, but more sarcasm in regard to opening their mind to seeing a much better way to look at things. I draw the line in regard to giving compliments at the place where it feels forced. If I don't have a ready compliment, then I won't force it, but I will go out of my way later to come up with something. My sarcasm is directed at the negative thoughts and actions, and never the person. We then redirect those thoughts and actions into a positive action item.

Managing the Can Do

The most positive and empowering thought you can have is 'I can do it'. It also functions as an objective thought as well, because as long as you are focusing on something that is at least somewhat realistic, then it's the best kind of input for your brain. This most fundamental thought is paramount to empowering athletic achievement. Dr. Gary Sailes, a Sports Psychologist then of University of Indiana Psychology Department, shared how our thoughts change our competencies. He showed a large group of coaches how saying 'I can' instead of 'I can't' actually made one athlete stronger physically, in an experiment right in front of our eyes. The ability to think through a problem is much better aided by a 'can do' mentality.

Armed with fresh and deeper understanding of having a can do attitude, I brought it home to my hard working, but under talented team. Their cognitive affective profile would never be the same. Dr. Sailes outlined that the words, changed the thoughts which changed the affect of the person. In psychological terms affect means 'coming from the emotions', and the emotional part of the player is strengthened with right thinking. This team I was coaching seemed destined to finish fourth in our league, or maybe third, if we pulled a major upset. Upon my return to practice, I announced, 'We can win the championship. We can do it, you can do it.' Repeat after me, 'We can do it, I can do it.' An amazing transformation immediately took place.

This group changed dramatically, they went from being the normal hard working team I expect to, easily the hardest working team I have ever coached. I also was helped by this thinking. This was a team that lacked power, so instead of trying to build power, we focused on speed. This team was so dedicated to the speed work, that doubt I have had a faster team. Our speed was used like a weapon, and every player believed that they could get to every ball. Our stifling defense that was unlike any other team in the league. As Herb Brooks is quoted in Miracle, the story of the 1980 USA Olympic Hockey team, 'Legs feed the wolf', became our rally cry. As it turned out, we won four dramatically against teams I expected to be ahead of us in the standings. Even though we lost to one team twice, also in real nail biters, that other team inexplicably lost to two teams lower in the standings, which meant we tied for a league title. It was a testament to the power of 'I can do it'. Any time my players found themselves in a tough spot, we just kept saying over again, 'I can do it, you can do it, we can do it.'

Look for the negatives, the 'I can't do it', they are sure to pop up, and replace them with 'I can'. Be sure to write down your best ideas, and think of them in a positive cognitive affective format.

Important Thoughts: Action Item(s):

CHAPTER TWENTY-SIX
Fixed and Growth Mindsets

**For to set the mind on the flesh is death,
but to set the mind on the Spirit is life and peace.**

~ Paul of Tarsus

People with a growth mindset believe that their abilities grow from challenges. Those with a fixed mindset define their abilities by the binary measure of succeeding or failing, proving that they have what it takes or not. Growth mindset folks move forward to overcome challenges, improving themselves, gaining new skills and synaptic connections in their brains. Fixed mind set people believe that they are already finitely abled, and either they are good at something or they are not, and there is not a chance to grow. Those who believe they can grow into new roles seeing possibilities and improve themselves and see almost everything as something they can do. Those who aren't growth minded feel like things that happen are fate, and they don't exert much control over the outcomes. A fixed mindset believes that people are either born with talents or not. Growth mindset people see a starting place, knowing that they can work to become better. Fixed mindsets are really a lie, because everyone improves in life simply by growth.

Shifting Mindset

Players with a fixed mindset believe that their own intelligence and talent are innate traits that don't change. When we or they say 'that's just how I am', we sell ourselves short. For example, these students typically worry about not looking smart, get upset by mistakes, and give up sooner on tough tasks. Students with a growth mindset believe that ability can change as a result of effort, perseverance, and practice. They might say, 'Math is hard, but if I keep trying, I can get better at it.' 'I'm shooting less than 50% of my free throws in, but I will work until I can make 60% or more.' Of course if a basketball coach expects a player shooting under 50% to become a 90% free throw shooter overnight, then they are not very realistic. Magic Johnson famously spent an entire offseason working on his free throws after an NBA Finals exposed him. He became a very good free throw shooter.

I had my own defeatist attitudes in life, one of them being 'I'm just not very good administratively', and so I failed pretty regularly to deliver paperwork, communicate on a timely basis, and show up to meetings that I should. It would be an understatement to say that it held me back in my chosen profession. I was not alone in the coaching ranks, for that I am sure. But then I decided that I no longer wanted to lose respect, business, and stunt the growth of players by my own lack of responsibility. I went from an utter failure to at least a B- grade administrator. Nowadays, when I call people back away they say, 'Wow, I can't believe you got back to me so quickly, the other coaches...' I am not yet an A+ in admin, but I'm continually honing my skills.

Students with a growth mindset see mistakes as ways to learn, embrace challenges, and persist in the face of setbacks. Whether or not students are aware of their mindset, a broad body of research has shown that what they believe about their own intelligence can affect their effort, engagement, motivation, and achievement as measured by test scores, school grades, passing rate in post-secondary education, and other metrics.

Important Thoughts: Action Item(s):

CHAPTER TWENTY-SEVEN
The Soil for Planting

The best day to plant a tree is 20 years ago, the next best day is today.

~ Chinese Proverb

Developing a program is much like planting, and the ongoing care is much like the cultivation of your field, or garden.

Farming the Present, Dig More Deeply Now

The only soil we will ever have for planting new growth in our lives is the here and now. It's common for coaches to have posters or t-shirts that say, championships aren't won in (insert month of playoffs), they are won in (insert off-season training). This is a great thing to focus player's attention on the activities that go into preparation for great performances. Part of the ills of youth is that the vast majority of young people have no vision of the future. Another problem, is that they don't often see how the processes of today's work feed into the growth that will be realized at a later date. Today in their minds can seem like a static and unrelated experience from tomorrow, next week, next year. Athlete Centered Coaches have a vision for each athlete to be more than they are, imagining a path, and readjusting that vision as the player responds with their own decision making. Sometimes adversity is part of the path, and a contingency plans need to be developed.

Develop Planners

The sooner we can have players thinking ahead for future seasons, the better. Everyone once in a while you meet the rare individual who has a clearly defined goal for life and a drive to move toward that from a very young age. When we refine that, teaching players to make the most of every passing moment, wasting fewer and fewer moments, we not only find much more enjoyment in life, but achievements simply seem to flow out of us as a natural manifestation of being fully engaged. Scott Ford in his book *Integral Consciousness for Sport*, discusses the flowing present, and the absolute present. Now, now, now, now. The first 'now' occurred in the present as you read it, and so did each 'now' after, but the first one was then in the past. So as your attention flowed from word to word, your attention was in the absolute present, that is the present that you take with you.

The Precious Moments of Life

I recently sat with a cancer patient, who was also an avid athlete, for a few hours while we discussed how his mindset shifted the moment he realized he has a terminal disease. He echoed these same thoughts. For my part, it was refreshing to let him tell his exact same perception of flowing time, and avoid the temptation to say anything that might hint at 'I know that'. Greg's experience with his own mortality he found to be a real blessing, as now he is really savoring every moment. His former athleticism has been wiped away by the ravages of multiple treatments as he looks to do everything he can to extend his life to be available for his wife, children and grandchildren. Keeping sports in perspective of mortality is important, since we can also think about what our legacy might be. Considering for a moment the temporal nature of our existence on this planet, helps us to give more value to every precious moment.

Moments to Memories

I love to tell stories about times my young players came up big, and delivered the goods at precisely the right time. I also tell stories about when the competition did that very thing, and my player could not overcome a magnificent performance. 'Sometimes you beat the bear and sometimes the bear beats you.' When we zoom back into the precise moments that exist within our mortal time on earth, there are some absolute things that occur in sports, the sweet spot on a bat or tennis racquet, an ideal release point for a throw, a bullseye target, each of these things exist more or less outside of time. The tremendous privilege of having a peak performance, or to be present for someone else's peak performance, are things we carry with us. These are indelible memories that we can hold onto and enjoy moving forward. Ideally we can find these perfect places, but so much of what makes sports great, is when players overcome adversity to write a new story and do something fantastic.

The Seed Dies Before It Grows

We bury the seed, then out of seeming death, it comes to the surface bringing new life. In the same way great coaches and great athletes use adversity to start something new. The immense optimism that comes with coaching and ascending as an athlete morphs into a new contingency when there is an injury, a bad outcome, or a personal setback. How to get back, how to rise up, and get back on the horse that threw you.

The ability to spontaneously make a play is to be firmly rooted in the absolute now, and not stuck on the past, or looking too far in the future. The ability to move past a set back, and return to what is in front of us, with little memory of failure, makes for some of the greatest stories in sports. Like Dan Jansen winning gold in his least favorite discipline, after falling in two consecutive Olympics in his specialty, after the tremendous amount of work mentally he did to prepare for that second Olympics. Overcoming another fall, so catastrophic, and how little hope anyone held for him to win Gold at all. How many times have you seen a football player on defense in position to make an interception, but drop the ball, because they had pay dirt in front of them. They were thinking touchdown, before they even caught the ball. They must immediately shift back into the present to be ready for the next play. One of the best cliches in sports is, 'What is the most important play? The next one!' Going ahead to the future takes our attention away in part from what we are doing. Coaches preach 'first catch the ball', but why are these defenders still oftentimes going ahead into the future? A better instruction might be 'stay in the present with the ball'. It would be far better to make the interception, and stumble on the way to a possible touchdown, than to drop the ball.

One of the most remarkable moments I have experienced as a coach was in a playoff match, when one of my doubles players suddenly ran 25 feet diagonally in front of her partner to take a ball that no conventional wisdom would say was hers. She then executed a low percentage shot which was equally daring, likely to fail and completely unexpected by all onlookers. She made the shot, won the point, as the opposition was flabbergasted, not at all ready to react to her move. Her play created a dramatic strong misdirection. One high risk play, the put the other team on their heals, because Stephanie had become so unpredictable all of a sudden, and they could not cope. What had been a tense, back and forth, very equal competition suddenly was broken wide open, and our players won the final three games to win the match. Afterward, I joked with Stephanie, 'That was awesome, I salute you, never do it again! I have not yet decided how serious I was about that comment, but I do recognize the genius of the moment. Great coaches free players up to play instinctively, and our training should mostly train those instincts like a musician plays scales, so that they can improvise later with great skill.

Picking the Fruit Early

Reflect for a moment on the errors that occur in your sport when players are living mentally and emotionally too far in the future. One universal problem with young athletes is when they come to the realization that a win is in sight. Especially if they are not in the habit of winning, or if they have assigned a lot of meaning to the competition. They start looking at the the finish line of the contest, dreaming about the final score. When their minds wander to that potentiality, as they often do, they have left the here and now where the game is played, and passively or actively move too far in the future. They then are prone to relax and stop actually playing at full effort level. This is why one of the all time great sports cliches is so meaningful. 'Play one game at a time, one point at a time.' Paired with the understanding that we have to be fully present while playing those points, helps athletes give more consistent performances all the way through. It's all we can do. We can only do what we are doing now, and affect change on what we are doing, so that we can accomplish something that will come in the future.

Planting 100% Effort Very Well

No matter which sport I have coached, every single team, position group or player I coach, I start with them giving 100% effort at all times. I stay on this topic of giving 100% effort regardless of the situation, until it becomes a deeply ingrained habit, and I have very high standards for that level. Starting anywhere else would be to neglect the most important element in my program. This is athlete centered coaching at its core, because the most important gift I can give my players is to help them understand the difference between their

95%, 98% and the 100% effort that I want. This then becomes a standard to be maintained, and at the first sign of a dip in intensity, I can address it immediately and my players know exactly what I mean, since it was the first core concept taught to the group.

So, there is a connection between the moment to moment work of helping players play in the present, with how they will perform at key stages in a competition. A team that has a lead, loses focus and quickly is scored upon, can quickly go into panic mode, but having that unshakable tree that was planted before that gives players something to hold onto, can help right the ship. Teams and players who are ready to continue maintaining high positive intensity no matter the score, are less likely to have a major dip in effort level. This type of effort can be monitored moment to moment in practices and games, and if we haven't planted the core tenets of the program before, then today is a great day to start.

Important Thought: Action Item(s):

PART THREE

THE COACH IN SPORT SOCIETY

Leadership is more about responsibility than ability!

~ Jim Tunney , American Football

CHAPTER TWENTY-EIGHT

Brains, Knees, Vital Parts

The most common impediment to improvement is injury.

~ John Jerome, The Sweet Spot in Time

The course of a person's life can take a major turn for the worse with a catastrophic injury. Our care for the full timeline of an athlete's life will give any of us perspective on the short and long term effects of a major injury. Maximizing general safety in every aspect of the sport from facility preparation, to rules of safe play, and eliminating as many risks as possible is essential. I would never want to be the reason an athlete was injured. Football is making great strides in first acknowledging brain injuries, and second in developing better equipment, while modifying the rules to make the game more safe. People might not realize that there are actually more concussions in soccer than in football. Soccer also is a leader in serious knee injuries like tearing an ACL.

Maximizing Injury Prevention In Peformance

There are many techniques that can be used to help players avoid injury. Do the research in your sport as to best practices for 'pre-hab', which is to identify most commonly injured areas and do the necessary mobility and stability exercises to try to mitigate those issues. One interesting example is that the National Italian Soccer studied knee injuries and found that players who had extensive balance training early in their career were less likely to have a knee ligament tear.

Injuries will occur and how we respond to those can become a part of our legacy as a coach. Athletes and parents will remember the care given in the moment, as doctors evaluate, treatment is given and throughout the rehabilitation process. Taking an out of sight out of mind approach can be ruinous to your reputation. Actually caring throughout the process and continuing to check in on a schedule that is shows enough engagement is vital. Of course, you can read the signals from the family about how much is too much.

The Bed Side Manner Athlete Centered Coaches

When people are healing from injury or illness, there is much data that suggests that the amount of interpersonal support they receive plays a role in their recovery. The psychological aspects of how the brain deals with healing and recovery are a bit mysterious, but we do know that people who have support from the people who should care the most do better, recover faster, and those that feel alone are less likely to recover quickly and sometimes at all.

After an injury the way we modify activity for the returning player on the mend is also an indicator of being athlete centered. Time and space come into play here as well, because it's tempting to rush athletes back for competition. Balancing the relative importance of a vital game or match in a team's history and the health of the players is a delicate thing to do. I have had players who played hurt and even ill to the point of having a fever at their behest, because of the historic nature of the event. We did all we could to manage the injury, made allowances for early removal from the contest at the first sign of trouble, having already checked with the trainer about the risk of making the injury much worse. I would never play a player when there was a risk of injury, beyond the normal chance, that could create a permanent issue for them in the long run. In 30 years, there have not been a many times that I have had to think about sitting a player out because of the risk of further injury, but I also have not coached as often in contact sports. If I am inserting injured or players into the lineup, it's with the idea that we will monitor the situation closely, and it must be for a championship. There is such a fine line here, and I know that I might sound contradictory, but when their is a championship on the line, that's when I allow players who are not at risk for further catastrophic injury play.

I will never forget the story of an NFL owner who referenced a player who had played with a severely injured ankle for a few years. That player had not received an accurate diagnosis of his injury, but was given pain killing injections. When later his lower leg was amputated, the owner said, 'It's too bad Curt didnt work out...', not really acknowledging the extreme sacrifice given by the player.

Take The Long View

Always keep in the forefront the long term of the person's life ahead of the short term of the game. If we are putting our athletes into situations where we know that we increase the risk of brain injury or other injuries that can affect our players futures, then we really need to reexamine that.

Important Thoughts: Action Item(s):

CHAPTER TWENTY-NINE
How Coaches Collaborate

**Cooperation isn't very difficult, because all
you need are common goals. True collaboration
requires trust. Trust that is not easily earned.
We as coaches need to develop these relationships
over time, building a better life with each other.**

~ Styrling Strother, Transforming The Practice Court

There is another side [to ego] that can wreck a team or an organization. That is being distracted by your own importance. It can come from your insecurity in working with others. It can be the need to draw attention to yourself in the public arena. It can be a feeling that others are a threat to your own territory. These are all negative manifestations of ego, and if you are not alert to them, you get diverted and your work becomes diffused. Ego in these cases makes people insensitive to how they work with others and it ends up interfering with the real goal of any group efforts. ~ Bill Walsh, American Football Coach

Coming Together in the Spirit of Collaboration

What better achievement can there be, to be a game-changer, an innovator who changes the way something is done? Bill Walsh is among the most innovative coaches of all-time, but he learned his offensive principles somewhere else. Sid Gillman, Al Davis and others poured into Bill Walsh's life and coaching, in the same way that Bill Walsh developed one of the most prolific coaching trees of all time. To introduce a Fosbury Flop, a Slam Dunk, a 5-3 defense, Zone Read, Trap Play, Triangle Offense, etc. to your sport is to have made a profound difference in the way the game is played. How do coaches ascend to the next levels of coaching ability or even the apex of their sport and make contributions in this way? These achievements are not often performed in a vacuum. Very rarely is there any kind of savant achievement in sports coaching. By far the greatest ladders of success are exactly that: ladders. Players and coaches work to gain a foothold, and each layer of lessons from the masters ahead of them, help propel those people to new heights. Peeking their head out of the clouds, those that achieve great breakthroughs are standing on the shoulders of giants that preceded them, and are helped by those close to them who help shape and refine an innovation until it is ready to be implemented.

There is also a fundamental difference in the attitudes of coaches and players who will ascend to the very highest levels, or at least fully maximize their own potential. As stated earlier, my friend Sean Brawley has shared the formula he uses for success: Performance = Potential - Interference. Many times, the attitudes and/or subconscious thoughts of players or coaches hold them back and are the greatest forms of interference that can be found. Another great friend and coaching collaborator, Styrling Strother and I have had many discussions on this, and it's our belief that we can achieve a lot with a very cooperative attitude, however, the greatest achievements stem from a highly collaborative one. Styrling is a trainer of coaches, whose guiding principle is to make everything in practice align with learning to win and life skills development. True collaboration does not come easily. Since true collaboration has some stringent requirements, it's not as easily achieved as is simple cooperation, which only requires some common goals. Trust is hard to develop, easily damaged and requires a healthy amount of humility from all participants. The final ingredient is what Napolean Hill calls, the Law of the Master Mind, where groups of people who all have a common goal and pledge to work together have a very high degree of creativity, but it only takes one person to betray the group and wreck the energy. That does NOT mean that their should be no dissent. In fact, dissenting opinions expressed respectfully can save the project from 'group-think' and unintended consequences. Scott Adams a social commentator of sorts says, 'It was a failure of imagination', to describe groups that don't to stop to ask what will happen next if they do what they want to do. High levels of collaboration help dramatically reduce the amount of interference in the creative process, and dissenting voices are a part of developing the final product, so don't mistake them for being disruptive to the process.

Simple Common Goals

When people work together to follow through on what they say, to support those common goals, then the proof of the cooperation will be found in their actions. For example, a group of coaches in a league may meet to discuss a rule change that will be more equitable, or somehow better serve the players. In order to do that, the only necessary ingredient is some kind consensus of agreement about the rule, and it need not be unanimous. All coaches will then choose to cooperate or not. They will choose to abide by the new rule or break it. I have coached in a few leagues where the coaches often seek to reinterpret the rules to suit them, and they break them fairly often. When the agreement on the rules and how they are enforced breaks down, then do you really even have cooperation? Certainly it will be very difficult to develop trust, so as to move toward collaboration, when coaches don't work together on simpler tasks. When cooperation breaks down, then true collaboration is not possible.

The Danger of Collaboration

To truly collaborate, each participant needs to trust one another because there is an element of vulnerability and risk-taking, with each party making concessions in order to make dramatic positive changes. Coaches may share some of their proprietary knowledge with each other, with the understanding that the other coaches will not seek to re-brand it as their own. Recently, it has come to light that some prominent online sports educators have been using material for which they paid a master coach, and did not ask permission to rebrand the material as their own. A fairly public conflict ensued which worked to damage the reputation of the one coach. Still others have inappropriately filmed copyrighted professional events without permission for another rebranding. So, those who are not really collaborating according to the rules of trust and propriety are harming themselves in the long term, even though they may make good money in the short term. Ultimately, a far better way for coaches to ascend is by sincere service to the master coaches, then at the best time, wait for the time of the delivery of a master work to be promoted. This close mentorship delivers amazing results.

Mentorship

In every coaching circle there are well noted master coaches who have a coaching tree that has been established by years of deep mentoring with long established proteges who then pass along the precious training. As games evolve, the coaches also evolve while making it their own, keeping up with the times. Sometimes the younger coaches bring an innovation to the master coach who then puts it to the test. Often small groups of coaches can come together to find a system that works best for their players, only to have discovered something that to the outside world looks like an amazing change in how the game is played. Necessity is the mother of invention. Highly collaborative coaches who have established trust between them come together to invent, not to steal and cheat. Collaborative coaches also extend that attitude to their athletes, and this is the where the true nature of athlete centered coaching is expressed. Coaches bettering themselves, expanding their coaching skill sets, and learning to trust become the source of this collaboration for their players.

Important Thought: Action Item(s):

CHAPTER THIRTY
Pathways to Collaboration

Coaching is a profession of love.
You can't coach people unless you love them.

~ Eddie Robinson

Perhaps the greatest roadblock to true collaboration is fear. It has been said that the opposite of fear is love. Some people say that love and fear are similar to light and dark. When the light goes on, darkness recedes, but there will always be shadows. Ultimately it's love of sport and the people involved in sport that will help drive away the fear. Fear comes from different places, but many times the root cause is either an over-inflated ego, or an unhealthy and weak one. When we think too highly or too lowly of ourselves, we easily can be afraid to ask for help. Trying to place ourselves on a higher level, seems to create an air of being guarded so as not be exposed. Great coaches stay in the present knowing that each day if they pay attention, they can gain one new item of information or skill, and that cumulatively over time, they can better themselves. That is the growth mentality at work. So little by little we can achieve greatness, but that will also be aided by the healthy admission that we will never know everything.

Too Much Future Thinking

Ego problems arise in coaches who rest too much on the successes of the past, or have grandiose visions of what they might achieve in the future, but have not yet achieved. When we say to ourselves, 'If only I had THIS, then I could DO THAT', misses the point of achieving all you can in your current station in life. Coaches who are fully engaged in the present are much more likely to experience a sense of privilege to be present when great things are happening, and to help facilitate them.

Even those with a so-called 'growth mindset', can trip up on taking in too much information too fast, or act out of a deficit mentality of trying to make up for lost time. Great coaches also then share with others, and have the patience to give one nugget at a time, rather than overwhelm their audiences with too much information.

Coming Back to Being Fully Present

When we are fully present in the moment we can get into a more collaborative way of being. Being 'in the now' allows for better listening, and a stronger ability to perceive when information has been received by the student. At the heart of collaboration is helping one another, and my experience with many of the greatest coaches in the world is that they are very free at giving and gaining help from others.

Deep Dive into Humility

Another great trait found in the greatest coaches is humility. The best of the best have a feel that they may never arrive at a place where they now know it all. In fact, much more likely is that they sat at the feet of a master coach, observing and getting many hours of mentoring prior to striking out on their own. The apprenticeship model demands a certain amount of being fully engaged in the moment, because without that, boredom, impatience, frustration and any number of other negative influences come into play. The more educated we are, the more we know how much more there is to know and we will never get to that place.

Being fully present with our thoughts also acts as a gateway to self-knowledge for the sake of our betterment. There is a saying that a person may 'Glance at themselves in the mirror, but as soon as they leave, they forget what they look like.' While we don't want to self-consciously self examine at all times, having moments to reflect on the events of the day can be a major part of a coaches growth toward mastery. Asking the questions, 'What did I enjoy today? What did the players enjoy? What went well? How could I have done better? What needs to be done next? Do I need to adjust the plan? Assume that there will be very few nearly perfect days.

Knowing Ourselves

If we don't have enough ego strength and self-understanding, then it's harder to develop an authentic thought, one born from taking the sum of our knowledge and putting our personal stamp on it. Having a balanced view of our own talents, capabilities, limitations, and level of experience is crucial to finding the right balance of receiving and giving back. Too often, younger coaches discount the influence they can have on their sport. Be brave, get out there and share. When we have an accurate enough view of ourselves, and we know our own strengths and relative weaknesses, then we are less subject to the fear of exposure. The more we learn about ourselves, the more ready we are to receive criticism.

We arrive at the pinnacle of collaboration when top coaches share some of their proprietary knowledge as part of a team, league, region, or national effort. This could be just a one-way street, as other coaches may simply consume the information. When coaches respond with their perspectives, providing feedback and constructive criticisms, then the entire product can be improved for all. The call to action to be more excellent still. I really appreciate the times that I have presented lectures, demonstrations and paradigms at conferences with the tough questions that come. What an amazing opportunity to hone my own understanding of my offering. Also, at times, it causes me to be more humble, because I have to answer that I don't know the answer to their question.

Talking Along the Road

However, coaches often remain silent. I want to challenge you that if you have not attempted to share your ideas, to share them. Also, when someone shares their ideas, question them with a purpose of trying to understand the concept. One harmful thing that coaches do to one another that destroys trust is that they criticize before understanding. Even when a coach does understand the other coach fully, the way they couch their comments with constructive criticism can hurt or help. I have put forward some online courses on coaching topics, and been amazed at how a younger coach will tell me something much simpler than what I am teaching without even questioning me on what the content is. They will limp through the early part of their careers limited by their own expert status in their minds.

Coaches ascend to a new level, when they create something, and open it up to criticism. Styrling Strother, author of '7 On Court Strategies', in writing his book, sent it out to various top coaches, who then have offered to critique and suggest edits. This work went through the same process. Frank Giampaolo, one of the most influential authors in Tennis also regularly sends out his pre-publications for feedback. Those actions take a very high level of trust.

Important Thought: Action Item(s):

CHAPTER THIRTY-ONE

Who Owns the Sandbox?

Alone we can do so little; together we can do so much.

~ Helen Keller

Moving toward greater collaboration with our players can take coaching to a new level. This whole book is really about moving away from a coach centered approach, and toward a player centered one. Including players in the discussion and phasing in their interaction with the program as they mature helps contribute to greater intrinsic motivation on their part. For those not familiar with intrinsic and extrinsic motivation, they can be summed up in the simplest term, although there is much more nuanced meaning to each. Intrinsic motivation comes from within and mainly centers around the satisfaction player feel from the performance. Extrinsic motivation depends on the outcomes, the tangible rewards of wins, trophies and prizes. As we work together to better our craft, do we foster more intrinsic motivation with our players by delving into the inner world of what drives them? Do we understand who is already highly intrinsically motivated, and who might need to make a shift away from being extremely extrinsically driven.

Collaborating with Players

Some key questions we can ask any player to help us navigate this great journey are; How do you see things progressing? What do you think is the next logical step in your progression? How does that fit with the long term plan of your overall development? How do you learn best? Are you more visual or kinesthetic in your learning style? Do you prefer to see and imitate, or be guided through the stroke and experiment until you think it feels right? Do you like to put ideas into action? Do you like to have things explained to you before we do them?

When we give information, there is a lot of research that suggests that smaller bits of information are more palatable for players to consume. We might give one big chunk of information, then break down the chunk into smaller bits that all fit together. Any one item of information is best framed in 10 seconds or 42 words for a person to have the best ability to attend to that detail. Lengthy lectures, especially in the heat of battle are almost certain to be lost because of the inability of players to attend to words for long when they are in a heightened state of competition.

This key question to players can help you, as a coach, discover a player's strengths and weaknesses in learning. If a player is more of a visual learner, look to explain your teaching concepts with words that paint a picture for the player to see the idea you are trying to teach about a stroke mechanic or strategy. Use great analogies like The Figure 8 Swing Path. If a player learns by doing, then we create activities to challenge the player's learning. At Styrling's behest, I have decided to align with a name change of these activities from 'drills' to 'challenges', as it sets a better tone, and players seem to more readily accept a challenge, because they see it as an opportunity for improvement. Visual, Kinesthetic and Auditory learning play a role, but we many times rely on the auditory, and tend not to have simple enough explanations that paint word pictures, or as Tim Gallwey said, 'To create feel-mages'. One of the timeless ideas in teaching is that of demonstration, as players can observe them imitate. An underutilized method in some sports is guiding the action to give the player the feeling of the path of the motion.

The Product of Reproduction

Ultimately, it's what the player can see and/or feel that will be something they can reproduce. But, do we check for understanding? How do we do that? It happens best in a collaborative environment. All three: Visual, Auditory, and Kinesthetic methods of teaching are like using the three primary colors: Red, Blue, and Yellow to allow for more color to be expressed on a canvas. Yes, some people love red more than blue or yellow, but that doesn't mean that blue and yellow are not needed at all. Players can have tendencies toward one learning style over another; learning to recognize those tendencies can build collaboration very quickly between a coach and their players. If we go back to the definition of learning as a relatively permanent change in behavior, then we can set parameters for acceptable mastery. We must however stop short of perfection.

I have a story I like to tell about a former player who is also now an accomplished coach. When Vinh was 13 he started with me on a tennis court. And every other shot he took a swing from the heals approach, which lead to many errors. It was easy to identify, but a pretty deeply ingrained habit. Within a few weeks, we had reduced his habit to one in ten shots, then in a few more weeks one in 20, and by the end of the summer it was one in 50. Skip ahead to when Vinh was 16 years old and he had not swung from the heels all summer. In a match against an 18 year old that I didn't think Vinh could beat he played amazingly well, won in straight sets and late in the second he 'swung from the heels', he stopped, looked back at me, we both laughed. After the match I said, 'See, it's still there.' The point of this story being that no matter how much effort we put into trying to achieve perfection, and work on new habits to replace old habits, the old won will still be there, even if it is diminished.

Shifting Perspective from Coach/Player to Coach/Coach

Guest Section: Styrling Strother

When it comes to building collaboration between coaches, this can be a difficult task. Tennis coaches tend to be very strong individuals, and very entrepreneurial, so forming this type of collaboration takes a bit of going outside the normal comfort zone of any coach who enters into collaboration. Bill and I sometimes battle, and struggle together to come to common understanding, but it's worth the fight, and we both take it in an "Iron Sharpens Iron" approach. Sometimes we throw sand. We ask ourselves, are we playing in the sandbox of true collaboration, are we only in the sandbox of cooperation, or in the sandbox at all? We want to encourage you to join us in the USATennisCoach sandbox of collaboration. A communal growth mindset is very important to avoid becoming defensive when our ideas are challenged by another's experience or opinion. "Without tension there is no hope for growth" is a powerful truth I discovered many years ago. I realized that in order for anything to grow and mature, it must be tested and go through a process of metamorphosis (a transformational process from immature to mature form in two or more stages). So the big question is: "How do I know which "sandbox" I'm playing in, Collaboration or Cooperation?

Maybe a good place to start is asking yourself these questions:

Do I become defensive when my ideas or perceptions of coaching are challenged?

Do I believe, 'I've arrived and have all the best answers to any coaching method out there?'

Do I hold on to, 'the way it's always been taught', or do I consistently strive to find the value in other ideas and   w a y s   t o communicate more effectively and efficiently?

Your Mission (if You Choose to Accept It):

Find a coach you trust, ask them to give you an honest assessment of what kind of coach you are, start in a   place   of   humility and discovery to become the best you can be on and off the court. A good question to   start with is, 'Hey coach, do I have a growth or fixed mindset?'

Important Thought: Action Item(s):

CHAPTER THIRTY-TWO

Sharpen The Next Generation

Iron sharpens iron.

~ King Solomon

Let's liken our coaching relationships to a fine blade we might use in the kitchen to create an expert meal. Coaches who are new the industry generally are rough around the edges. They use their relatively dull blades, which require more effort to cut, and might not be able to produce necessary precision. Unescessary tension is created in the coach, and some collateral damage is created in players and relationships, when the precision is lacking. Coaches who work the trade of coaching, to refine their abilities become more and more sharp. Taking more time in preparation for coaching can deliver a much better experience for everyone. Sharp blades are not as dangerous as dull or dirty ones. Razor sharp knives bring a certain fear and responsibility for their use, giving the user pause, because a careless swipe could do a lot of damage. Even so a clean cut mends so much more quickly and better than a comparable gash.

Measure Twice, Cut Once

In the working trades, where sharp saws do the work, the axiom, 'Measure twice, cut once comes to mind.' So it is in coaching, we smooth out our rough edges by creating friction with the other rough edges, until we have made ourselves into very useful tools. The need to mindfully use our abilities give us pause to consider that some things that we do or say cannot be undone, or unsaid. Things that people see or hear from us, cannot be unheard. No matter how sincere the apology, every day that we coach, there is a chance we can do damage. Blades that go untested, unused naturally go back to dullness. Too many coaches rest on their laurels with old bad information that is actually harmful to athletes, but was once the pinnacle of conventional wisdom. Coaches used to think that 'water was for the weak'. Methods used to gain flexibility, unstable surface training, and some other very new techniques are actually quite harmful, or harmful when done at the wrong rate of speed, or without fundamentals. It seems that at least once a month I am reminded of a time I believed something that was flat out wrong, or am learning something new that exposes my incomplete knowledge on a topic that I felt I was quite competent. The periodic sharpening of our skills is necessary if we are truly going to be athlete centered coaches. When the flowing present of today's lessons meets 25 years of absolute present, then there is a good chance that you or I may become a master coach.

Rust and Decay

Regardless of any pinnacle of achievement we may have attained, we all succumb to the rust. It takes time and energy to work the iron ore of raw coaching ability slowly and methodically removing rough edges and shape those skills into a strong set of tools.

Everyone starts as a raw product and I am not a stranger to that. In fact, in the stories I tell here, I see some glimpses of my former self and it's not a great feeling, but we must accept ourselves, acknowledge our flaws, and continue to work on them. After over 30 years of coaching, I do believe that the work from so many years of learning and working to refine has produced some tools that others can use. Yet, I will welcome feedback and additional information to enhance future editions of this book. If you have made it this far, feel free to email me at 720degreecoaching@gmail.com to give me your feedback or great information. I want to give back and hope that I can save you the difficult lessons I have had to learn the hard way. That's what it's all about: giving back. The older rusty coaches still have a wealth to offer, those with the shiny tools are maybe better equipped to translate that knowledge to the new generation, and the new generation should speak up, but also be eager to learn and be molded by those with sharper tools than their own. We want to work with up-and-coming coaches, collaborate early and often with everyone, especially our peers, and all lean toward the deep coaching knowledge of the all-time greats.

What to Do With Legends?

One of the topics that came up in our talk was reaching out to the venerable giants of our sport, the rusty ones if you will. The coaches with immense experience have seen all the trends and fads and now their metal is weathered, but tried and true. While they might be behind on current trends, these wise old masters might be exactly the true north that so-called innovative coaches might use as a touch stone to be sure not to drift too far away from the fundamental truths of coaching. Our mission is to reach them and mine those vital truths, so we can share them with the next generation.

The Questatement Challenge

A few years back I spoke at a coaches workshop in Southern California and I was pleased that it was so well received. There was an interesting moment in my 'player centered coaching' presentation of *How to get your players to the net*. I was going through the hardest part of the talk, the part when coaches work to execute it, players will have difficulty. There is no escaping the struggle of going from unconsciously incompetent to consciously competent. Some players may have extreme difficulty and want to stop. There is no getting around the fact that when you challenge players with a difficult drill, that it could get pretty ugly for the first few minutes of their performance, and maybe longer. Some fundamental actions may not be performed well, while they struggle to master a new level of challenge. We must allow our players to struggle under assigned challenges. Seeing this struggle, a coach in his mid-twenties or so asked me with a challenging question. I made up a word to describe the way some people ask pointed questions, I call them a 'questatement', it's a question that is really a statement. Coaches often do this to challenge one another. His offering was something to the effect of, 'I have a problem with when you say the player MUST perform this certain action. They should have to make a decision, on their own, right? So you really force them to perform that? It doesn't seem realistic.' His tone of voice was a bit testy.

Stop and think for a moment about how you might react to that moment, when you are speaking to a group. Do you want someone to do that? Would an interaction like that be a problem? Do you want your ideas openly tested in front of 60 coaches, many of whom you don't know? I do! I have tremendous respect for a young coach who will put themselves out with their opinion, like that. Internally, I had to put away my reaction to the tone and body language of this young coach. I was focused on the content of the question as a service to everyone present. I welcomed the question because if he is thinking that, then there must be others, and many people will learn how to respond to challenges as well. So I answered the coach:

'Yes, absolutely, I put the players in a position where they have no choice because I know that given the choice, they won't do it. The decision has been made for them, and all they need to do now is execute. It's freeing, rather than restricting. And yes, you are right it's not realistic, but in the next step of the progression over a number of days, it becomes more realistic. They then will progress to a stage where they have to actively decide to do this action at the right time. Players then learn automatically to recognize the situation that allows them to perform a skill, attacking the situation.'

The Aftermath

Later, a few different veteran coaches said things to me like 'Way to put that young buck in his place.' I responded, 'That's not what I was doing, I was engaging with his challenge, answering it fully, and I am thankful he did that because without it, no one else would have seen the answer to the objection of doing the most crucial step of the progression, so without his challenge, the talk would have not have been as valuable. I hope my tone was not punitive and I expressed my appreciation to that guy for his great challenge.' Perhaps he was a little rough in the way he expressed it, but let's say the way I responded showed him a more refined approach, just as it did the veteran coaches who still have their barbs showing. So I was glad that these experienced coaches said that to me, even though I was initially disappointed by their superior attitudes. I answered because I liked the question saw value in it for everyone. I hope that clipped the edge of a barb right there.

Coaching Arrogance

Quite commonly when I am at a coaching conference, I will hear people who stand back and criticize the poor level, mis- and dis-information being presented, or observe about the coaches at all levels. They say things like 'This is just flat out wrong and harmful', or 'look at the poor level of play among the coaches participating. No wonder we are having such a hard time in this country.' In the next breath I greet them with:

We need coaches of all types at all levels. Great, you are a so-called High Performance Coach, but we need coaches who are moms, we need grandmas and grandpas, we also need inexperienced high school kids and those fresh from college athletics or the professional game. The kids need this mix. For some reason we like to glorify the higher level coaches and players, losing site of the base of a healthy community being filled with players and coaches at every level.

So I don't waste a breath, when I hear this, I tell them right away. We see these levels. Young coaches emerging, experienced coaches working with well-polished tools together or using still unfinished tools to make imprecise cuts, and finally someone to bring them together to do the same work all together in community. The work is never finished.

Important Thought: Action Item(s):

CHAPTER THIRTY-THREE

Modern Complaint Society

There is a national problem of student complaints in collegiate athletics. Coaches seem to refuse to want to set standards for behavior and it ends up costing them in the end.

~ Tom Newkirk - Civil Rights Attorney for Coaches

As the speed at which information can spread multiplies at a new rate almost every day, the time honored traditions of teenage misinformation has not changed. From seemingly the beginning of time, teenagers have gotten it wrong! You can tell them something very specific and many of them just seem to miss the point a little, simplify things, or hear what they want to hear. Great coaches help players to think critically enough to consider their sources of information and communicate in the best possible way. When instituting my program on a high school team, the effort that goes into teaching them how and when to give and get information is one of the more frustration jobs for me.

You have freshmen who listen to other freshmen for their information, and they invariably mix something up between the two. Then when they do the wrong thing at the wrong time, they blame that other kid.

Drifting Away From People Connections

As people drift more and more away from the community of having people they feel a strong connection with, moving more toward a cyber connection to the internet world of social media their seems to be a certain empowerment of anonymity. As people who were raised on social media begin to assume positions of authority, there is a normalization of bad social media behavior that is becoming more and more acceptable.

Cyber bullying, conspiracies hatched in near anonymity, a whole team of kids can hatch a revolt against a coach. The school I am currently coaching at has a very strong social media policy, and they will summarily expel a student for egregious cyber bullying. At our parent's meeting our athletic director explains fully the policy of the school, and it's history of actually expelling a student in recent years, but also gives friendly advice on how to manage it.

Every player should know that anything they ever post on the internet is permanent. Everything on the internet, or in a text, or any other electronic communication can be captured, screen shotted, subpoenaed, etc. I know that many young people today are sending lewd pictures of one another. This kind of behavior can affect your athletes. As a positive role model in your player's lives, it's a great thing to talk about how to approach social media in a positive uplifting way.

Bringing Them Back Alive

A coach can make it one of their top objectives to help teach players how to connect with people on a personal level. This skill above many other skills can help them along their timeline of success. We can also help them avoid being connected so deeply to 'The Matrix', that they can be more alive enjoying so much more the people they encounter on a daily basis.

Important Thought: Action Item(s):

CHAPTER THIRTY-FOUR

Gender Bias: Athlete Complaints

The ends you serve that are selfish
will take you no further than yourself,
but the ends you serve that are for all,
in common, will take you into eternity.

~ Marcus Garvey

I want to be careful to frame this discussion of the complaint culture and gender bias in coaching in the most broad parameters. Let's begin with what is not necessary before going into what is necessary. It's not necessary for a coach to prescribe to an ideology in order to take gender bias seriously. It's not necessary for a coach to call themselves a feminist, nor is it necessary for them to go all in social justice in every aspect of equality. Every coach can and should decide for themselves, and model independent thought, but when it comes to protecting every coach's right to coach within the parameters of acceptable behavior we all need to band together in some way. Some coaches are all in on social justice in every form it takes, and more power to you, but it is necessary to advocate for the equal respect of women in the coaching workplace, even if you aren't trying to fight for everyone else's idea of what justice for all looks like. On the most fundamental level, we can and should get behind the equal treatment of female coaches. Maybe you are like me and you dislike being labeled in any way. Perhaps you enjoy certain labels attached to you, because they affirm your identity and that's fine. I like many don't want to be labeled, because then it seems those applying them don't allow certain behaviors.

We have a choice as coaches what kind of legacy we want to leave behind us. My goal for my legacy is one of developing equality and opportunity for those who might not naturally have been given a chance. Maybe you are the coach who has been the one given a chance. We must advocate for others and advocate for ourselves. I may never be recognized beyond these pages for any efforts I give, and yet that's not the point. Every action large or small can make be pivotal in retaining a coach, advancing them, and/or defending them from undue criticism.

I recently learned of the plight of many female collegiate coaches. There is a problem now of women leaving the coaching ranks, when really we should be seeing an increase. It's a complicated problem, but at it's most simple, female coaches are being criticized for the same behaviors that male coaches are praised for. My very simple theory is that male coaches tend to be given reasonably favorable comparisons to fathers of athletes. Coaches can be seen in their temporary and not 24/7 role as being more altruistic than an athlete's father. Women coaches however naturally would be compared to a mother, and that is a tough comparison to win, especially when the behavior of a successful women coach more closely resembles her male counterpart coach.

No Need For Labels

Every coach needs to take gender bias seriously for a few different reasons. First, I want to make clear that I don't call myself a feminist, and I do that because, you like me might be put off by a militant approach to solving this issue. My goal for this chapter is too bring a common sense approach. First, the number of female athletes is staying steady if not rising, yet the number of female coaches has fallen over the last few years. These words won't be without pain, and that is fitting. We as a coaching community and the sports world in general is beginning to see that women's expertise in coaching is just as good as men's and many women are superior coaches.

Education Of The Institutions

According to Tom, there is a need for education, and he is willing to do it for a small fee or sometimes for no fee, but when a situation gets out of hand, then he has no problem taking a school to court for wrongful discipline or termination. The problem of gender bias in coaching is connected to the modern complaint society. Mr. Newkirk finds that the more elitist and monied a school is, there is a higher likelihood of mistreatment of coaches, and particularly women. In fact, female athletes complain about female coaches far more than any other combination of coach and athlete. When I asked Tom if the problem has to do with unfair comparisons to an athletes parents, Mr. Newkirk indicated that is the simplist way to think about the core issue. So female coaches suffer from an unfair comparison to a player's mother, while a male coach may have an equal or more favorable comparison to a father. It seems like common sense that all coaches should be compared to other coaches. Of course, there can be more complexity in every situation, but in general, male coaches usually draw favorable comparisons to ones own father, simply because there is less time on task, and the coach does not sit in the seat of lifelong disciplinarian for that athlete. Also generally, with obvious exceptions, the coach may be viewed as being more selfless altruistic than the father. As my wife says, good luck with having a female athlete allow her female coach to win a comparison with the athlete's mother. A female coach who does any sort of discipline, or an intense fitness regimine with her team will most likely suffer a very poor comparison the nurturing mother of the athlete. So, something has to change. Of course, many many athletes love their female coach, and there few, if any problems, but when there is it's often a problem of unfair comparisons.

Advocating For Fair And Equal Evaluation And Treatment

When the program has an expectation that all coaches will be judged equally for their character, professionalism, and care of the athlete's long term and short term outcomes, regardless of gender, race or any other characteristic, then that school will be better prepared to qualify complaints in order to proactively deal with the legitimate ones. A school may also hold at bay or vet the frivolous complaints born purely from a bias against the individual that is undue under the circumstances. Some complaints could and should be dismissed if no particular behavior can be identified. This requires some burden of proof. Again according to Newkirk, many complaints come through to administration where the athletic department heads can't or won't identify a behavior or an incident that shows unprofessional behavior from the coach. It would require a description of events, time and day, a close representation of things said and done. It would exclude the subtext of attitudes and feelings. Tom says that usually the coach can start to build a strong case when the school can't or won't identify a standard that was broken, and the behavior that did so. Many schools fail to investigate, that they almost certainly did not even ask the athlete to state the behaviors that are causing the problem. I have faced this in my own career, when anonymous athletes complained about a feeling they had, but could not connect it to an actual incident. So, unfortunately, without that information, I don't know if something needs to change. When the school does not ask for any specifics, then they are really falling into a sort of trap sprung by the student athletes. They can easily misinform the school and their parents, when they are not pressed into sharing specific details of what actually happened.

Developing Institutional Standards

Whatever your organization, league, or institution, it's vital that very specific standards are set for all coaches to abide by. Again, Tom Newkirk indicates that for some reason coaches fail to set standards of behavior for which they will be held accountable. This though will empower them when they put forward a common sense outline of where the line is drawn between great coaching behavior and maladaptive. Get together with your group, set the standards for behavior, and make sure they are applicable to the male and female coaches. This type of standard setting must be reaffirmed annually, or whenever their is turnover in your coaching ranks. When male and female coaches unite to say they all stand for the same principles, then that will protect all of them from undue criticism. Similarly identifying student/athlete behaviors that are in line or out of line with the mission of the organization will help solidify the overall educational mission of your group. This way any undue criticism of male or female coaches will be easy to identify. Without developing those standards, there is no basis of comparison. So, the next time you have a coaches meeting broach this subject. If the standards are vague, work to make them more specific and explicit.

Important Thoughts: Action Item(s):

CHAPTER THIRTY-FIVE

Good Coach Citizenship

Failure to prepare is preparing to fail.

~ Gen. George S. Patton

Preparing to succeed in the long term requires the development of good relationships with our fellow coaches. Coaches in our league, conference, region, or those private coaches who teach specific skills to our our players in or out of season, those are the ones we are best served to create as much collaboration with as we can. Some coaches are potential mentors, and others might benefit from being mentored by us. How we engage our fellow coaches in the direct community of competition in our region creates a strong learning model for our players. Being friendly, organized, professional and cooperative for the sake of all the players in the league and beyond helps set the tone for great sportsmanship. Create community, by being a community leader. Speaking into existence a better environment in which your athletes can grow to see the bigger picture of life after competition. It would be hard to say you are an athlete centered coach, if you poison the atmosphere with other teams and coaches. As I write this, some coaches come to mind who have done just that, making the competitive experience less one of fun and enjoyment, and more one of jealous and hateful rivalry. I'm not saying that you aren't going to have an 'Us v. Them' approach on the field, simply that outside the lines and whistles we will do our best to be as friendly as is wise. Some coaches have tried to take advantage of my fairly easy going nature to try to fool me, or pull a fast one with the rules or what not. It's at that point that I stop being quite as friendly with those who begin to prove themselves less trustworthy. Honestly, I am not above meeting the challenge head on with those coaches, fighting fire with fire (inside the rules), but keeping all of my interactions civil and diplomatic.

Don't Make It Personal

Sometimes my players know when the other coach has been abusive to the relationship, and when I ask them NOT to make it personal, they almost always do, and tend to play great in those moments. Even so, I strongly recommend not making the difficulty with another coach personal, keep it as professional as possible.

Diplomacy, Civility and Responsibility

Being a professional coach means communicating in a timely fashion, showing up to meetings early, helping make the meeting flow, and pushing forward agendas that are good for the most possible players in the league. Learning to express your ideas in a very concise manner is key to helping everyone save time. Too often coaches think only of what is best for their own team, instead of what is best for the league overall, they also look to serve mainly the elite players, and not what is best for the most players in league. Of course, we do need to promote and facilitate for those who have made the greatest commitment to the sport, so we do need to seek balance in that way. I have seen leagues that seem to punish good players for being elite, and with a ghetto mentality seem to want to circumvent their success out of jealousy. Other leagues put the top players first in all things, and the interests of most players are an after thought. Bottom line, look for the best outcomes for the most players while not blocking the progress of the best, and you can find yourself in a position of leadership in your area. Create synergy with all like minded coaches in this regard. Being mentally prepared to grow into new roles of service in your sport is helpful in growing your influence and career.

When you seek to do the best for the most, you are sure to encounter some push back. Be mentally prepared to do the work of creating consensus for doing what is best. I promise you that when you take an established practice, and try to make it better, there is a high likelihood that someone will get upset. It's been said, "Good is the enemy of Best', and sadly too many coaches settle into being satisfied with low level of service to the athletes. Ultimately, my main argument that I use when we are discussing these things is 'aren't we all here for the players, all of them?'. That rhetorical question brings to light how easy it is for forget that simple fact, that coaches are there in service to athletes to promote their best opportunities to play, learn and have access.

Important Thought: Action Item(s):

CHAPTER THIRTY-SIX

Ups and Downs

Two standing back to back can fight off a crowd, and three cord strand is not easily broken.

~ King Solomon

When athletics are at their best, 'real life' inserts itself into the competitive atmosphere. I know I can be fairly obsessively dedicated to my team or players, and I expect that same kind of approach. Real adversity strikes players and coaches. Some tough choices need to be made. I recently wrote a blog post about hitting the wall mentally and emotionally. One of the grim realities of coaching is that we are going to have moments of weakness, we will have situations that are outside of our control. A great example is the De La Salle High School football team, which faced the death of a star player's mother, and the death of a recent graduate who would have been on his way from very difficult conditions in the inner city to play for a premier NCAA football school. Moments of weakness are part of the landscape. It's the community support structure that we coaches create, that determines whether we can overcome together. How else will a team deal with intense levels of grief and still soldier onward.

Feedback and Comfort Level

What was refreshing for me was that these coaches felt compelled to discuss that blog with me. The feedback was that the way I presented the blog sounded like complaining, but I had no problem with that. Part of developing community is authentic dialogue with people sharing their true thoughts. The fact that this coach took the time to reach out, connect, show concern, and interact on a dark topic was helpful to me. Interestingly enough, I had been going through a time of considerably low energy, due to exhaustion from a lengthy trip, followed by a pretty tough illness that laid me out for over two weeks. The result of all these things working together was amazing. First, I wrote the blog, then the feedback came, then I (mistakenly?) did not post the blog onto the WordPress, I only sent it to our email list.

We Might Create Confusion Before Clarity

This coach responded wondering what the message was, and what the lesson was, as he was confused by what seemed to be a negative tone. My good friend Styrling chimed in, after that email came in, and we had a talk. I responded to the email explaining the lesson of experiencing these negative outcomes, even when I thought I was seemingly doing everything right. I pursued my processes the best way I knew how, and was willing to adapt, but those I wanted to collaborate with were determined not to work with me.

The Law of the Master Mind

We are still dependent at times for the success of any group to have people with genuinely common goals. Ideally when we meet fully like-minded people with an aligned mission, amazing things can happen. When I had hit rock bottom with low energy, and was really depressed to a degree, I shared that with Styrling, and that's when the magic happened. When I shared that vulnerable moment with a fellow coach, he proceeded to pick me up. What he did not know is that I had delayed in calling a potential new client because my energy was low, and I knew that if I called that person to make a sales pitch, that there was very little likelihood of success in gaining that client. Styrling's energy became my energy, I was able to shift my mindset back on a growth track. Shortly thereafter, I called that potential new client and we had a very good conversation, which led to an easy sales conversion. Now, that was over a year ago, and that client became a steady source of income over an entire year.

Looking back on this, there were some very positive outcomes. Obviously I gained a client, but how can I be sure that it wasn't the experience that I had, that created the synergy with her? Also, I put out a message that I am not invincible and I do believe there must be a coach out that can be helped by knowing that putting on a false front is not the solution. The more mature and experienced coaches, many times put on an air of invincibility and that may not help younger coaches in our field to acknowledge their own. It's not easy to create empathy with the seemingly impervious.

Opening Up Possibility for Engagement

My moment of weakness create a chance for greater understanding with that coach who reached out to me. By opening up my experience to the coaching world, then the possibility exists that someone will reach out to me in their time of need, or to someone they trust. The outcome of my 'complaining' was awesome because now people know much more about about who I really am, which only enhances the authenticity of my coaching relationship with them. Finally, the coaching synergy between Styrling and I was increased as it came to light, we had a larger purpose beyond what looked like a failed blog post. So, the jury is out on whether it was a failure, but it lead to a great conversation, so in that respect the outcome was positive and uplifting.

The Seemingly Impervious

A while back, I was at a coaching conference and I met a coach who was a multiple time NCAA National Champion. We talked for about 10 minutes, he told me to look him up on Facebook, which I did. We interacted a bit more and I invited him for an interview on my podcast. What happened next really surprised me. He told me how great it was to feel valued again, that for years he had felt left out and no longer a part of things. He credited our 10 minute talk and FB follow up with encouraging him. I was blown away, as we naturally assume that people who have achieved lofty goals in their lives and careers will always be surrounded by friends, that they don't have any dark moments. This is when athlete-centered coaches, reach out to other coaches to get them back on the rails, as then the work can continue better and stronger when we look out for each other. So, right now I want to challenge you to reach out to a coach from whom you haven't heard anything in a while. You might just be catching them in a low spot, lifting them up. Bottom line: never underestimate your value in another coach's life, and never underestimate your value in the same way.

Important Thought: Action Item(s):

CHAPTER THIRTY-SEVEN
Handling Pushback

To announce that there must be no criticism of the President,
or that we are to stand by the President,
right or wrong, is not only unpatriotic and servile,
but is morally treasonable to the American public.

~ Theodore Roosevelt

Character development is a two way street. In order to gain the most growth as coaches, we also need to allow for the pushback that comes from players and even parents. If we are going to dish it out, we also have to take it. We are going to be challenged, and questioned on the how and why we do things, it's extremely valuable to have great answers, and when we don't to find them quickly.

Where Does Dissent Come From?

How do we handle pushback from players and parents? Often, the pushback is not coming from a good place, but many times it is. I wish we could have an open dialogue, so that you can share with me how you deal with dissenting views in and around your program. I call pushback any time players or parents seemingly have a divergent view of any part of the mission, objectives, goals, or activities of the team, players or coach. Inexperienced coaches can be prone to interpreting a little dissent with an attack on the program or the person of the coach. Many times things that are misunderstood, twisted, undiscovered, or otherwise unknown can be discussed in a collaborative setting and become powerful bonding moments that bring greater cohesion to the program. We all see things from our own perspective, yet we always need those who can see our blind spot. So, it's very important to patiently listen to anyone who has a question or concern. This can feel very irksome, especially when you know that the person who is approaching this is only thinking of their own selfish interests. Even so, moments like that create an opportunity to win or lose them. We can reassert, reassure that person about the strength of the program, or that the issue will be addressed.

Styrling and Bill: Fire and Ice

Just prior to writing this chapter, my main collaborator on this book, Styrling and I were having what is normally our Monday morning meeting and in it, we both expressed gratitude that we each have each other's blind spot. Our nickname for us is 'Fire and Ice', because Styrling comes across a bit more passionate, and I come across more cold and calculating. Although the some items call into question whether I am icy or not. Together we cover each other's blind spots as much as possible, and we each count on others to help make us better. One of the areas where players and parents question coaches often is on the need for top players to play against inferior opposition. That is a legitimate concern, so here are our answers for that.

Styrling's Take on Pushback

This past week, my high school team, which is made up of state ranked junior players, played a team that was weaker at every position. I talked with my players, letting them know that they had a great opportunity to push themselves and experiment with a new strategy, to try different ways of winning. They could go outside their normal comfort zone to use a tactic in which they previously did not have much confidence. I challenged my #1 through #6 singles players to be more aggressive, after the serve and the return. I challenged some of them to come to forward to finish points at the net.

Seizing Opportunities That Most Don't See

I had a particularly interesting conversation with the parent of one of my top four players. She was just coming off a shoulder injury, so I decided to play her at #6 singles position to get her back in the groove. Her father came up to me before she took the court and asked if I was going to give her an opportunity to play more 'competitive' matches? (He knew this team was a weaker team in our schedule, so his concern for his daughter playing a much weaker player was understandable), I calmly explained to him that I had spoken to her before the match about the strategy I'd like to see her use against her opponent. I encouraged her to play as if she was competing against a high level competitor. I wanted her to look for and attack every short ball, on the rise, to her opponent's backhand side, with unrelenting force. I asked her to knock the cover off the ball and then approach and finish with a volley or smash. I told her I wanted her to end the point quickly and take every opportunity to do so within her confidence level. Even if she missed, she should go at the next ball with even more confidence. She finished the match in only twenty-four minutes with a decisive win. Most importantly, she was excited about the way she played and had executed tactically and forcefully. So while parents may pushback, or give suggestions, really the coach should give the most weight to the player's experience.

The Follow Up

The father came up to me and was extremely pleased at the way his daughter played so confidently, finishing the points decisively. I believe that I was able to open up his mind to the other side of the coin, which is, a player can make something incredible out of any opportunity (even if that opportunity seems less than optimal at the time). Over the years, I've realized that a coach can affect his players and parents in a positive way by first listening, then offering perspective about underlying opportunities. It's similar to a great painting that is covered partially by a sheet and you can only see just 1/2 of the picture and then someone comes over and pulls away the sheet to reveal the best part that was hidden, they removed the blind spot that revealed the complete masterpiece.

Five out of our six singles players finished that day in less than an hour, they actually showed mercy to the other team by playing all out and competing at their best, and finishing the match quickly, so that everyone could go home and do homework. My team learned a valuable less about competition: always give it your best and respect your opponent in this way.

Player's Question My Timing

Another instance of pushback involves the training for a high school team. I maximize my pre-competitive phase of training and it continues through the beginning of pre-season matches. In the short term, my team's results can be affected, easy matches might become more difficult as players who are sore and tired are already competing.

It's even possible for the team to take a loss in the early going, instead of win, if we had not been training so hard. Players and parents have complained to me, questioning, 'Why are we working out like this, when we have a match tomorrow? If we lose tomorrow, that will affect our seeding in playoffs.' To which I respond with, 'What is more important, being seeded higher, or being more prepared for success at the end? Would you rather have a higher seed, feeling the pressure of that higher placement while less prepared, or be the lower seed primed and trained to upset the higher rated team?' My teams seem to regularly pull major upsets. Most recently Amy as a #3 seed beat the #2 and #1 seed in the same day to win the first ever tennis championship in the 60 year history of the school. She thanked me for the conditioning. In an 18 month period, three consecutive playoff seasons, boy's and girl's, my #9th seeded boy's beat #8 and #1, my #10th seeded girls beat #7 and #2, and my #3rd seeded boys beat #2 and #1 in 97-degree heat to win a section title. The girls went on to win the section title the next year without me. I think it had something to do with being ready and not early season results. Their new coach called me after they won to thank me, 'The girls wanted to thank you for showing them the way in terms of work ethic and what it will take to win a championship.'

Future Proves Past

If you are seeing improvement, then what you did in the past is working. You will have little in the way of disruption from players or parents when they see the results of what you do, but it takes time. I set the goal of having the most improved team in my league, and sometimes I can claim to have among the most improved teams in my region. Sometimes, the result is not the score on the scorecard, but instead the feeling of accomplishment the player has inside them. The intrinsic value of improvement is something that can't be calculated. Winning is easy to see on the outside, but if you look for it, it's not hard to find on the inside also. No matter what the results are on the scoreboard, going forward with a strong process will reap the most improvement, and thus the most satisfaction. Who can argue with that?

Important Thought: Action Item(s):

CHAPTER THIRTY-EIGHT
Athlete Centered Coaches

*When we honestly ask ourselves which person in our lives
mean the most to us, we often find that it is those who,
instead of giving advice, solutions, or cures, have chosen
rather to share our pain and touch our wounds with a
warm and tender hand. The friend who can be silent with
us in a moment of despair or confusion, who can stay
with us in an hour of grief and bereavement, who can tolerate
not knowing, not curing, not healing and face with us
the reality of our powerlessness, that is a friend who cares.*

~ Henri Nouwen, Out of Solitude

I took a trip to Southern California to meet with a few people that I consider to have among the great mindsets for athlete centered coaching. I spent three days with Dave Borelli, who in 25 years of Division I level coaching won 18 Conference Titles and 7 NCAA National Championships. The amazing thing to me is how fluid the subject of athlete-centered coaching is when people first encounter the phrase. It seems that when people hear the phrase, it excites them, but they might not have heard it before and when they do, it fires their imagination. It's fun to see the moments when players are quickly processing their interpretation of it. It's a powerful thing to declare to your players, coaching staff and parents, 'I am an athlete centered coach'. They then will look at you a little differently, you then are in 'prove it' and 'define it' mode from then onward. That's the first thing I see in my athletes when I use the phrase, is the effect it has on them. After a little more challenge, people necessarily have to consider that athlete-centered coaching may mean something different to someone else. Some people wrongly assume that it means pandering to a player's whims. It's a timeless concept and has always existed, I did not coin the phrase but it describes the best of what we do. The concept is yours to mold and shape for you and your players. The way you manifest it will be uniquely yours, and it will create a unique relationship with you and those you train.

Empathy

It also brings the empathy back into play, because there seems to be an unspoken expectation that if someone is going to be athlete centered, then they necessarily have to know upon whom they are centered. Quite often, we begin with what something means to us, then we tend to project it out on other people. We then turn that around, thinking first about what it means to them, then we have a better view of how to guide them. When we listen and become more empathetic and understanding of other people's mindsets, then we have a choice to adapt what we do for that person or not. While there are exceptions where we don't adapt to the player, we force them to adapt to us, we first ask the question of why is in the best long term interests of the person we coach.

Knowing the Intra-Team Relationships

I interviewed Adeline Arjad-Cook, author of I Love My Doubles Partner, and one of her main points was that our coaches should know the relationships between players. An athlete-centered coach knows their team and the dynamics that exist between players. They will know how to put the complimentary personalities together. Great coaches also cull players out of their personal comfort zone and help them to play well with teammates with whom they might not be the most comfortable. This is one of the greatest life skills to be found in sports, being a good teammate with someone that you might not choose to be friends. Maybe the partner is non-communicative, or perhaps they are very abrupt or forceful in their style of interaction on court. Great coaches help players to branch out into a wider range of possibilities in their relationships, teaching the social skills of interaction on the most civil level. I know some doubles teams I have had created some comedy because of the 'odd couple' dynamic, but those teams found a way to succeed. Early on team captains can become tyrants when they are new to the role, because they assume that they have to boss their peers around to gain their respect. Poor coaches accept a fixed mentality from their players and have rigid guidelines, some players may say 'I only play well with ____ as my partner', but we know that isn't true. Great coaches foster a growth mentality, and the team grows closer together because of it.

Team Only Meeting

The story about a group that needed a team only meeting lead by captains points to a difference in mindsets. Some players wanted desperately to succeed, others wanted to succeed, but were not very driven. A few girls wanted their own way, their own mind. The pivotal moment came when the girls who wanted to win, created a new agreement about mindset among their teammates. That mindset remained after those leaders and I both were gone. The following year, they won the section title, which was not something that the school had come close to achieving in school history for that team.

National Champion Vision

Dave Borelli a great college coach of men and women, but mostly women's teams, spent time at USC and TCU. He would tell his players, 'It's not that we are much better than our opposition, but let's just act like we are better.' When I asked Dave to describe how his athlete-centered coaching helped cultivate these championship performances, he told me that there is no way he could give a simple answer or even answer that in an hour's time. Bottom line, it was the close relationships he had with each player that allowed him to know when to make a technical change, boost up their confidence, ask for more discipline, help a player through a tough time of life, etc. When players did not buy into his program, he also faced some difficulty. He expressed the difficulty in putting people first who are not honest with you. As a college coach, you recruit your players, but sometimes you get some unwelcome surprises. Dave is happy that he had great relationships with 99% of his players.

Detailed Observations

The image that keeps coming to my mind is a horse trainer and the keen sense of observation and the training of minute changes in behavior until maximum speed, balance, and maneuverability are achieved. Of course, people are not animals, but there is an element of knowing when to push, chide, wait, question, listen, and all the other small activities that go into coaching a player for many hours over what can be a years long relationship.

In each case, the athlete-centered coach is mindful and takes the time to know who they are dealing with, as well as helping them find avenues of success. There is also an element of not always being in absolute control of everything, allowing the players to show leadership, developing stronger relationships amongst themselves. Sometimes the athlete-centered coach knows when to step aside, not involved in something that they can't help, allowing players to solve their own problem. I know that in every one of my most enjoyable and successful years as a coach, the captains on those teams were also great leaders. As you have seen in previous chapters, the captains can also make things more difficult for a coach to work on those relationships with the team at-large.

Coaches V. Teachers

To conclude, perhaps the most important aspect of being an athlete-centered coach is learning when to move a relationship forward and closer, knowing when to stop, and knowing when to pull back, giving players room to establish their own identity on the team. There is a reason why coaches tend to be more influential than teachers or professors, and it mostly has to do with the the many hours of time on task, and the much longer relationship that can be up to five years and beyond.

Important Thought: Action Item(s):

CHAPTER THIRTY-NINE
Crazy Tough Coaches

**What vulnerabilities do we have and what can
we do to minimize them, to get around them, to survive
them—and give ourselves a better chance to win?**

~ Bob Knight, The Power of Negative Thinking

People toss around very intense words like sociopath or psychopath with way too much ease these days. I will not share the true definitions here, but those definitions are at risk of losing their meaning as people apply those words inappropriately. Sometimes among the most intense coaching circles, there are coaches who are seen to have psychopathic or sociopathic tendencies. Because these coaches also have lengthy track records of success, there is a transaction that occurs mentally and emotionally among the players and parents who seek out these coaches help. If they go to this person, they will have to be ready to absorb what might feel like abuse. An all-time classic example is Bobby Knight. But what lurks under the surface of the true facts of Bobby Knight? Sure, people remember Coach Knight's worst moments, and they are not excusable by any means. But it seems to be a shame that people don't realize how fiercely loyal he is to friends and former players. Additionally, why does his outstanding graduation rate, which is the greatest in the history of the NCAA not get enough attention? What is the whole point of attending college? Is it to become a professional basketball player? Is it to do 'one and done'? The strange system of basketball where coaches knowingly engage players who might only stay one year, so that they can leap frog into the NBA defeats the purpose of collegiate athletics. It also sends the wrong message to a generation of hopefuls, that they really only need to do minimal school work. Or is the whole point to get an education, learn about excellence, and carry those lessons forward? I might counter that there are basketball coaches who might seem more kind than Knight, but some are known for having horrendous graduation rates, so what does that mean in the greater scheme of things? How athlete centered is a college coach if they are not prioritizing the academic success of their athletes? Coaches that do not require or even aid in assisting players in attaining the most important benefit of a university are not athlete centered. In reality, the coaches who on the surface seem to be pleasant and helpful are the true sociopaths if they take advantage of young men and young women for their own success, while not ensuring that they will have the best opportunities for future success in their student athlete's lives.

World Class Tennis Success at a Cost

There is a case of a Southern California tennis coach that I won't name. He has an amazing track record of success in molding top tennis players. Many, many great players were molded by this man. He himself lived a traumatic life in his youth, which may have served to give him a completely different perspective on life than many of us have. Surviving among the worst conditions of World War Two is a life changing experience. This coach is known for being brash, curmudgeonly, and for sometimes saying things that are inappropriate for young ears. So, knowing all this, a parent would have to know their child, their make-up and wiring, to see if they are fit and/or resistant enough to stand up to the comedic acerbic bullying of the coach.

Tough Love

In reality, this coach has a very big heart and the love he expresses in his voice is unmistakable, but the form of the words and the force with which they are delivered really pressures the player, really draws excellence out of them. Children sometimes cry at these lessons. Not uncommonly, they cry in the first lesson. Sometimes, they never return. I sat with this coach for hours, talking about the method to his madness. He mentioned that his first job is to create an early first impression, so that there is no wasted time on his court. Players should make the best of every moment. There is a built in discipline to every thing he does. Prior to meeting a new student for the first time, he arranges with the current student on court, 'As soon as you see the car door open, I want you to make a mistake, then I am going to yell at you, don't worry, you are doing fine, but I'm just going to yell at you, and you take it seriously and do better, ok?' The new player arrives near the end of the proceeding lesson, coach yells, and the tone is set. 'I want them to know that they have to want to do well all the time.'

After a full day spent with this coach, the next day, I had a chance encounter with a player at a professional event. I asked him where he was from, and one thing lead to another and I discovered that this player in fact had one lesson with this great coach, cried, and did not come back. He later went on to become a Division 1 scholarship player on a National Championship Team. Later, I joked with the coach 'Great job coach, you gave this young man one lesson and he became a college player.' He laughed and made a derogatory comment in good fun, and we continued our conversation. So, now, while this offends some people's sensitivity, other people have larger filters that allow them to weed out any of the apparent negatives. It was also told to me that some conversations that have happened with young children were of an adult nature that could put parents in a very difficult position of explaining things they don't want to explain.

What is Fun?

I don't recommend acting the same way as Bobby Knight and this other coach. But if you are a coach who believes in helping athletes learn to be disciplined, then you are going to get some criticism from the other end of the spectrum who view that as abusive. There will be those parents and administrators who simply want to the kids to have 'fun', but their definition is vague, and they might not have any concept of how fun it is to play at a high level. I guarentee you that those who have played for the two tough coaches, developing a great relationship with them, have gone on to achieve amazing successes because of the discipline they learned in their lives that can be applied to any arena. For myself, it wasn't until I became a much more disciplined and determined athlete, that I was able to apply that to my studies, become an acceptable college student, and a minimally acceptable graduate student. The tough love I was shown, have helped me to become an author, and you as a coach have the opportunity to build these kinds of things into your students lives.

Important Thoughts: Action Item(s):

CHAPTER FORTY

Mental Skills v. Therapy

Mental skills are a more long-term solution than therapy as it teaches us coping skills that prove to be necessary and give us the tools and the foundation of our everyday lives.

~ Dr. Michelle Cleere

We can do a lot to inform ourselves about the key components of sports psychology from a performance aspect, taking a more holistic life skills approach to how we coach and teach. I encourage every coach to get themselves an 'unofficial' masters degree in sports psychology as I jokingly call it. We get so many practical mental issues to solve, it's a shame we don't get the piece of paper that goes with it.

Get yourself an introductory textbook for a masters, then read up on the most influential sports psychologists in your area. We have the opportunity to be the first person to lay out fundamental structures for our athletes. Our credibility with parents can take a pretty big jump when we bring in a well noted Sport Psychologist to talk with our players. Our roles will be more limited when we have more athletes to deal with on a daily basis. At some point it becomes time for a professional referral to a Sport Psychologist, like Dr. Michelle Cleere, one of the best in the business.

It's good to do some shopping in your area for someone who can work face to face, but the internet age actually allows for coaching more or less face to face from around the world, so maybe look up Dr. Cleere. This all is a preface to this guest chapter by Michelle. There are no cookie cutter approaches here or solutions given, but a general discussion of why a referral to a mental skills specialist can be a great idea for your athlete or team.

Reprinted and lightly edited from michellecleere.com

MENTAL SKILLS VERSUS THERAPY
IN COMPETITION, CONTROL, EMOTION

It's ironic that therapy has grown in popularity but mental skills still seems to be creeping along. There was a period where therapy almost seemed like a fad. It was the cool thing to do. When will mental skills training become the cool thing to do? I think the time is now.

Mental skills are a more long-term solution than therapy as it teaches us coping skills that prove to be necessary on many levels and give us the tools and the foundation of our everyday lives.

Therapy

There are many types of therapy and I am not here to knock therapy. I was in therapy for many years of my life and without it might not be where I am today. However, when I was in therapy, I was a bit broken. I needed someone to listen and help me to understand why I was dealing with life the way I was. I suppose at that time I needed to get to the root of what was troublesome and realize I didn't need to be that person anymore. While I recall sometimes transitioning my thinking to reflect conversations in therapy, I don't remember consciously changing any behaviors. Sure, the behaviors came along as my thought process was changing but it took a very long time for that to happen. Although I was VERY broken at that time. I advise that you refer a player to a mental skills specialist, who can help deal with issues that may be misinterpreted as mental illness, and let that mental skills specialist make a referral to therapy. My experience is that parents sometimes feel like their child is mentally ill, when really they simply lack skills.

Mental Skills

There is some overlap between therapy and developing mental skills. The biggest is that during the initial assessment the client does share their story. I ask a lot of open-ended questions to learn information about the whole person. I ask questions to explore when things started changing and what was going on during that time. From that point, mental skills training starts to diverge away from therapy.

Every individual is different. How they learn is different. And their current situation is unique. After I get to know them, I begin to determine what they need and how I can help:

* develop a deeper awareness of what's happening
                        (who, what, where, when, and how)
* develop a new coping skill
* practice developing the new coping skill while performing
* introduce sport coping into everyday life
* tweak the new coping skill if necessary
* reinforce it
* repeat the process for other new coping skills
* transfer skills to other areas of life
* put a plan together for further development

Mental skills development is, of course, about listening to a client tell their story and their changing story. However, it's largely about helping them to figure out how effective their current coping skills are, re-develop them, and/or develop entirely new ones. The re-development or development of the right mental skills is entirely based on what's going to work for every individual.

Each client walks away with an individualized plan based on their needs. Developing the plan in the absence of the coach or team, can bring a new clarity to the situation.

Coping

Coping is learning how to deal with and take control of situations and thoughts. Many of us cope just by reacting and responding. The problem is, we don't often think about how we are acting and responding and sometimes how ineffective it is. In this scenario, coping is often seen as a struggle but it doesn't have to be.

Coping might always be a challenge, but more so in certain situations. When you have the opportunity to develop mental skills that are more effective and have more than one way to deal with situations, you discover how much easier it becomes. Learning how to deal with certain situations in the relative safety of a one on one interaction with someone not extremely close to the situation can bring better perspective.

You have more control and then can be more consistent in whatever it is that you are doing.

Mental Skills for All Areas of Your Life

In sports, rather than allowing your nerves to get the best of you prior to competition, you can learn to understand what nerves mean, how and when they start and how to deal with them. Being overly nervous can be debilitating and effect how you start a competitive feat. That then can snowball and impact an entire performance.

In business, rather than allowing your fear of not being good enough effect you prior to giving a presentation, learn to understand what the fear is, how and when it happens and how to deal with it. Fear is debilitating and will affect how you start a presentation which then can snowball and impact our entire presentation. This is an obvious way that practicing mental skills in sports can aid us in our future professional lives.

In school, rather than trying to be what you think everyone else wants you to be, caring too much about what everyone else thinks about you, understand who you are, learn how to be OK with it and realize that you can't please everyone, nor do you have control over what anybody else is thinking.

In music, rather than worrying about whether you'll win the audition before the audition even starts, learn to stay present and just play. You only control the process of your performance. If you stay in the process, that means you've done your best. It's the only way to get the outcome you desire.

In life, rather than just reacting to situations, stop to think and understand how you are responding to them and why you are responding that way. For most people who have never had the opportunity to develop optimal mental skills, they discover that their 'why' is usually because it's the only way they know how, or that they've never understood the fear and doubt behind how they are acting and responding.

I work with many clients in all of the above areas. Coaches do a better job to branch out the thinking of what they teach to reach the other interests and goals of their athletes lives. We don't necessarily develop new mental skills for all areas of a person's life, but we talk about transitioning mental coping skills from one area to another. For example, many of my younger clients need a way to cope with nerves before competition and tests. The way to do that is the same or similar when dealing with other situations that arise in life.

Mental Skills Empower You

My passion is to help clients develop mental skills; not treat people as though they are broken. It's about building the coping mechanisms they need so they can deal with their environment in the most optimal way. Until you have the proper mental skills for you, the way that you are dealing with your environment is the only way you know how to deal with your environment. You really don't have control over what's happening.

Mental skills give you the ability to have more control over how you compete, and how you deal with negativity, doubt, nerves, stress, and how you view mistakes. These coping abilities allow you to perform more consistently and learn to enjoy the process – enjoy the match, public speaking, and that audition, or any other performance.

Let's take the stigma out of developing mental skills because they are an equal part of the equation, (physical being the other part) in anything you do. Let's make developing mental skills the new fad. My hunch is that once you realize that you could be much more effective and feel so much better about whatever it is you do, you will be happier and more successful.

You may wonder if a athlete is mentally ill. Making a first referral to a mental skills specialist who is professionally certified can be a great first step. Many times the person who learns new skills is fine in no time. The mental specialist then may make a determination if that person has much deeper needs, and at that time you the coach are insulated from the social ramifications of making that referral. In the long run, there is a greater chance that you may continue a coaching relationship with the player, and you avoid the consequences of a parent or athlete accusing you of 'calling me crazy'. The mental skills coach will retain the client confidentiality which is so helpful to the athlete moving forward in their lives.

Important Thought: Action Item(s):

CHAPTER FORTY-ONE
Hazing

Hazing (verb)
Usually part of initiations into a group of some sort. Commonly done by pouring nasty food over people, making them do humiliating things, and other ways.

The cops showed up right when we were done hazing the newbies with sardines, mustard, and marshmallows.

~ The Urban Dictionary

I have been accused of hazing.

Before I tell that story in vague generalities, I want you to know without any equivocation, that I do not support hazing in any form. Athlete centered coaches do not succumb to traditions of abuse. The notion that 'We had to go through it, and so must you' is really outdated, and does not really add anything to the experience of the athlete, and is at best annoying and at worst dangerous to life and limb, or psychologically scarring.

Let's turn to two different dictionaries to try to define this word: Merriam-Webster's

Definition of hazing
: the action of hazing
especially : an initiation process involving harassment

There is no clear cut definition of hazing, and yet when its defined by a school and coaches or players are found guilty, then it creates a pox on the program. Other definitions include the word ritual. I state early in my program that there will be no hazing ritual, and while I look for signs of it, there have been incidents that could be called hazing that have occurred behind closed doors, or out of my sight.

The Straw Man

I have been burned by this, and it was at a school that had a reputation for pretty intense hazing for a high school. The swim team was known for having a complete shave down ritual, and the shaving was complete, and done by classmates. This of course violates the privacy of the person. Another team at the school was known for concocting vile liquids for a player on their team to drink that included human hair of different types. This would induce vomiting in the athlete. The school was extremely embarassed when these stories would become public and I am not sure if a coach was ever fired over these things, but the principal at the school certainly wanted to appear to have things under control.

My case was interesting, because at what point does teasing become harassment? When is celebrating a player who makes a breakthrough become a 'ritual'. During one season I had three very troublesome freshmen players. One was a bit rebellious, another was extremely flaky with equipment and uniforms, and the third was a liar and a cheat. Early on, I informed my athletic director that I was having a problem with the three, and I kept him appraised of the situation as it developed. Within a few weeks I had dealt two of the players and they were with the program and fully integrated. The third player had a strong reputation of being dishonest. I took him at face value, even when there were times I knew he was lying. When something went wrong for him, he seemed always to try to blame someone else first, and each time it turned out that he was throwing someone under the bus. My team captain assured me that he would take care of this kid. I was at my wits end.

Team Leadership Misconstrued

So my captain took over as the trouble player's counterpart and main practice partner on the team, and was constantly in his ear. Over a couple weeks, I saw a dramatic improvement in the troubling players attitude, commitment to the team, and truthfulness with me and others. So, impromptu, I decided to have a ceremony to welcome this player to the team. It lasted under 5 minutes, and while there were a few awkward comments it was fun, and meant as a backhanded compliment. A few minutes after this was over, I went directly to the player to check on him. I specifically asked 'How are you? Are you doing ok?'. To which he answered yes, and I kept my eye on him, during the rest of practice, and all seemed fine, until…

On the way home from practice I got a call from my athletic director stating that I was to meet with him and the principal at 11:00 AM the following day, where I was informed that I was suspended in lieu of an investigation. All of this was happening in the final week of the regular season before playoffs. I was shocked. As the meeting went on, the principal bragged that she had helped get her daughter's division I college fired. I offered to quietly resign at the end of the season, since my team did not need the distraction in what could be a sectional championship year. The principal would not accept that, and I would not accept going through an investigation during this sensitive time. I weighed my options, and resigned that night, writing the story to hand to my friend who was the sports writer for the local newspaper. I was ordered not to have any contact with my players, but my captains kept calling me, so I gave them one final chat.

Team Responds To Adversity

The captains would have to practice the positive energy that we had talked about for two full years. They would have to keep the team on track without me.

My assistant coach and the athletic director had a talk to find out the rules of sectional playoff matches, which are open to the public. I was not barred from attending events. I attended each playoff match, and since tennis is an interesting open air event, there is no defined sideline, there are no rules about coaches communicating with outside observers. I would watch matches, and whisper in the ear of my former assistant, who was now the acting head coach and my athletic director and they would do the coaching. It all worked out incredibly as the players were the ones who showed incredible leadership in one of the worst disruptions you can have in a season. In fact, in the sectional finals, they made an amazing and spirited come back winning the final 4 sets in three different matches to come from a 3-1 deficit to win 4-3.

At the the end of that competition, the parents of my former trouble player complained about my presence, even after their son was in the match that clinched the championship, and my guidance assisted that team. I was barred from communicating with the team at the regional championship level, even though we had a legitimate shot at making the finals of the regionals.

A Great Ending

Ultimately, the story came out well for the players and created a more dramatic tale. For me, it was needless drama that meant even if I was found innocent of all charges, the culture of that school was not a good fit for me. So, did I approach the borderline of hazing? I would have to say yes, because someone had it in their mind that it was. Do I agree with their assessment? Absolutely not.

It's something surprised me, and I don't mind telling the story in order to help protect you from similar folly. I strongly recommend that if you have a hazing ritual to stop, and also to consider that some moments that seem innocent enough, even playful teasing, can me misconstrued and turned into something to fit an agenda. Someone could try to make you a straw man that is easy to knock down to show that they are in charge, and doing something about larger deeper problems, even when really they are not and those problems continue unabated.

For my part, I forgive the young man, and hope that he learned how to be a great teammate in life. As for the parents, I forgive them, but will not forget as it seems that they were the ones who initiated this effort in a misguided way. I realize that that you the reader may interpret this story any way you like, but let it stand as a warning that someone else's standards for what is considered hazing may be different than your own, and it can affect your timeline!

My Stance

I abhor hazing, but I do believe in working with players to mold character, and in this age of deconstruction of the meanings of words, anyone is capable of labeling anything anyway they like. It's part of the new danger of coaching. It harkens back to the modern complaint culture and the importance for programs to define exactly what is and what is not an act of hazing.

Important Thought: Action Item(s):

Bill Patton

CHAPTER FORTY-TWO

Friendly, But Not A Friend

Familiarity breeds contempt. ~ Chaucer

A head coach can be friendly with their players, but it's not a good idea for them to be a friend. That role can be played by others in the athlete's team, when there is an entourage style training team. Assistant coaches can be appointed to have closer bonds with players. Of course, the coach player relationship can be quite close, but friendship can make the ending more difficult, and the tough messages of a coach harder to deliver. I like to have fun with my players, and set a tone of enjoyment, AFTER I have set a tone of hard work, attention to detail, and learning about the process of improvement. The moment joking gets out of hand I zip it right back up to where it needs to be. Every team that I coach seems to have a player or two with whom my personality meshes, and because they 'get me', it would be easy to start playing favorites. I tend maybe to be a little harder on those individuals to steal my resolve not to play favorites with anyone on my team.

Your Situation is Unique, Act Accordingly

The way you deal with this depends a lot on whether you are coaching an individual player, a small group, are a head or assistant coach. In a private skills coaching situation that also has a different dynamic. Ultimately, deciding not to try to be a friend of your player is a healthy choice. There are some organizations that use the phrase 'professional detachment', but I find that a bit too cold and distant. Obviously a head coach must be the most aloof to some degree from the group as a whole, although certain players in leadership roles may be invited in more to the head coach inner circle. When I say aloof, I don't mean that they won't interact with each player, but it's tough for a coach with 50 players to really know each one incredibly well, that would fall more to the assistant coaches.

Balancing Attention

Be fully aware that having relationships that are too close with some players, and too distant with others can create a perception among the team and their parents of favoritism within your group. Problem players will make issue of this. Sometimes I respond, 'I'm not here to be friends with anyone on this team, but it's only natural that I am going to gravitate slightly more to players who have great attitudes and make attempts to be friendly, doing what they should. Conversely, it's not as fun to work with players who have bad attitudes or consistently give a poor effort or have low commitment level. It's not rocket science.' That seems to settle it every time, in terms of the conversation, although I can't control the inner thoughts of the player. They will have to choose to understand and act accordingly or not. It's not something a coach can enforce, but they can work to win the hearts and minds of everyone on the team. If a problem player persists in acting divisively, making issue out of unfairness, then they and I will have a one on one meeting to discuss their shortcomings and why they don't feel so much favor. Having said all that, we should account for the fact that it's easier to gravitate to the more talented players regardless of how much an example they are to the rest of the team in terms of work ethic. More extroverted players of course get more attention than introverted ones. A great coach makes sure to take some time to engage introverted players, or have someone do that who plays an important role on the team. No matter how hard you try, it's never going to be perfectly balanced the way you give your attention, but it's worth the effort. Your players might not even notice it, but they will appreciate it.

Important Thought: Action Item(s):

CHAPTER FORTY-THREE
Today

Today, confidence is my biggest weapon.
I will give 100% effort, enjoy the competition,
and show myself strong and wise.
I learn from every circumstance.

~ The Mantra

We repeat the above mantra in a very matter of fact tone, and it's amazing how these words can transform players ability to perform, no matter their level. Your principles, my principles ought to be made of stuff that averts fears. We can set a tone of mindful awareness of what matters, and maybe not even talk about what doesn't matter. Today means just for now, it's not a high pressure promise to always be confident. It's hard not to say 'I am confident' and not smile. We also can talk ourselves into it. What comes first, behaviors or psychological states? The interaction between the two is inseparable. The way we feel will dictate how we think and act, or how we think and act can influence our feelings. We are far more in control of our thinking and actions than we are our own feelings.

Speaking Confidence into Existence

Many times with young athletes, I ask them to repeat after me: 'I am confident', 'I feel very confident', 'I will play with confidence'. Quite often their can be an immediate improvement in their play. I don't really even try to hard to delve into what was plaguing that player, but I do know a lack of confidence when I see it. Any one of a multitude of fears can affect our confidence. Growing our confidence is like turning on a light switch, when we do, the darkness recedes behind shadows. The shadows remain, but now the room, our minds are full of light.

Paying Attention to the Joy of Athletics

When we talk about enjoying the competition, then we are training our minds to see the fun no matter the outcome. Of course it can be more fun to win than lose. Sometimes though, when facing extremely good competition that draws out your best possible performance, coming out on the losing end on the scoreboard does not feel like a loss. It feels like a win because of the high level of play. High level play is it's own reward. Players can begin to identify why they are having fun or not. Keeping sports in perspective for the temporal passing pleasure that it is can be exactly what empowers athletes to go all out, and play while taking the best risks at the right time. To 'risk all your winnings on game game of pitch and toss' is the ultimate in having the ability to seize the moment. It's Franz Klammer winning gold in the downhill at Kitzbuhel, its Derek covering home plate against the A's tagging out Giambi at the plate, it's Joe Montana saying 'let's go see John Candy in the end zone in the super bowl. It's Pete Rose after an amazing World Series Game that was lost by the Cincinnati Reds, saying 'Wasn't that a great game!?'

The Outcome is in Doubt

The best and most exciting competitions are the ones where the outcome is in doubt, the match up is a close one, each team has strengths and weaknesses that create uncertainty of how it will turn out. The fear of the unknown can be exchanged for an excitement of discovery about which team is better. It's an amazing opportunity for a seemingly random lightning strike of a player or a group of players playing the best game of their young lives. It's the opportunity to take what might not be a player's best performance, teaching them to manage mistakes and turn to competing for every kernal of space, ball possession, leverage or whatever it might be.

Anxiety can certainly curb enjoyment, and lack of engagement with the game will likely create less enjoyable outcomes. So for the athletes that taket the competition too seriously because they assign too much meaning to it, learning about enjoyment can improve their longevity and outcomes. For those who have no problem having fun, but shy away from actually working to defeat the opponent, they can be the source of others not enjoying the sport, because they can't rely on the competitive spirit of others. This is were teammates can blend together, rubbing off on one another learning from each other and playing in the moment for each one. When your athletes can band together along the vast continuum of high strung highly competitive natures and the utter joy of running in the sun making a play, then you really have something.

Strength and Wisdom for Now and the Future

I will show myself strong and wise is a sacred trust and a lifelong mission to be a better person through sporting endevours. The ultimate of the four pillar goals I present to my team is learning. Ultimately it's learning that will determine the future of each player maximizing their potential. There are many players labeled too small or too slow who learned a certain set of skills that enabled them to become among the best players in the world. The world is full of players who have or had amazing talent, but failed to learn even fundamental play. Then the story goes, woulda', coulda', shoulda' been a contender, a champion. They simply did not do what they could have done. Every athlete deserves a coach who will teach them to learn everything they can at every possible moment that they can.

Gleaning Each Moment

The effort level allows us to maximize the moment and sets us up for being fully physically, mentally, and even spiritually engaged with the moment. Exploring the joy of play, and the struggle of meeting a challenge while staying fully present with it, not running from it is an amazing life skill that can benefit us in so many ways. Having a wise, positive and strong presence in the meet, again is something that will help in a debate, a job interview, a presentation, a sales call, or many other of life's moments when we can win the day. The growth mindset individual is open to receiving all of these gifts. The fixed mindset person is locked out from moving upward, missing out of the grace of every improving moment by moment.

Important Thought: Action Item(s):

PART FOUR

THE COACH'S INNER WORK

No one learns as much about a subject
as one who is forced to teach it.

~ Peter Drucker

CHAPTER FORTY-FOUR

Inner Work Comes First

**We would accomplish many more things,
if we did not think of them as impossible.**

~ Vince Lombardi

I believe in the law of attraction to some degree. Birds of a feather, flock together. People with similar values are drawn together, players and coaches with ethics that are aligned, same thing. I know that as a younger coach in my 20s, I had no clue about really going into personal development, and deep thinking about what I wanted to do. As a direct result of that, there were many problems, much friction and wasted energy. The pool of players and parents who would buy into my system was smaller than it might have been. Over the years, as I have done the work of self development, and following the path that I was made to walk, my circle of influence has grown, but it still has its limits. Doing the work of developing our core beliefs about coaching, learning, adding to them, and refining them, increases the breadth and depth of attraction for those who might learn from us. Our relationships can be compared to the solar system with the Sun and planets in orbit, or like the hub of a bike wheel and each player a spoke. The central figure needs something with reliable strength to it, to support the orbits and/or the function of each spoke for an efficient use, the stronger the nucleus, the more gravitational pull, the more stable the orbits.

Athlete Centered Within Definitive Parameters!

Is it advisable to free up a player into more self-determination, if you don't have a well-defined coaching philosophy? In a word, no. What are the parameters for players within which players are going to work? Without a well-defined coaching philosophy, then you have few. Your core is missing, your gravity is reduced, the strength of your hub does not support all the spokes of the wheel. Without well-defined limits to exactly how athlete-centered you become, there are no limits to player behavior. **This is perhaps the most important chapter in this**

book, and I want you to take it with the full weight of conviction to build this foundational piece. It would be foolish to read onward, as we begin the process of placing planks of major structural pieces of coaching in place, if you have yet to create your coaching foundation.

The Starting Place

Everything we have discussed up until this point leads to the discovery of 'where we are now'. It is necessary to build upon foundational truths and principles. Without a strong foundation, the house will fall. When players in developing higher level skills, abandon fundamental play, then it's time to regress back to building them up from the ground. I had a young tennis player that I coached privately, who had some very odd notions about how to play. He seemed to want mimic Federer's Forehand, Nadal's Backhand, and Andy Roddick's serve until he decided that he should try Federer's serve and Nadal's forehand, etc. His game could be described as 'technique in a blender'. He wanted to play like anyone but himself.

Empowering Good Fit, Exposing Bad Fit

I had expressed to this player over and over that he would be best advised to learn his own strokes rather than imitate others on a whimsical schedule. Since he was unwilling to discover his own style within the parameters of the rock solid fundamentals, he found that he was not a good fit in the program and he left. So being athlete-centered does not necessarily mean kowtowing to the whims of a player at any given moment. It doesn't mean being codependent to maladaptive behaviors. What it does mean is giving voice to a player's dreams, goals, and maybe even their preferences, while not letting them off the hook from learning the non-negotiables of good play.

Idiosyncracies Within Parameters

We do necessarily have to have room inside of proper parameters to allow some freedom for self expression. How will you know if a player is a good fit with your program if you don't have a program? If I didn't have well defined standards, I would have been frustrated for longer in dealing with a player I could not serve. He would not know to find the exit to find a better fit. How will you redirect them in their stated desires, if what they want exceeds, or does not meet the parameters of a program that has no limits? That sentence doesn't make sense, it's rhetorical in that the player can't find a place in or out of the program if the coach's program philosophy is not well defined. Forgive my nonsense there, as I am making the point that it really does not make sense. **Without the necessary grounding in clearly defined philosophy, to be a rock-solid influence in the work of a player, in developing their foundational plan, in how they want to play, then there are no boundaries.** Read that over again out loud. It's a hard sentence, but it's precisely what I want to say.

Make the Big Decisions First

As with most things, making the big decisions first helps guide the smaller decisions. The biggest decisions have to do with the major principles of a coaching philosophy. The next biggest decisions have to do with fitting inside the school, club, or facility culture, followed by what are the overarching long-term goals of the program. The next pieces after fitting into the mission, or building the mission are developing the objectives, and then the goals that support the objectives.

Rocks, Pebble and Sand

There is an awesome analogy whereby you have two containers of the same size. Next to it, you have some sand, small pebbles, and larger rocks. If you first put the sand in, then the pebbles, then there is not enough room for the larger rocks. If you go in reverse order first placing the larger rocks, smaller pebbles, shake a little to let them settle into the lower places, then add the sand, then it all fits. So it is with first developing your largest pieces of your program, before getting into the objectives, and finally the details. Developing the details is fine, but they have to be connected to larger principles. So it was when I explained my four pillars of 100% effort, Enjoy the Competition, Showing Yourself Strong and Wise, and Learning from Every Circumstance. You, of course, can use those as a template, but it will be even more powerful when you make them your own somehow, or align them more with your values.

Take the Time

I would recommend getting away for a few hours to really think and write out four or five principles that are the basis of what you do. Expressing the physical, mental, emotional, the process, and the outward behavior of everyone connected to the program is essential. Focusing too much on one of those would be a mistake.

Important Thought: Action Item(s):

CHAPTER FORTY-FIVE

15 Mindful Things

Think

~ The IBM Motto

Being Mindful is a Great Way to Rule One's Own Spirit

Here is a list of 15 things you can do to become more mindful.

1. Listen

Mindful people are masters of awareness, an art that escapes many people. They engage eye contact with people when they speak. They enjoy the music of birds chirping while they enjoy their morning coffee. They enter conversations only when they have something valuable to say. Take a look around during your time as a coach, many of us are blessed to be in beautiful surroundings with the people we want to know. Pay great attention to those blessings.

2. Day-dream

Concentration is a good skill to have, but it becomes even more powerful when combined with imagination. It can be hard to stay interested in a complex project like writing a book, building a team, or helping a player craft their game. Mindful people let their thoughts drift to how happy and accomplished they will feel when it is complete, which reminds them that it is worth the effort. Give yourself time to create vision.

3. Go Outside

For most coaches, that's easy! Imagine all those people who are chained to their desks. I like to brag about my 10,000 square foot office with views in every direction. How many CEO's are stuck with just a corner office?

It is not healthy to spend every moment of your day chained to a desk in a zombie-like state, without any opportunity to escape. Mountains are meant to be climbed. Rivers are meant to be canoed. All of the wilderness in this world is a playground that is meant to be explored. It's also smart to go explore a bit on road trips, so that you aren't simply in hotels and athletic facilities. Find a great restaurant, a scenic or historic park, etc.

4. Take Breaks

When you were a student, you probably noticed that your ability to focus on studying diminished more and more with every passing moment. Mindful people take mini-breaks every hour or so, because they know the brain can only concentrate for so long before it needs a reboot. Break time in practice can be a great time of building chemistry. There is nothing productive about forcing yourself to work beyond that breaking point, and many of the very best programs abide by that principle. It's an old-school and not necessarily productive notion that you should take your team to the breaking point for the sake of learning a certain play.

5. Pause to Reflect

How do you think you will ever accomplish your purpose without pausing to consider your place in the world? Conside yesterday's practice, the match that ended today, what was learned from it? How does that inform future practices, do you challenge your team to new heights or regress them to more fundamental play? Keeping a journal will help you make sense of the feelings swirling inside you, and you are more likely to capture the essence of your next logical step. You will also identify toxic influences in your environment that need to be addressed. Discovering what your next area of growth as a coach can be is immensely powerful step toward mastery.

6. Laugh at Yourself

There will be moments when we say the wrong thing, or make a clumsy move. I sometimes spill the tennis balls all over the place. Our sense of humor at the right time can help create more of an atmosphere of acceptance, thus enabling your players to have more of a sense of humor about their own games.

7. Nourish your Body

Think brain food, think cleansing food. Find a list of foods rich in anti-oxidants.

Eating shouldn't be viewed as an act of deprivation. Instead, see it as an opportunity to nourish your body with healthy foods that will make you feel positively alive. Mindful people pay attention to how different foods influence their body and mood. If it causes an upset stomach or wrecks your energy, then you probably shouldn't be eating it. I know what it's like to be the coach who eats and drinks too much. I started to look like Bullwinkle, and if you don't know who that is, do a quick search. We must do our best to model healthy lifestyle choices for our players.

8. Express your Feelings

With your team, you might want to be careful with this one, you might have to hold things in during important moments, or really let it all out. Think first!

The longer you bury an emotion, the more intense it will become. Putting up barriers can temporarily prevent difficult conversations. But hiding the truth for too long could cause permanent damage to trust in your relationships. Speak your mind without filter. If a person can't handle the real you, then they don't deserve you, but that doesn't mean we shouldn't measure our words careful to say everything we really mean and nothing we don't.

9. Have Great Eye Contact With People

Mindful people don't make a habit of staring at their cellphones during a conversation. Some people look around as though they would really rather talk with someone else. Fully engage with the one that you are working with and you will develop greater levels of trust. Make sure all of your non verbal cues line up with what you want to convey. When our physical presence is at odds with what they say, then that incongruence will affect relationships with players.

10. Be Quiet At The Right Time

Silence is nothing to fear. When you ask a question of your team, there can be a silence while they think. If they have learned to wait a moment, and because of the coach's impatience, he or she gives the answer right away, then they learn not to have to think. When they do give answers, putting them down for an imperfect reply will not help you in the long run. Give them time to think, speak, and refine their thoughts as a group. In fact, waiting for a longer time through silence will show that they really don't know anything about the topic, so you then know that they will be curious, and that you can give them the most fundamental knowledge.

11. Tap Into Creativity

Don't always do things the same way, come up with wrinkles to keep things fresh. Change up the drills, create new rules for games, turn things in different directions. Find a new way to communicate. A few years back the University of Oregon Football team started sending signals in from the bench with large signs with four different images on them, each image had a meaning. Then players would signal which of the four actually meant something. It was quite interesting, and they were an explosive group offensively, partly due to their sophisticated signals.

12. Embrace Opportunities

Zig Ziglar once said, 'If it doesn't challenge you, it won't change you.' Mindful people don't pursue comfort, because they know this road inevitably leads to complacency. If you can't remember the last time you fell short, then you're probably not aiming high enough. Say yes to more things, especially those opportunities that will take you out of your comfort zone.

13. Focus On The Task At Hand

Most people stumble through life like a drunkard, without any awareness of their surroundings. Driving to work with no recollection of the trip. Eating a food while paying no attention to their body's signals that it has had enough. Performing a task in the midst of distractions that cause them to make inexcusable errors. Mindful people do one thing at a time. Do each thing to the best of your ability, and pay attention to the details of what makes each thing great.

14. Challenge Your Own Preexisting Beliefs

Everyday we read, everyday we learn something and we can either deepen our nuanced understanding, or change our minds about something.

Opinions worth having should hold up to scrutiny. Only an arrogant person would be unwilling to consider the other side of an issue. Engaging in a thoughtful debate probably won't change your mind, but it will introduce you to new ideas that grow your perspective. I like to bounce ideas off of my staff, and let them explain to me the pros and cons of a certain way of doing things. I also love to hire people who have their own opinions and can share them with me. There have been major paradigm shifts in the program from concepts taught by an assistant coach. Innovative line up changes were developed by assistants, and players inserted into the lineup that I would not have guessed would work so well, but trusting my assistant it worked great.

15. Dwell On Encouraging Thoughts

Mindful people let thoughts drift in their consciousness without any judgment attached. They travel through this mental chatter with the caution of a soldier walking through a battlefield covered in landmines, carefully identifying the thoughts that empower them and discarding the rest. Since we know that the default position of our minds is negative, framing our perceptions and beliefs as positive, or even simply as objective becomes a struggle.

CHAPTER FORTY–SIX

Know Your Brand

Think Different

~ The Apple Motto

Your values help establish your brand, and yes it's similar to creating an identity in the marketplace, but more importantly it functions as a self assessment to know more about yourself and who you are right now. Yes, you are THE brand, and you offer products. Understanding your brand will help you develop higher quality products in line with your identity. I know that this may rub someone the wrong way, coaches tend to be humble people, and they might not relish the idea of 'being the message', or doing self-promotion. Mistakenly, even though all the work is about the players, when the coach knows his own brand very well, communicating it to others well, it creates the first engagement between player and coach. A well developed branding may help the right player to find you, and the wrong one to move along to the next coach. Branding functions in part to help with attraction, and good fit initially.

Invest Time Into Developing Your Brand

The catch is that you have to invest. Making an investment of time into developing and understanding our own brand helps us differentiate from other coaches. For each of us, this led to an immediate rebranding in our messaging. What is your profile? The test is very short and very amazing. The other opportunity is to spend an hour with Bill for the cost of a private lesson to go through 'The Values' exercise. It may take about an hour of work, and up to 30 minutes on the phone in two 15 minute segments, but when we truly assess our values, the potential for great empowerment in goal-setting is wide open.

Time Value

One particular concept that is universal to coaches is the use of time. How do we express our value of time? There are deeply ingrained cultural factors that come into play when we discuss our attitudes of about how we choose to spend each moment. Some cultures are all about burning the midnight oil, others are about maximizing daily family engagement, and others still about efficiency. I want to urge you to value other people's time as much as possible. This means to communicate, plan, make and keep commitments, be early, leave late, and do everything in your power to make the minutes spend together have the best possible outcomes.

Why do we resist following up on these things? I have found that commonly there is a lot of resistance in the area of doing the work of discovering and refining values. I can relate to the resistance, I have been a victim of my own, let go of victimhood and began to own my own resistance. Now that I have worked out my values and slowly refined them over the years, they are more and more. From a place of authenticity, I can now guide others to find and refine their own values, for use in affirming goal setting. I recommend creating five different statements that capture the essence of what success really means to you. Your highest ideals will be captured, expressed and used as sharp tools to get work done.

The unexamined life is not worth living. ~ Henry David Thoreau

Developing your five values statements is a way to keep your work and goals grounded in what is line with who you are and your core beliefs. I believe that not only will you be blessed in your coaching by defining your values, but your general success in life and relationships can be enhanced as well.

A Little Self Love

Let's start with a little love for ourselves. When we start with ourselves, we become grounded, and our players sense a strong basis underneath us, even if they never acknowledge it. We aren't talking about Whitney Houston's "Greatest Love of All", we are simply talking about taking some time alone to really work by ourselves a bit, to create more efficacy in what we can do for others. If only we could get off the hamster wheel.

Some of you have already read this and decided that:

A. I don't have time.
B. I don't need it, I know myself very well.
C. What's going to change if I do?
D. A myriad of other subconscious blocks that hinder us on a daily basis.

If you avoid these things because of a fear of the unknown, don't worry, the results will probably not shock you and reveal that you are living a double life, but their is a very likely epiphany coming your way.

Guided Decision Making

The benefits to you from developing your authentic approach also benefit your team, players, and relationships. When you take the time to establish, refine, and/or rediscover, you will be more likely to find yourself making more mindful decisions. Take time to measure a decision against the things that you really find profitable in life, and what your team will find useful. Do your planning in line with activities that are worth your time. When you have five statements that reflect your moral code, each decision you make, goal you write, or activity you plan should support at least one of them. My best goals support three or more of my 'ethics', and any goal that supports all five values is golden. Of course, if you are writing a goal like 'withdraw all the money from the bank and move to Brazil', chances are it does not support your values, unless of course...

I used to write out my goals and become immediately scared by them, because I didn't have a compass pointing me in the right direction, I felt like my goals were a reflection of greed, selfishness or some other negative part of my personality. Now my goals don't scare me at all. After I wrote out my five value statements, some goals went right out the door, and others that had previously been frightening, now were seen to support four different value statements, and thus became much more rooted in authenticity, than in simple achievement for achievements sake. Many have heard the analogy that someone climbed a ladder quickly to the top and had a momentary sense of satisfaction until they realize it was leaning against the wrong wall.

Take some time, consider which wall you want your ladder to lean on, developing your brand, your identity, your values, and understand yourselves better, and your influence with your players will be multiplied.

Important Thought: Action Item(s):

CHAPTER FORTY-SEVEN
Self-Discipline

Whoever is slow to anger is better than the mighty, and he who rules his spirit than he who takes a city.

~King Solomon

It's a great fantasy to think of ruling with an iron fist. We become far more powerful and effective when we rule our own spirit. Movies and TV love to portray coaches who seemingly get everything their way, giving orders, their foot soldiers follow them. Many times they are portrayed as angry people. The story usually goes that someone did not follow orders, so that player had to learn a life lesson to accept the coach's way, or hit the highway. A prodigal son story may ensue from there... Unfortunately this is just not the reality for most us of the athlete centered coaches, but that story might not sell as well at the box office.

Digging Deeper Into the Real Story of Leadership

The appeal many times is to the conventional wisdom of leaders as commanders, even though the best commanders were often the greatest collaborators as well. General George S. Patton, to whom I am not directly related, was famous for saying, 'If everyone is thinking alike, then someone isn't thinking.' He wanted dissent, all views, complete analysis, because he knew the damage 'groupthink' could do. An important aspect of a battle could be missed, a vulnerability created, an opportunity missed. We as coaches need to rule our own spirit and conduct ourselves in a way that fosters the strongest possible message of collaboration and self discipline for our players.

Life is Complicated, Sports are Complicated

Life can be a tangled ball of string. Everyone needs help on some of those knots. Those that are less mature may trying pulling hard on a piece or two and actually tighten some of the knots. When the string is very tight, maybe all we need is someone to hold one piece for us while we pull the other direction. Without a helper we might consider cutting some strings, but the damage to the full length of string may be too high a cost to pay. This is an allegory for unraveling the problems faced by a difficult team program situation. Lord knows I have had my share of those, and mostly the first year coaching in a new program includes doing some untangling. Over time, we learn to find the end of the string and patiently learn to pull it through a loop there, and unwind it from a knot there. You can't really hit it with a hammer, that won't really accomplish anything. When frustration builds, we can put down the ball of string, coming back at another time to take a few more actions, then before you know it, the whole thing is undone.

As is fairly common with those who have a background in psychology, I like to straighten out paperclips. They never really come out completely straight, but very quickly you can get them into a crooked line. The artistry comes in the form of gently smoothing the remaining curves. And so it is with working with our players. Before going about that work, we need to do our own inner work, and when we show a growth mindset, improving over time, then we create an ethic that translates to our players. Coaches who seem to have arrived, do not have the same impact with players.

From Expert to Collaborator with Experts

The greatest influence comes when two whole people come together to collaborate. For my 720 Degree Coaching business, I selected an infinity symbol to be prominent in the logo. 720 degrees is twice around a circle, or once around two circles. A friend shared with me his thought that he had heard the origin of an infinity symbol is two circles that intersect in one place. Thats good enough for me to latch onto. Being whole, does not mean being perfect, it simply means being in a place where we can grow. This is a pure coaching model, where the coach is a person with a growth mindset, and the performer has a similar mindset. The coach may aid the player to develop a better mindset. As the relationship improves so does the level of collaboration, and soon there is a private language developed over time and not everything needs to be spelled explicitly anymore. The collaboration continues until a time when there is nothing more to explore.

Dr. House?

The more prevalent model used is the medical model, where the coach is the doctor. The student is ill, something is wrong. The doctor does and exam, looks for symptoms, providing therapeutic solutions. The student takes their medicine, or not, and gets better, or not. Then like an episode of Super Crazy Doctor like you see on TV, the drama continues until at the last possible moment before the patient dies, they are cured by the wild genius coach. While I wouldn't say this never happens, because I have had my Super Crazy Doctor moments, over time I have learned to treat people who are well, as though they don't need anything from me. So, in my own mindset, I have had to capture those SCD moments, putting them away, so that I can give my student the place of expertise in their own game.

So I discipline myself to help the player be the problem solver, they are not the problem, they have an issue they want to address. They are the expert, and we can enhance their expertise by showing them how to use tools, helping them perform surgery on their own technique, mental game, fitness, team relationships, and any other salient factor that needs to be addressed. Ditching the idea that I am perfect and they are not, or I am in control and everyone needs to do it my way, can help relieve a lot of inner pressure from the coach to put on a phony lab coat, playing a role that is hard to preserve. Before we move on to developing discipline, we need to start from a better place, a spirit of collaboration. We don't have all the answers, and many times our clients do. We simply help them uncover their answers.

My Take Away: Action Item(s):

CHAPTER FORTY-EIGHT

Retaining Athletes: Appropriate Training

**70 percent of kids in the United States stop playing organized sports
by the age of 13 because,
'it's just not fun anymore.'**

~ a poll by National Alliance for Youth Sports

Very young athletes want to have fun, be with friends, improve and feel a sense of accomplishment, among many other reasons that they play sports. Very low on their reported list of what they want is anything to do with winning or being a professional athlete or Olympic medalist. Very few little players start with that kind of dream, but that doesn't mean they can't foster that idea later in their development. It means that maybe one or two kids on your team have that goal in mind. While early sports participation is great to help create healthy children to open up their options, pushing the idea ad nauseum about being a professional to 6 year olds is really not a good idea. Although there is nothing wrong with telling the kids once or twice that they could be a pro. Keep in mind, athlete centered coaches realize that they are characters in the athletes story, not the other way around.

When It Kicked In

The interesting stories of different times when an elite performer decided to go for it, are uniquely theirs to tell. The place on their timeline when they made the fateful decision happens as a matter of fact, a bolt from the blue, or something in between. The here and now of the sports experience as they see it, includes these things. For some that don't have the dream, or the goal is foisted upon them, being in the program can feel like a prison term. Because of their own enslavement to the notion of developing future professionals, and in a misguided 'work ethic' approach, coaches focus too much on a 'time on task' approach, to which the player is a captive. That coach might neglect the relationship building between teammates, and the player/coach relationship. They may view fun activities as a waste of valuable time. On the other end of the spectrum, some coaches spend too much time trying to make it fun, but leave out the essential training that will help the players to be successful. Sure, fun is number one on the list, but improvement and developing skills are as well. The social aspect of being with friends is almost an automatic, as the players will find the time to talk with each other. It's simply a matter of whether the coach sanctions it, or tries to squash it. Finding the balance point on the relationship building, while using practice time efficiently and including a fun activity almost every practice, that's when the magic happens. Discovering the tipping point of overall experience for the person who plays, and their ongoing development will make the coach successful on many levels. The coach with a great sense of being fully present, who notices when players are not having fun will begin to deftly strike a balance between these things, or identify that in the short term the activity is not meant to be fun.

Including Social Time

When coaches include time for friendship, they help each player to improve and celebrate each other player's accomplishments. This is also a vital piece in the mental health of your players long term. People are far less connected than they used to be due to time spent with screen time on devices. When you help your young athletes connect as teammates face to face, they become part of something larger, and that can have a life changing impact on them.

The most practical way to address how you allow players to connect is to ask, how long is your break time? Another practicality is pay attention to break time. One thing I started doing a few years ago was to observe my players during break time. Are they really enjoying each others company and building relationships, or were they really collectively more interested in getting a quick water break and getting back to the activity? Both are good. Is someone left out or not with the group when we take a break? Can I find one of the players who will go out of their way to connect with a teammate? Going out of your way to show a youngster how to go out of their way to draw someone in can have an amazing ripple effect moving forward. Like the analogy of a butterly flapping it's wings in China starts a hurrican somewhere else. Hurricanes are not good, but you get the point.

Not a week goes by when I don't allow the players to have a bit extra time between activities, because I can sense that they are getting along great. When my players are having a particularly good time of bonding, the scheduled five minute water break can be extended by a minute or two to maximize the time of team chemistry creation and frankly, increasing the fun. Taking one or two more minutes to allow players to wrap up a conversation can really pay off when the time comes that they really need to play for one another and root each other onward. Contests can be won or lost because of better chemistry or not.

Focus on Processes

Athletes want to get better, and when you create a process oriented program, they might not even realize how refreshing that is compared to coaches that focus solely on outcome goals, placing more pressure on teams to win the big one.

At every level of the game, teaching and refining what it means to give the best possible effort is not simple. 110% effort is not really process oriented, but it is nonsense. Avoid that which really lacks common sense, and it runs counter to what young players intuitively want from their sports experience. They can do without the pressure, as they already put enough of that on themselves to succeed for their team. Don't be fooled by a couple of kids who such people pleasers or are fairly driven themselves who will agree to 110%. Ask yourself, are they only telling me what I want to hear? Do those who say 'give 110%', want things to happen faster than the normal course of time. I'm guessing that they do. In kind, they are training players to want improvement faster than it can naturally come from an honest amount of 100% effort. My experience with trying to reach into the future to try to make it come more quickly is how I have wrecked myself with anxiety and impatience for the results. Acting and talking that way also seems to spoil the present moment, which then never seems to be quite good enough. In my minds eye, I don't see those coaches affirming players when they reach the mythical standard, but instead chiding them when they are far below it, which they invariably will be.

Make the Shift to Accepting a Challenge

Get into 'the now' and stay in it. When we are too future focused, then we it's tempting to be not OK with temporary set backs in training. When we are actually OK with a temporary lack of fulfillment of objectives, taking a growth mentality, players are more likely to take on the challenge and find it more interesting. We all have to accept our path. Every coach, every athlete will need to deal with adversity. When we accept those challenges at the right time, then we are more likely to make better choices furthering along our path. The road we follow most likely will not end at the Super Bowl, a World Series, or a Grand Slam Championship. We can find some very meaningful achievements in other directions. Taking on new hurdles to overcome, that require us to grow and simply become better, is a far better model, than the ceaseless striving for more, bigger, faster and stronger than today attached to unrealistic standards. When we follow our processes today, then tomorrow we experience better performances.

Giving Only Your All

Another problem with attempting to give 110% effort is that people are asserting that players can give more than what they have, they can give more than what they are. Perhaps they are guided by a vision that when you really give 100%, then you grow, and your capacity is increased, but that's not what their language says. So, if that is what you really mean, then why not remove the confusion and simply ask for 100% effort. I certainly never accept anything less than 100% effort. If that is the case, then why not teach that? In this case, I do strongly believe that players are better served by communicating more accurately what we want to have happen.

My 30 years of experience in gyms, fields and courts tell me that giving 100% effort is tough enough for players to achieve at all times. A large cross section of players who buy into the 110% myth get themselves so bothered, that they will only end up giving 90%, because they are pressing so hard. Trying to give more than you have can increase muscular tension, mental worry slows them down, or causes mistakes that need to be corrected. Fun is diminished by the thought, the program, the coach of this player, and one strong factor for their burnout is now firmly in place, established by the coach who asks for too much. It is far better to learn to play in a flow state, where players don't feel pressure, beginning to approach 100% more and more. It's more something for us to facilitate, than to enforce in a player or a team. Developing a culture of maximum effort is perhaps the most important building block for any program. All these things are best facilitated in the here and now, and giving only all that we have, and all that we are. Sometimes all we can do is observe. Stop and look at how hard players will try when they are having a lot of fun, they will amaze you. More players will stay, and they will play better, and it will be a self perpetuating cycle of improvement.

My Take Away: Action Item(s):

CHAPTER FORTY-NINE
Developmentally Appropriate

Pre-PHV (pre-adolescent) should focus on 'mastery of fundamental motor skills, sport sampling, general physical preparation, development of muscle strength using a variety of implements, introductory sport skills, physical literacy, attention to volume of training/playing, rest, and nutrition.'

~ National Strength and Conditioning Association

There are too many coaches who are insane or nearly insane, who risk ruining children's future in sports with workouts that are not at all developmentally appropriate. There is an epidemic of young baseball pitchers who need Tommy John Surgery because they lack fundamentals. Who are these coaches who took a high risk approach to technique, allowed young kids to throw too much, or the wrong types of pitches? Who are the parents who sign their future major leaguers up for a coach who will then hurt their chances of ever going pro? I occasionally meet idiotic parents who believe that using small equipment is not a good idea, because 'that's not the game', 'you have to do it right from the beginning'. So they want their child to play football on a 100 yard field, and use an adult size soccer ball. They want their child to only use yellow tennis balls on a 78' court, instead of smaller frames with slower bouncing balls and shorter courts that allow players to develop requisite skills before moving up to greater challenges.

Those approaches are out of sync in time and space with the developmental level of the child. The developmentally inappropriate behavior of parents and coaches may explain the damage that is done with pre-adolescents, and might possibly explain why so many kids quit sports by age thirteen. Training inappropriately is not as fun as using best practices for everyone.

Compromising Health In Search Of...

Youngsters with compromised systems due to the overuse, inappropriate intensity, and incorrect use of high level training aids are getting more common. Throwing the curveball too early, the kick serve in tennis, unstable surface training in the wrong sequence and with poor fundamentals, these types of activities and many more lead to more problems, some of them can be debilitating. Young athlete's shoulders, elbows and low back can be injured in a chronic manner from which there is no real long term recovery.

Social Media Perpetuates the Myths

People love to fawn over videos of little savants, prodigies, seemingly enormously talented children who seem to be 'can't miss' in terms of being an elite athlete. The fact is that very few of them make it. For every Tiger Woods, and Andre Agassi who exhibited rare talent early on, there are hundreds of thousands, if not millions that do not make it to the highest levels of sport. So let's stop pretending that we can magically predict with early talent identification who will make it and who won't. It's actually far more fascinating to find someone who seems under-talented but has the right attitude, work ethic, growth mentality and coachability to be more than anyone every imagined.

Look Instead for the Underdog

One of my favorite hockey players is Joe Pavelski of the San Jose Sharks, who was always told that he is too small and too slow, but at every level below the NHL his team won championships and he was a captain. He is now the undisputed captain of the Sharks, and they have been a threat to win it all, maybe they will during his tenure there. Joe has honed particularly helpful skills to become a great face-off man, has incredible hockey sense to be in the right place at the right time, and is the best player in the entire league at tipping pucks into the net. He spends countless hours working on tipping the puck which requires incredible eye-hand coordination. He is making his mark in that way, and may be one of the best of all time in that regard. But he has had to face up to those who discounted him, and he was not a high draft pick but is easily one of the top 20 most influential players in the league at this time. He has the ability to take over a game.

I will stop with this one prime example, but I will encourage you to look for the players who have the desire to become better, and always believe that they can overcome their so-called limitations. There are many more professional athletes who started from rather humble beginnings, but stuck with it to become a pro. Referring back to a previous chapter, think on how many more opportunities are granted to players who stick with it, and how many more stick with it, when coaches create programs that make sense. The programs not only need to be social, but appropriately challenging mentally and emotionally.

My Take Away: Action Item(s):

CHAPTER FIFTY
Overtraining and Balance

That fear of missing out on things makes you miss out on everything.

~ Etty Hillesum

One of the laws of success set forth by Napolean Hill in his all time classic The Laws of Success in 16 Lessons is the Law of the Chief Definite Aim. So, it's about having one major over arching goal that is above all others, and excludes any other goal that might interfere with it. Our society celebrates the coach and/or the athlete who seems to have an absolute obsession with sport. The narrative that is promoted is one of working 20 hour days, sleeping in the office, watching film past until midnight. There is almost no discussion of highly successful coaches who leave the work at work, and don't bring it home. There is almost no talk of coaches who are also devoted husbands, wives and parents. It's easy to get sucked into a mind set of worry. People can become anxious about being outworked, out-thought and outperformed. Striking a great balance of recovery, time off with time on task is an important part of longevity.

Chronic injuries, over training syndromes, and compromising the auto-immune system come with training too hard, too long and without enough recovery.

Taking a Break

One of the greatest soccer players in U.S. History Landon Donovon took a lengthy break in the later stages of his career. He stunned soccer fans, citing mental and physical exhaustion as the reason for a respite from training. Landon made public his lack of motivation. He expressed that he was feeling mental and physical fatigue, which clearly are signs of overtraining syndrome. Fortunately, after several months of rest he was able to return to the soccer pitch. Here we discuss how overtraining effects an athlete's performance, cognition and mood.

Overtraining is Common

Overtraining syndrome occurs frequently throughout athletics, regardless of sport. Studies have shown that over half of professional soccer players will experience overtraining syndrome during a season, 60% of distance runners will experience overtraining syndrome at some point in their career. One case study of athletes found that at a six week basketball one third of the players at camp experienced overtraining syndrome. Overtraining occurs in both high volume training regimens, like swimming programs, and high intensity training regimens, like weightlifting. Overtraining refers to training above the body's capacity for recovery which results in overtraining syndrome. While it's very difficult to prepare athletes to perform at the highest levels of sport without bumping into the limits from which athletes can quickly recover, it is important to read the early signs of overstepping a player's capacity so as to rest enough at the right time. As with any disease or disorder, the first question to ask is what are the signs and symptoms of overtraining syndrome?

Signs and Symptoms of Overtraining Syndrome:

* Decreased physical performance
* General fatigue, wake up feeling tired
* Insomnia
* Change in appetite
* Irritable, restless, excitable, anxious
* Loss of bodyweight
* Loss of motivation
* Lack of mental concentration
* Feelings of depression
* Low Grade Fever

Overtraining seemingly can take one of two routes depending on the style of training, through the sympathetic nervous system, or via the parasympathetic nervous system. The sympathetic nervous system is responsible for fight-or-flight response: elevating heart rate, releasing adrenaline and blood vessel constriction at the digestive organs among other functions. The parasympathetic nervous system is primarily active while at rest and essentially slows down the heart rate and activates the digestive and other housekeeping organs in the body.

Commonly high volume aerobic training can bring on parasympathetic overtraining symptoms such as unmanageable levels of fatigue. High intensity training more often can lead to sympathetic overtraining symptoms such as irritability, anxiety and insomnia. Whether through high intensity or high volume training, understanding how to prevent overtraining syndrome is naturally beneficial to athletes and their coaches.

Finding Balance

Maintaining a balance between training at a sufficient intensity or volume to generate increased performance without leading to overtraining syndrome often requires that coaches and athletes have open lines of communication that allow those doing the work to report the early signs of overtraining. I once had a meeting with my three team captains, because the schedule called for an intense workout, but I noticed that some of our players were looking a little fatigued. Two of the three captains agreed with the schedule, perhaps out of duty or a 'group-think' with the coach, or even out-right to give 'the right answer'. The third captain expressed that he was feeling fatigued and knew for a fact that others on the team were feeling that way. So, I asked them, 'What is the verdict?'. They assumed that we would do the tough workout because it was a vote. I showed them something about leadership, and that it's not always about majority rule, pleasing the coach or 'doing what you should', but really paying attention to the possibility of losing players to fatigue.

Neither undertraining nor acute overload produce the desired performance improvement. To produce an optimal improvement in athletic performance the athlete must train by over-reaching: stressing the body through muscle overload, but with proper rest for recovery. Training above the body's capacity for recovery is detrimental to performance and leads to overtraining syndrome. (The Unknown Mechanism of the Overtraining Syndrome, 2002. Armstrong and VanHeest), demonstrates the effects that increasing training intensity or volume has on the body and performance.

Another Mind Body Connection

Overtraining seems to be more related to psychological pathology, than having purely physical roots. The way the body reacts to overtraining follows the pattern laid out by general adaptation syndrome: alarm, resistance and exhaustion. Shifts in hormonal balance during the process of training and adaptation affect mood. A ten-year study found that college swimmers' scores on a Profile of Mood States Test rose with a close correlation to the differing levels of training volume over the course of the competitive swimming season, only returning to baseline at the conclusion of the season (Psychological monitoring of overtraining and staleness, 1987. Morgan, et al.). Perhaps the most compelling item from research shows the psychological connection with the physiological nature of overtraining syndrome is its similarity to major depression.

Many of the characteristics of overtraining symptom overlap with depression. 80% of the overtrained swimmers in Morgan's study were found to be clinically depressed, according to diagnosis with their signs and symptoms. Besides the signs and symptoms, biochemical markers are similar as well. Blood cortisol levels are decreased in both overtraining syndrome and major depression. Epinephrine levels are also altered in both. Adrenal glands produce less epinephrine, and the indicators run in multiple different brain chemistry components that indicate clinical depression, but I will spare you the scientific terminology. Athletes seeking treatment for clinical depression have found some relief. Anti-depressants have successfully been used to treat both the physical and psychological components of overtraining syndrome in elite athletes.

Knowing The Limits Of Stress and Fatigue

Recently, much excitement has been generated in the neurology and physiology communities over exercise-induced neurogenesis and brain plasticity. While exercise increases neurogenesis, overtraining and major depression alike result in reduced brain plasticity and neural retraction in animal models. Thus strongly underlining the caution to pay close attention to pushing athletes too far. Winston Churchill famously said, 'Fatigue makes cowards of us all', as he admonished the British people to sleep and eat normally, to not succumb to the terror of German bombing raids. Athletics are far more trivial than that, but the concept is clear.

How do we best treat overtraining syndrome? It is important to realize that outside stressors play a role in overtraining syndrome. The best defense is to keep outside stress to a minimum. If this is not possible due to occupational or family obligations, it may be a good idea to reduce training volume or intensity during periods of high outside stress. Keep the body healthy: stay hydrated, maintain caloric balance, and keep up on sleep. Whether an athlete or the athlete's coach or doctor, be aware of the psychological state of the athlete through conversation or mood questionnaires. Finally, treat overtraining syndrome with rest. The longer the overtraining syndrome has occurred, the longer the rest treatment needed.

Going Off-Balance Can Lead to Problems and Poor Performance

One of my better teams was a group of girls who were quite good athletes, but also very active students academically and with many extra-curriculur activities. These girls seemed not to have an 'off button'. During spirit week at school, girls in each graduating class on this team were up late at night finishing floats, practicing skits, singing and dancing. Immediately after that event, many of them became ill. Everything still looked good on court, we were playing well, but the girls had created a high pressure outcome goal to win all 84 individual matches during the season. Two girls who were sick lost a match, so we finished 83-1, and they cried. It didnt bother me, but looking back, that was the beginning. These girls were tough, they recovered almost fully, and we headed into the post season. As the 10th seeded team, we beat the 7th seed and the 2nd seed in very close dramatic matches. Each match was very tense and emotional. The first was on a Tuesday, and we followed that with a light practice, then the second one was on a Thursday, and the semi-finals were scheduled for Saturday. We were up against the 5th seeded team, that was a bit underrated, as they went on to win the tital. What happened though in the semifinal is that my girls had collectively hit the wall. Where previously they could increase their intensity, and they could listen and work collaboratively as we problem solved their matches, this day was different. Few players reached fully competitive intensity, and when I tried to fire them up and talk with them about problem solving the strategies, I got a sort of glossy eyed look from them. They had checked out mentally. We hit the wall of overtraining. Most likely that 5th seeded team was just a bit too good, but we will never know if we could have beaten them while fresh. The good news is that at the end of the year, at our celebratory banquet, I made sure to give the lesson about living a more balanced lifestyle. The training for the team was not going to be reduced much, but they would have to get to bed before midnight, eat well, and manage their stresses better. The result was that they won the section title the following year in dominating fashion.

Researchers are just beginning to understand the complexities of overtraining syndrome, this young exercise physiology frontier will yield new discoveries through cross-disciplinary research, so do some of your own research, and future editions of this book may become more detailed in this regard.

My Take Away: Action Item(s):

CHAPTER FIFTY-ONE
Big Planning Tools

Most people get excited about games,
but I've got to be excited about practice,
because that's my classroom.

~ Pat Summitt, Legendary Basketball Coach

Use Big Planning Tools, Reduce Learning Curve

When we plan, we are giving 100% effort, without a plan, we are sure to miss something. When building something large, many times our mental landscape needs to change. In the example of a large building on a plot of land, huge amounts of soil need to be moved, compressed, dug out, and very large tools are used for that, backhoes, graders, etc. Luckily for sports coaches, the job of preparing to build something large can begin with pencil and paper or a computer. When making the overall plan, use your cement mixer, put down some strong groundwork from which you will not budge. When laying concrete, consider that you want to only add to it, and not subtract, because using a jackhammer creates a major distraction. Laying out the groundwork for a great season really starts with planning the largest most permanent fixtures to the program.

The permanent fixtures of any program are the conditioning and fitness, reteaching and reaffirming fundamental play as needed, and making at least one incremental improvement in each player during the season. I look at Bob Melvin a multiple winner of Major League Baseball Manager of the Year award. He is expert at preparing his teams, and every player goes through a process of refining what they do. Melvin's best miracle season came in a year when the Oakland Athletics began the season where initially the A's were batting so poorly that they were a legitimate threat to set an all-time low batting average record. What did Melvin do? He helped each batter go a few percentage points higher, and focused much more on drawing walks, fouling off pitches, taking a very conservative approach to minimize strike outs, and extending at-bats to tire pitchers out. Soon other teams would dread playing the A's because a four game series meant that they would have to go deep into their bullpen. The A's did NOT set a record for all-time worst batting average, and they MADE THE PLAYOFFS in one of the most remarkable runs in MLB history. All made possible by the impeccable planning of Mr. Bob Melvin.

Contingency Plans

How well we plan and have contingencies in mind will determine how nimble we are to solve problems. We can save ourselves a lot of problems by anticipating them ahead of time, coming up with solutions ahead of time, or planning a course of action with less chance of errors.

As a tennis coach, an example the kind of planning I needed to was predicated on a very unique group that I was dealing with in my lineup. My team was made up of some diminutive young men, few of my boys were taller than 5 foot 8, most of them were in the 4'11 to 5'4 range, and I had only one player on the team who could serve over 100 MPH. What was I going to do with all these small and not very strong servers? We needed a plan. We were not physically offensively gifted to win short points, my team was the tennis equivalent of the Oakland A's mentioned above. We were going to have to work for everything.

In that season, I planned two things, that my players would dramatically improve their speed on court, and also that we would learn to spin our serves in many different ways, while placing them extremely well to set up their position on the court. I knew absolutely that I was not going to change any part of the plan to build speed. Most every conditioning segment had a speed building element. My assistant coach and I absolutely had to do everything we could to get every last bit of quickness out of those players. We knew our players' serves were going to be returned, and that our players may have to dash quickly over to get to a hard hit, well-placed return from a bigger strong player. The plan worked, because during that season, I saw many frustrated opponents wondering why they couldn't hit the ball past our players. They were used to the other teams in our league that did not have the amazing court quickness. The longer grinding points that out players were used to and trained for took a major toll on the quick point trained offensive players on other teams. Their relative lack of fitness compared to my teams was exposed. There were quite a few times during that season that opponents would reach the end of their fitness, and 'the wheels came off', as I like to say about a player who could not run the same way at the end of a match. If you want that as a result, then it has to be part of your plan.

It's A Grind, Avoid Grinding Them Down

High School Sports in the spring time can be quite stressful for the players. The high school athlete's experience of overtraining is different than a fully grown adult athlete. Whatever age group you are working with, try to figure out what the issues are in the players lives that are universal. As a young coach, I did not account very well for what seems to be a relative grind at the high school level. Coupled with a teenagers perception that 10 to 12 weeks is a long time (some team seasons are much longer), their academic schedule gets more intense as the season goes along. The academic demands increase especially in the spring time, as testing becomes more important. Some states have very rigorous standardized testing. Your seniors are thinking a lot about graduation, and all the year end activities. Throw in SAT, AP, ACT tests for your Juniors, the ramping up of projects, then finals, and you have the potential for having a very stressed-out group of players.

Stress Release, Rest, Late Season Preparation

Part of the reason I send players home with a fun end to every practice is to relieve the stress of the practice day, helping players head home to dinner and homework with a smile on their face. That can set the tone for their evening! If we don't help alleviate stress in our players, it most certainly will mount up on them, and create problems. When we help manage our player's stress levels, or even simply attempt to understand mostly by checking in with them, and listening to how they are feeling, we can respond by making subtle or even major changes to the practice schedule on the day as part of our decision making. While I don't recommend kowtowing to the wishes and whims of players or parents, paying attention to the real needs of your team will require some nimble contingency planning. As our seasons move along, the amount of mental, emotional, and physical energy the players will have is less, unless we plan very well to allow enough time for rest and recovery. The early work of conditioning at the beginning of the season, can be pivotal in helping players with recovery times from competition to competition and become a great source of stress reduction and confidence to lay it all out in an effort to win.

I love to give players the most difficult conditioning of the week on a Friday, so that they can come back from the weekend stronger. Your sport might not allow that, but be wise in how you schedule your workouts. When that work is done well early in the season, then it allows a coach to allow for days of rest later in the season, thus creating greater gains, and better performances by your team of fresh players. My teams often play against others that haven't prepared themselves well by doing the more difficult conditioning in the beginning. I imagine that they either never do a complete conditioning routine, or continue to work at the same intensity all season long, and end up paying the price in burnout. I plan into my season schedule at least two fun only days during the season to allow players to recover from a very tough competitive stretch. Working our players too hard and/or too late in the season, can push them over the edge in terms of the energy they have available for the toughest competitions at the end of the year. I want my players fully rested ahead of the most crucial time, the end of the season approaching playoffs.

When we set our players up for late season success, then the momentum of our programs improves and they come back for the next season with more excitement.

My Take Away: Action Item(s):

CHAPTER FIFTY-TWO

Criminal Abuse

Destroy the seed of evil, or it will grow up to your ruin.

~ Aesop

How can a parent, coach or a program be called Athlete Centered if they wittingly, or unwittingly allow athletes to be physically, sexually, mentally or emotionally abused?

They can't!

This is going to be a difficult chapter to read.

Long Term Systematic Sexual Assault

2018 saw the sentencing of Larry Nassar, a doctor who worked for many years with U.S. Olympic Gymnastics athletes. He sexually assaulted them again and again. In recent years, the many abuses of adult coaches on youth athletes have come to light, and sanctioning bodies have been all too slow in responding, or moving to prevent such abuses. Too many programs allow their players to bully one another. Many times the bully is the coach. Sometimes the bullies are the parents, and yet the coach does nothing to teach families how to deal with competitive stresses. Even the somewhat stringent background checks on coaches are far too permissive. In reality, we all need to be much more vigilant, and create a watchful community. Recently, I became a coach for a private Catholic school, and I was impressed by the depth of the vetting that I had to go through in order to coach. The training I was given put me on notice that the school is well trained in the indicators of likely abuser's behaviors. Anyone who claims not to have noticed that bad things were happening, simply were not paying close enough attention to the athletes, or they turned a blind eye. It's that simple. Any phony outrage by parents should be directed at themselves, for the disconnect from the reality of what their children were facing.

It's Everyone's Responsibility

Everyone in sports should know about grooming behaviors, and other indicators that something is not right. Those in leadership must create an environment where players, parents and other stake holders can freely communicate about abuses, or allegations of abuse. In turn, that same leadership, must take measured steps in following through in dealing with coaches who have been alleged to have been abusive. Navigating these things carefully to prevent innocent coaches from having their lives ruined by public accusations that are found not to be true is paramount, but the highest level of thoroughness must be examined to assure the safety of many children in the sporting sphere.

Coach and Program Horror Stories

In recent years, I have heard stories locally of a coach who has had inappropriate contact physically with players. The behavior what was explained away as being for the safety of the player, or accidental. That coach create a program culture with a deeply ingrained fear that players will be ostracized with a vengeful attitude, if they question it. Should they become a threat to the culture of permissiveness, the players that enjoy that would make them pay. I'm certain that if some parents knew the behaviors exhibited on team road trips with these high school kids, that would summarily remove their child from the team, and/or not permit them to play in the first place.

I know of one such case where a player who I had worked with privately, was touched inappropriately, and attempts were made by her teammates to silence her. Players who witnessed the event, who sensed something was wrong and wanted to back up their teammate were warned not to speak up for fear of vengeance from the team leadership. In reality, some programs can become so sick and twisted, that abuse and lack of propriety seem to go hand in hand. The established players who are in the coach's favor enjoy certain benefits, while anyone who questions the established order is punished directly or in a passive-aggressive way.

Another coach with whom I thought was a casual friend, is actually in prison now for having preyed on his players. I feel like such a fool because when he was first charged years ago, I supported him, because it seemed like it was a witch hunt against him because of his sexual orientation. While I agreed that what was reported was inappropriate, it did not seem worthy of prison. Now I realize my own error in coming to the support of someone who would later be discovered as a serial abuser of young athletes whom he had groomed for years, even maintaining years long 'relationships' with those he was supposed to serve in purely a professional manner.   So, I understand the interpersonal struggle to come to grips with the fact that your friend or your rival may be an abuser, and it takes a lot of courage to report what you see. It's too late for the friend, and he is paying his dues to society. In the wake of the Nasser Trial, I called the school district in charge of my former rival to report what I had known. They responded very professionally, and now they are on notice to pay closer attention to that man.

Coaches Seem to Be More Prone

The nature of sports coaching creates a more dangerous dynamic than academic settings for a number of reasons:

* Longer school relationships between players and coaches
* More opportunities for a coach to be alone with a player
* Athletics can create compromising positions due to athletic gear
* Injury situations can create awkward situations in assessment
* Passionionate pursuit of excellence ramps up into arousal

Make a Stunning Admission

As a coach, I have had players who were attracted to me in a way that goes beyond the player-coach relationship. Admittedly, we, I find some of our players attractive. On the face of it, it sounds egotistical, but it most likely has happened to every coach at some point in their career. I'm happy to report that I have always acted appropriately with my players. I had a player who attempted to give me a full frontal hug, while the two of us were alone outside an athletic facility. At the moment she attempted this, I practically batted her arms away from me, using a light martial arts move, so as not to injure her. A moment later, my team captain came around the corner catching the very end of that encounter. I called the parent to inform them of what their child had attempted, and had a very frank and honest discussion with the parents at that time, and they knew that their daughter was wired a little differently than many and had a hard time understanding why others were not as affectionate as she is. It's critical that all coaches admit that it is possible for an attraction to take place, and to have a plan of action to avoid problems.

Not a Complete List Guidelines

The guidelines of what a coach needs to do to protect themselves from impropriety and even the appearance of it are very real:

1. Never stay in a closed environment with a player alone.

2. Communicate with your superiors at first sign of inappropriate behavior,   follow their directions as to how to proceed. You can be protected by policy   and early reporting.

3. Avoid touching players except possibly as a high five or very brief pat on the   shoulder.

4. Reject any and all sexual innuendo in speech or action.

5. You may need to talk to the player's parents as I did.

Boys Will Be Boys?

One of the worst excused for bad behaviors in sport coaching is the 'boys will be boys' approach, which seems to excuse the worst of boys toward each other and girls. Misguided at best, evil at worst, some coaches seem intent on teaching these boys how to be a man, while exhibiting chauvinistic, misogynistic and other abusive behaviors. In many programs bullying is allowed by star players or team captains toward the less talented less powerful players. At one high school where I coached a member of the football team came by the tennis courts and exposed his bare buttocks to the girls on my team. He got away with only having a stern talking to, by one of the assistant coaches, but I also brought this up to the head football coach who did not seem overly interested in finding out exactly what had happened. Players on that team routinely engaged in staged teasing and sexualized wrestling in the parking lot of the school. It was beyond embarrassing.

In another instance, my athletic director and I were appalled by the behavior of another team who during the introductions for a sectional playoff tennis match shared their overtly sexual nicknames witnessed by a mixed crowd of players, parents and siblings. My athletic director followed up, and their coach was later fired. That program ended for a period of time after my Athletic Director made contact with his counterpart at the other school. Recently, a friend of mine brought program back to life with much better behavior.

We all can call on every coach to nip all inappropriate behavior in the bud, crushing the evil seed before it can sprout. Put out the match in our players, programs and even their personal lives before they become a forest fire.

My Take Away: Action Item(s):

CHAPTER FIFTY-THREE
Playing The Long Game

In our view, it is of utmost importance for the competitive coach in the early ages of development to establish a culture where players and parents are consistently motivated by the effort, the act of play, not by wins.

~ Michael Paduch

Developing successful, advanced junior tennis competitors is a difficult, multi-year engagement process that requires fine structure over chaos, and long term orientation over short term gains and cheap tricks. The famous 10,000 hours rule or a 8 to 10 year period is usually quoted as a norm and we have not seen anyone being able to shorten that cycle in any country and in any system, or to make it more predictable and linear.

Those who win tournaments early, especially those who win before age ten or twelve, are not necessarily the ones who will stay on with the sport for a very long time. At least there is no clear correlation at large to indicate such a trend despite obvious edge cases that show the opposite where a youngster wins early, stays on with the sport and keeps on winning.

Attempts at predicting tennis success future based on early age success proved to be as reliable as trying to win at lottery and worse than trying to invest in high risk stocks. If you encounter a person, perhaps a self-usurped guru coach who makes claims about the future pro career of your U10 child, run as far as you can. You are just being sold a snake oil. If you are a coach and you encounter a parent of a U10 who talks about his or her "financial investment" in their child's tennis, let them go elsewhere. It will only lead to troubles down the road and you do not want that.

Those who are open-minded to constantly expanding their game, who see themselves today, tomorrow and the day after tomorrow playing tennis with increasingly robust tennis toolkit are the most likely to reach the highest level of competency and will succeed when it really matters: during their teens, where plans for what is to come start to formulate with more clarity.

So, does winning early has an impact on long term development of a player? Is there a problem with not winning early at all? And why the urgency if we aim for a long haul? Let`s address these extremely important points.

Winning Early And Setting (Wrong) Expectations

As players, when we lack experience and maturity because of our young age, every time we win, we set internal expectations or hopes that next time we play a similar event or this particular opponent, we will repeat the feat and will win again. We may feel pressured by subtle or not so subtle signals from the outside – from parents, supporters, team mates and from misplaced coaching – that we need to repeat this result naturally as we did it in the past perhaps more than once.

But repeating wins naturally is against the very nature of this game and against the principle of any sport to begin with! Have you ever caught yourself thinking that Roger Federer should win this match against Rafael Nadal because he had beaten him on this surface before at this level event? If you have, as had millions of tennis fans every time tennis champions had played against each other, rest assured the same happens in the minds of the little kids who compete, and it is an entirely wrong type of thinking. Here is why:

First, the expectation to repeat the wins assumes that tournament draws and the levels of play in each event are the same. They are not. Draws are supposed to be completely random with a computer assigning who plays against whom in all OTA and Tennis Canada sanctioned events. In some UTR events, draws may not be random but the competition is set to be level-based, so that means players with very close UTR ratings are manually matched to play against each other leading to a lot of very close matches resolved in tiebreaks.

So not only you have no control over who signs up to play a tournament any given weekend, you do not even know in which round you will face a certain opponent. In larger tennis regions and in events with bigger draws it is almost as bad as playing roulette in a casino or choosing a chocolate like Forrest Gump: "you never know what you are going to get". So how can you expect the things will go as easy as they did a week or two before? It just makes no sense to assume so.

Secondly, an expectation to win against the past opponent just because we beat him or her once or twice before assumes the opponent's game is not improving while everything else is being constant. Well, these two assumptions are or at least can be just plain wrong: opponent is changing and nothing is constant including our own game.

Our form may not be consistent during each match for a myriad of reasons despite our best efforts. A player may be coming out of a minor cold, a girl may be at a certain time of the month and does not feel 100% energized, a drive to a tournament in Toronto was unusually long and impacted the player, there were no courts available for proper warm-up and more.

On top of all that, our opponent's form and the level of play may oscillate as well. They may have improved one particular type of shot that they used to miss a lot before with just a few private lessons dedicated to it. They may have learned from past mistakes and decided to change tactics against you throwing your entire game style into a disarray. Combine any of these factors and you see very clearly that no assumptions about the win can be made until the match is truly over.

Motivated By Wins Versus Motivated By Play

Some super-ambitious young players get motivated by wins, these early wins we are talking about, the ones that are years away from any relevance, the wins that may not even be counted towards national rankings. In Canada, the U10 results do not get ranked nationally at the time of this publication. I even recall reading an ITF paper that advocated for results as high as U14 to not to be nationally ranked.

In our view, it is of utmost importance for the competitive coach in the early ages of development to establish a culture where players and parents are consistently motivated by the effort, the act of play, not by wins. The wins should be congratulated on but only in the context of the effort expended to secure a win.

The winning player should know they won because of the team they train with and because of the hard work he or she put in during practices and during the matches. A competitive coach should offer a mute or very little enthusiasm for wins achieved by opponent's medical withdrawal or because a match was won against an absolute beginner who was signed to a wrong type of a tournament.

Congratulate on wins that involved hard work, effort, combat and strain – not ones granted by defaults or some other administrative decision. Such wins are on-paper only, they do not matter at all and should not even be talked about with the players. They are really just a waste of time in a grand scheme of things as far as we are concerned.

Similarly, if effort is all you praise, then what you really celebrate and reward in the psyche of your players is completely independent from the score. A 2-6, 2-6 loss by one of your players may be the best, hardest fought match in his or her entire career and it may as well be worth celebrating.

It all depends who you play against and how well. A well played match against much higher ranked junior is worthy of your praise regardless of the score.

If you create a culture where players are motivated by the level of play they demonstrate, you will automatically create hope and desire to strive to get consistently better and better without a futile pursuit of short term wins and the emotional feeling of boom and bust between one win and one loss that kills motivation and damages team and individual player morale.

Is Early Winning Important Or Not?

With all the talk about rewarding the effort (the level of play) and not the outcome (the score) you are probably expecting an answer along the lines of: well, it does not matter really whether kids win early or not. The real answer is unfortunately more complicated than that...

Some early wins, and especially the wins that repeat from time to time, are very important. They demonstrate to a child that:

a.   It is actually possible to win!

b.   Winning feels good, certainly much better than losing!

c.   What led to a win was me doing things right, just the way I was taught!

Point a) gives a child confidence that he or she can be among those who win from time to time. It creates a vision of what is actually possible if everything aligns on court correctly.

Point b) creates a psychological hunger for competition: if I won once, I want to try doing this again and while I know it may be tough, I also know I did it before, so I will keep trying over and over to get that feeling of being a winner again. It is like a pursuit of a certain psychological state of elation, a certain high.

And finally, point c) serves a purely didactic purpose: I did what I was trained to do and it led me to a win. I will try doing this again to repeat this feat. It also creates an elevated sense of trust in the team and the coach who leads me as if it was not for them, I would not been able to secure this win.

To sum it all up, some early wins are useful and important. Too many wins early create a sense of expectation or hope that may not be sustainable as a child grows, enters higher levels of tournaments, experiences body changes and encounters peers who may be developing faster. Early winning children not conditioned mentally for what is to come often become disillusioned and lose motivation to pursue the sport because they think they are no longer "any good", which often has no basis in reality but too many times leads to early exit from competitive tennis.

What If There Are No Wins, Ever?

Children who never win anything will invariably ask themselves, their parents and their coaches some important, and sometimes sad, questions: why am I not as good as him or her, is this coach really helping me, am I good at anything at all…

A child who never wins against anyone at any level usually requires some major intervention. Often, if this situation repeats season after season a child will withdraw from competition and eventually from the sport. The trick is to find the level of competition that is adequate for this child, so that he or she does not feel belittled (relegated to a lower rank) and actually starts flourishing and winning a little against those closer to him or her at that new level. This will give them the a), b) and c) points they have been waiting for all along to earn, and thus the player will remain with the sport.

If this intervention is not done in time, however, or if a suitable level of competition is not found, a player may develop certain mental disposition and attitudes that will make them unsuitable for this particular sport in a long run. In other words, they will start hating competitive tennis and the player is lost.

Long Term Orientation vs. A Sense Of Urgency

At first sight it makes no sense: we have a young kid, let us say a girl age eight. She has a decade ahead of her before she turns eighteen and gets accepted to College to compete on a full ride Division 1 team. That is our hope. So where is the sense of urgency? We have all the time in the world to get things right in her tennis development.

Well, it is not that simple. There are some cascading dependencies in a generally nonlinear development path which we discuss in detail later. Some things need to be firmly in place by a certain age while some other things can wait until later but in general, there is always a set of skills, competencies or abilities – physical and mental – that have to be in place by a certain age.

There is some room for the slippage but not a whole lot of room. If a child is slipping in some area, an intervention is needed to rectify a problem. If no action is taken to rectify it urgently, we will have a much harder problem to solve down the road and the player will be exposed in the most brutal way: by not being able to compete at a certain level because of his or her developmental deficiencies. These deficiencies at some point become too difficult, too costly and too ingrown into personal habits to undo.

In many cases, players who pursued pro tennis careers have had developmental deficiencies they had to work around to build their game in a way that can mask these weaknesses as fixing them later became an impossible task. We are thankful to Gabriela Dabrowski and Tony Milo for discussing these important topics with us.

My Take Away: Action Item(s):

CHAPTER FIFTY-FOUR
Setting the Tone

*To solve big problems you have to be willing
to do unpopular things.*

~ Lou Holtz

As with any aspect of athlete centered coaching, there is a fine line between the responsibilities of a coach and the responsibilities of the player or team. Especially with younger athletes the onus is on the coach to set the tone for the day, every day. An easy error would be to assume that if the tone was good or great yesterday, then it will be the same today. There is no resting on yesterday, or any expectation for tomorrow. Today has its own unique challenges.

Protecting the Plan Takes Mental Toughness

Coaches who mentally prepare to set the tone in the moments leading up to a match or practice are more likely to execute. I know from my own experiences that if I don't have time to mentally prepare, or something happens which has me preoccupied when I could be preparing, I am more likely to slip up in this area.

Tone Built on Coaching Philosophy

What is the tone you want to set? It all comes back to the pillars of your coaching philosophy. If your philosophy is not well defined, then the tone of each practice can be all over the map, and not by the choice and intent of the coach or even the committed players. If you are not establishing the culture of your program according to rock solid principles, then someone else will set the tone at times. Establish three to five principles of doing the work each day, and it will be your touchstone to come back to when things get a little crazy. Your best players who are most dedicated will be the first ones who are disappointed when a poor tone is set for the day. It's a daily battle.

Over time, as players become familiar with your philosophy, these pillars might not need any reminders attached. In the early going however, there could be considerable amount of effort expended in simply explaining what these guidelines are. I find it amazing that teenagers many times don't realize that giving 100% means every moment, it means moving quickly from one thing to the next, and finishing strong the last few feet, instead of taking your foot off the gas. I stress that giving 100% effort for 95% of the exercise is 95% effort.

Like Eating Your Vegetables

We have certain activities that are necessary, but we don't enjoy, that is a great time to set the tone within ourselves to make the best of those moments. Mostly, the fitness aspect of training is going to be the hardest push for most players, but when you can show how the conditioning gives them a competitive edge, motivation Remaining fully present with the activity until its done, can be easier said than done.

Dealing with Resistance

Setting the tone gets more difficult when you face push back from players, parents or other coaches. 'Why are we doing this?' is the question they ask. You must have a quick and concise answer, and those pushing back must know that they are not going to derail your objective by turning it into a conversation, a negotiation or even a debate. On the other hand, there is a lot of risk in not allowing players and parents to express what they are thinking, so making yourself available after practice to fully explain the rationale behind what you are doing can win the day. It's quite common and to be expected that in your first year with a new team, that there will be some dissent as you install a different program than what everyone is used to from the year before. However, those types of discussions need to take place at a time that allows for better planning. The plan for the day must never be negotiable, unless that is what you want, but there is risk associated with negotiating on the day. Because I know that the players feel more empowered when they have choices, I might give them a choice in which type of plyometric exercise we do, or at the end of practice I will let them choose between two large group games that have the objective I want in them. Once we open up a discussion that allows players to divert the plan that creates an opening for chaos, and there the less motivated to voice their opinion and exert influence on the decision making.

Is Setting the Tone 'Coach Centered'?

Why is the coach setting the tone 'athlete centered'? It's really a way to teach the maturity of leadership, modeling what needs to be done in order to bring about improvement in a group. I like to compare being a coach with being the hub of bicycle wheel. This centerpiece must be strong and reliable, or the wheel will wobble. The athlete centered approach comes in as the coach then works to adjust each spoke, each individual athlete, until the tension is uniform around the hub, leading to a well balanced wheel. The hub allows the spokes to be tuned. This evenly rolling wheel of a unit is the whole point behind developing disciplined habits on the team. In another chapter we will discuss an athlete centered approaching to teaching personal and team discipline. The coaches strong leadership shows the limits of player directed activity, keeping it in line with the goals and objectives of the program is the greatest service the coach can provide.

My Take Away: Action Item(s):

CHAPTER FIFTY-FIVE

Seize Opportunies

I coach everyone the same way, differently.

~ John Wooden

Our coaching philosophies must be rock solid, but our implementation will change based on who we have with us. Each player and team has it's own unique personality. Even at the same school, when a few seniors graduate and some new freshmen come in, the personality of that team changes, especially when those seniors were great players and/or leaders.

Back Up the Truck, Park It in the Right Spot

What kind of team do you have? Where are they in their development? Are they on the cusp of a first championship? Are they developing, but raw? Do you have to start from the beginning with fundamental play, because of what came prior to your arrival? Making an honest assessment about where your team is now, helps you to make a long term plan, and effectively go along the path developing each piece of training for them to overcome the next major hurdle in their development. I can relate to it all, since I have coached recreational soccer with 7 year olds, middle school players, not so great high school teams through elite level teams, and athletes. From those experiences I learned that you and I as coaches can never take a cookie cutter approach. As our teams change year to year, protecting the culture with the new players is a high priority, but the personality of the team will certainly change to some degree.

Do you have a veteran team that is expecting to surge, or a young team that might have to take its lumps and learn the hard way? What kinds of activities are needed with that type of team? Do you have seniors who languish and you can't wait for them to graduate because they poison the water? How much recovery time is needed by your group after a tough stretch of the season? How will the team react to a tough loss or a major win? As coaches, the better we know our team and can begin to anticipate our team's likely reactions, then we can also be ready with solutions that fit them. It's been said that good coaches have a system and look for the players who fit their system, but the greatest coaches adapt their system to meet the strengths of their team. One of the greatest things I hear coaches say is, 'We just try to put our players in position to be successful'.

Coaching Wisdom v. Negativity at Home

Not everything is planned, but when we have a plan in mind, then we are better able to seize the moment. A friend who coaches a very good and fairly well known high school football team and I were talking about how his team changed so dramatically with the graduation of his starting Quarterback who later would play in the NFL, along with some very good skill players. He really needed to simplify his offense for a new QB. This meant more reliance on the defense, ball possession and strong running. Parents whose youngsters had been used to an intricate high flying offense were suddenly critical of his approach. My friend stuck to his guns, methodically installing one or two more plays each week to diversify the attack. Dinner table discussions continued, and he knew that he was being criticized at his player's homes by mothers and fathers who knew better, even while he was doing what his team needed. His week by week faithful work while facing unending criticism all paid off with a trip to the section championships against a legendary team about whom a movie was made. That legendary team was having a down year and was beatable, but the cumulative effect of so much criticism all year long seemed to be the deciding factor in the game, as the team played poorly in the championship game. The culture of that school was rife with complaining parents, something that the administration never seemed to get ahead of, even though strong leadership can help quell this kind of negativity.

Managing Negative Perceptions with Team Leaders

Our plans will come under scrutiny with parents, and I have no easy answer as to how to manage negative perceptions. Mainly your best conduit to develop trust with the parents is to gain the full trust of your players. Getting your players fully on board with the plan means investing some time in getting their thoughts about where they think the team is in it's development. Teenagers often have an unrealistic outlook on the state of the team, but all you need are one or two leaders who understand. It's been said that positivity and negativity are highly contagious, so create a core of highly positive leaders, and let them spread that outward to everyone. Developing a solid relationship with a sensible team captain who thinks for themselves and feels free to push back on ideas that they don't accept, creates an avenue for solidarity of purpose on the team. When teams think of the captains as only a conduit for the coach, and have no real voice in representing the players, then they are not going to be as influential with their teammates, especially the most skeptical. Having a parent or two who really know your sport, who come without a personal agenda can also be allies in helping with the battle for hearts and minds among the parents of the players on your team. Be creative, develop as much consensus as you can, and be prepared to teach early and often.

Good Planning Allows Us to Seize the Day

I had a young team that lost a tough match because they did not have enough experience pulling through in tough circumstances. They didn't even give a true 100% effort, partly because they felt the match outcome was already decided. We also had some negative forces on the team who created anxiety about the outcome among their peers. Strangely enough, after the loss, players stayed around and were playing a social pick up game, messing around. They were playing great! I watched this for a while and wondered where this performance was an hour prior when the real competition was happening. I decided not to talk with the players about this immediately, but to get a few more minutes to truly soak in the experience. After a while I called them together:

'Gentlemen, are you having fun?'

'Yes, coach'

'You guys are playing great! Where was that during the match today?'

'We don't know.'

'Do you think you now the pressure is off, so you feel free to play well?'

'Yes, maybe that's it.'

Moving forward, that team which had been a bit of a disappointment in terms of results because they played below their ability, played a great match at the end of the season, pulling an upset over a team higher in the standings. That moment created some awesome momentum in the program and lead to that team making a few leaps in the standings until we won a league championship. I find that team tennis is fairly predictable and there are not a lot of upsets because the better player and teams almost always win. The ball doesn't bounce funny, one hot player can't take over a contest, official's calls don't have a catastrophic effect on the game, and there are an average of 487 hits in two sets, so any 'lucky' shots seem to even out. So, when one tennis team upsets another, it really is a special moment, it has to be a team effort through and through. So in my plan, I had known that my young team would face adversity, and while I did not know when it would hit, I knew I had to be ready, but also not to overreact to it. At the moment of our very short interaction that team was in 5th place out in a 9 team league. The next year we would finish 2nd, and the following year after that we won our 2nd title in a 44 year span of no championships. The seed of that was one day, and one brief conversation with no shaming. We simply identified what the problem was, and decided together to do it differently. Seizing opportunities can begin with making one simple observation, and having one simple conversation.

My Take Away: Action Item(s):

CHAPTER FIFTY-SIX
Phases To Maximize Opportunities

*The concept of periodization for athletics is not a new concept,
but its usage is of fundamental importance to anyone looking to
make
systematic improvements in their training and involve the
often-forgotten variable of individualization.*

~ Coach Ninja

Aspiring great coaches must understand how to create a periodized training schedule to put their athletes in position to perform their best when it matters most. Periodized training is Athlete Centered, because it looks at the schedule of the athletes, to set them up for having the very best chance of being fully prepared prior to their most important competitions. Realize that there is absolutely no cookie cutter approach that will work, especially because the demands of every sport is different. Macro periodization for a team, can also be blended with micro periodization for a player. The needs, desires and dangers of training are different with different kinds of athletes at varying positions on the developmental spectrum. As stated earlier I have seen coaches performing adult level workouts with 5 year old and younger children that could qualify as child abuse, if the child and parents did not willingly go along and even celebrate what their little monster can do.

Do your homework, study not only the demands of your sport, but also developmentally appropriate workouts. Dr. Mark Kovacs recently said in an interview with me that reducing the intensity and/or scope of the work can allow for more to be done within developmental parameters. We may also have athletes who are the same age, and inside the parameters within we believe they should perform a certain exercise, skill, or drill, but when it hurts them, then we have to stop and take notice. There can be a wide range of ability within a tight band of age group and level based play. If for whatever reason athletes are not able to perform the task with proper form, then it's worth more study.

Preparation Phase

Baseline exercises that establish fundamental strengths and capacities necessary for the sport. Building in pre-habilitation and injury avoidance happens mostly in this stage. Ability testing, and conforming to parameters of acceptable ability before going on to higher levels of intensity is wise. For many sports this means establishing a range of flexibility, aerobic stamina, and learning fundamental movements that mitigate the chances of injury. Finding the best balance of mobility and stability for your athletes is a key building block for success, and safety. Returning players may learn next phase skills in slow motion or in very controlled environments. Year around athletes will have more time for this phase and it will pay off. High School Sports Seasons are so short, this phase may be compromised slightly to make room for later phases. Once I have build a strong culture of belief in my program, athletes are more likely to pursue this in the weeks ahead of our first day of practice.

Pre-Competition Phase

This phase includes ramping up the speed and intensity of work outs and performances. For some sports, an emphasis on explosive anaerobic capacity and skills come to the front, while some aerobic exercise may phase out of the routine. In the words of former Olympic Wrestler Dan Brand, 'Many times simply playing your sport a lot gives you want you need to be prepared.' In the case of Tennis which is a dominant hand, upper body dominated sport, it's important to work out the non-dominant side for injury prevention. Understand the particular common injuries in your sport, and use rehabilitative action to protect your players from acute or chronic injury.

An example of a counter-intuitive plan that I use as a tennis coach is that I only test my players' aerobic base by asking them to run for 12 straight minutes. Once they meet that threshold then they can participate in the pre-competition phase, if not, then they will complete 12-minute runs while the others train anaerobically. I know many of my fellow tennis coaches will scoff at that idea, but my team's track record in long matches, and especially in third sets shows that we had emphasized the anaerobic which helped us at the end.

Another characteristic of pre-competitive is situational drills that focus on one aspect of the competition. Like in football when tackling drills are done, or offensive linemen and defensive linemen focus on the hand fighting and balance to gain or hold a position on the field, fast break or lay up drills in basketball, or any number of situational play.

Adding new layers and more complexity to the competitive situational play until the pieces come together should culminate in being ready for the transition to the competitive phase.

Keep up with the latest exercise research, and don't be afraid to go against conventional wisdom, when it's outdated. Sport Science is discovering many new aspects that can help your players train smarter in this area of explosive movements.

Note: take great care with unstable surface training, and consult a professional on the proper use and progressions so that you don't compromise your athletes speed and quickness.

Competition Phase

The Competition Phase can be a few days or up to few weeks. For my uses I like my competitive phase to be under 10 days. For those at elite levels of sport this may go on for many weeks., like during a World Cup, or Olympic Tournament which can be quite lengthy. Essentially all the training has been done, it's all about dealing with a few nuances of game planning and keeping players healthy and sharp. Warning: I have seen many coaches who violate the principles of the competitive phase and when they do, they sabotage their teams ability to rise to the occasion. So called leaders who load extra work, new plays, exhausting conditioning, and create high pressure situations will find that their players seem to play with a heavy weight on them.

Creating practices that allow their bodies to recover, have elements where they simply play the game the way they want to play, with messages of confidence in their ability can be just the empowerment they need. In this phase, don't give the players any new information, tail off the conditioning, play points and practice matches, and be ready to compete with a fresh and competent team. You may even want to shorten your practice schedule a bit without compromising the ritual aspect of it. Of course, there might be some fine points, and a little tuning that goes on, but making any major technical changes to their game can be disaster. The message is, 'You are as ready as you are going to be, and it would be unwise for you to be unsettled before these upcoming competitions, so let the fur fly.' Their game is their game, let them play.

Active Rest

One of the smartest things you can do as a coach is hold to the promise of active rest. As your team moves toward the most pivotal regular season competition(s) of the season, let your players know that as soon as they get past that stretch of the season that you are going to have an active rest day. It should be fun, and filled with players favorite activities. I don't necessarily recommend giving the players a day off, but in sports like football, that might actually be needed and appreciated more than a 'goof-off day'. On an active rest day, it could be fun to play a different sport with your team like basketball, soccer or tennis, or use the most entertaining drills and games that they enjoy. A light refreshing jog can be used in place of a grueling run. Give more time to longer breaks to enjoy the presence of teammates. Spend some time reflecting on the lessons learned during that competitive phase. Allow some time to process those lessons and it can build your team up to a higher level.

Can I Trust My Coach Not To Kill Me?

Strong morale is built when players trust that after they give every last drop of effort during the competition phase that they can have a time of recovery. When they know that there is something easy on the other side, it helps them give all they have during the crucial moments. Again in postseason play, especially in high school sports, I am much more likely to have a very light practice or an easy one the next day after a playoff win. Managing energy becomes the key to gaining the best advantage moving forward. Again, my teams have very good post season records for this reason, because I don't push them harder, when the competition does that on it's own. Less successful teams and programs do the opposite, they seem to ramp up effort at the worst possible time, pressurizing the situation. When my teams haven't managed their own energy, because of the 'fear of missing out' culture, then they find themselves with an empty tank at the worst time of the season. I have had to teach my high school players to lead a somewhat simpler lifestyle, because the planned mediocrity of trying to do everything means they might not have the energy to compete when they need it most.

Repeat

Study up, your sport, your season, your players, may be need through all the phases again before post season, or maybe you have club teams, high school teams, travel season, etc. Make sure there is some down time for athletes to recover in between club seasons, travel teams, house play, and school team seasons. Go back to building that base, the core, and you can take it up a notch from the last round. In season, an active rest day can only be one day, but when it's on a Friday, that's great because the players will have 3 full days of recovery.

This phase is 1-3 days, any longer and the team will go on a mental vacation that they might not return from. In a 12 week high school tennis season, the most rounds of periodization I have done is three, but with most teams I only have done two.

In conclusion, think about your team, and plan for these phases of training. Seize on opportunities that arise to build your team up according to the principles you want to teach them. Plan each day of practice to have an ideal balance of activities for the phase of training you are in. This should give you a general idea about periodizing, but we will get into more detail in a future chapter, and my ideas are very general here, so you are advised to study up on all types of periodization to fit them to your specific sport, level and athletes.

Micro Periodization

Commonly you will have some outlier athletes who do much more work than their teammates. Just the other day one of my seniors let me know that he had done 'leg day' in the gym. Some of your athletes will really work and play hard on the other days that you don't see them, so pay attention, and it may mean resting a player, or putting another player through a different phase than the team, because they are coming back from an injury. Essentially, I threw that in there, because their will sometimes be exceptions to the macro periodization schedule of the team.

My Take Away: Action Item(s):

CHAPTER FIFTY-SEVEN
Air Tight Daily Plan

Time management is an oxymoron.
Time is beyond our control, and the clock keeps ticking
regardless of how we lead our lives.
Priority management is the answer
to maximizing the time we have.

~ John C. Maxwell

There is an art to developing a great periodized schedule. As with any great piece of art, the artist makes many erasures, corrections, edits until they get it exactly right. Many times the creation takes on a life of its own. So, when you put down a schedule periodizing your workouts for an entire season, there will always be an upset. Rain, injury, missing players, other disruptions to the schedule will come when you least expect it. The technology you need is pencil and paper, so that you can erase and start over on a certain day. If we ignore the mitigating factors that get in the way of our teams or players achievement, then we take the risk of not maximizing our time, prioritizing properly.

Progression/Regression, Mastery/Challenge

The performance of your team may require you to regress and re-teach some fundamentals. It would be unwise to continue to progress, teaching more, when the foundational skills are lacking. This will only lead to frustration. In my 30 years of coaching sports, I can't remember a season when I did not have to repeat a certain lesson, or build a missing skill that did not allow my players to execute the challenge I was presenting. Creating an acceptable amount of discipline in players in regard to executing routines for practice are needed in order to progress. Every once in a while you meet that athlete who tries something one time, and with a tone of self-fulfilling prophesy cries out, 'See! I knew this wouldn't work', after they finish giving it an intentional poor effort. To this I normally respond, 'Drills don't work, people do! It's your job to figure out how to make it work, with my help.'

Developing routines and rituals that players can ease into, because practice always starts the same way, helps create a nice flow at the beginning. Allowing some rituals at the beginning will help a certain cross section of players who like to know what's going to happen. Players then can ease into a higher challenge level. It would be a mistake to begin a practice with something brand new or at a dramatically higher challenge level than what players are used to doing.

Practice in Reality, Two Variations from Two Coaches

Next up, I will share an example of my sloppy work, and the more clean presentation from my friend Styrling. Cryptic notes are easy to follow when you have the full plan completely written out, and/or your team knows the routine. Veteran coaches can simply have one word written on a piece of paper to guide them. Newer coaches might want to have more detail, and some instructions for things to do or avoid. So if you are new, or you have an assistant for whom you plan activities, you might want to get more detailed. Some of you might look down on me for making notes the way I do, but some of you might find it refreshing.

Example One   *Pre-Competition Phase Practice*

2:15pm Warm Up is 15 minutes
2:30pm Players are assigned courts and either work on Loops and Angles, or doing the   transition challenge.
2:55pm It's not written but we will take a short break for water and explain the next   segment.
3:00pm A quick 15 minute segment of poaching to build the habit, with a diagram showing   diagonal movement.
3:15pm All Players Lob and Overhead for 7 minutes each.
3:30pm An intense bout of exercise. Previously we had not done 15 sprints. I can explain   side sprints if you like.
3:55pm a full five minute REST after sprinting.
4:00pm Kamikaze is a doubles game where the net person must attempt to touch the first   shot from the returner. If they do, then they cannot lose the point. If they make an error on the volley the point is replayed. A regular set can be played or just 4 service games to allow each player to be the net person. Variations: Serving team can

have a bonus point for net person making first volley, or return team can get a bonus point for ___ net player failing to touch the ball. (I said I would explain below, but really I am explaining above)

4:30 Cupcake is fully explained in my book The Art of Coaching High School Tennis. Three groundstrokers hit big forehands at three net players. The game goes to five. If the groundstrokes win they become champions, run to the other side for volleys. If the volleyers win, then a new team of three groundstrokers comes into the game. For the sake of space here, let me know if you want the full rules. Three players on each side make spaces to volley smaller, and places to pass smaller, creating a challenge of precise placement. It's a fun large group game.

4:45 Practice ends, completely. No extension of practice because of poor play or as punishment for bad behavior. It's over. Parents will learn to trust you. If you want to be hated, and have a lot of negativity in the parking lot with parents whose late afternoon and early evening are being ruined by your extension of practice beyond its normal time, then have at it! You can really make a busy mom angry if you disrupt her afternoon ride schedule.

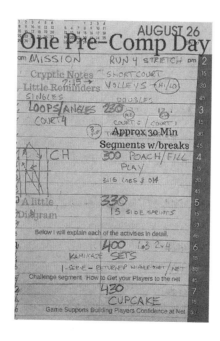

Example Two *Pre-Competition Phase Practice*

2:00pm Practice Begins with a low movement drill, no running, no stretching, but a low stress activity.

2:15pm X-files is a short court game played crosscourt, and balls cross each other from two   games on one court. Works short angle shots and concentration due to another pair on the same court.

2:30pm An intense bout of exercise. This one is more explosive than the one before.

2:55pm a full 5 minute break.

3:00pm S/R - Serves and Returns for 30 full minutes. 6 players per court, two servers for every one returner. Servers take turns serving two balls to the returner, who gets more continuous practice while servers learn to slow themselves down to a more realistic   speed. Every 10 minute (9, to allow a minute of walking), rotate, each player should get 20 minutes of serving and a slower pace with 10 minutes of returning. As the season progresses this becomes 21 minutes, then 15.

3:30pm Players assigned to courts and have specific challenges bases on singles, doubles, and skill level. This is where a lot of magic can happen if we give them good challenges. Beginner players can get stroke work. Singles players will play challenge sets for the ladder. Doubles teams play one bounce doubles, and others have a stroke to work on.

4:00pm   Singles players have a challenging footwork skill to develop. All other players work on lobs and overheads.

4:30pm   Game: Stations, where the first shot must be a lob or overhead. Game: Cupcake   for dessert?

5:00pm Practice ends. Rarely do we have 3 hour practices.

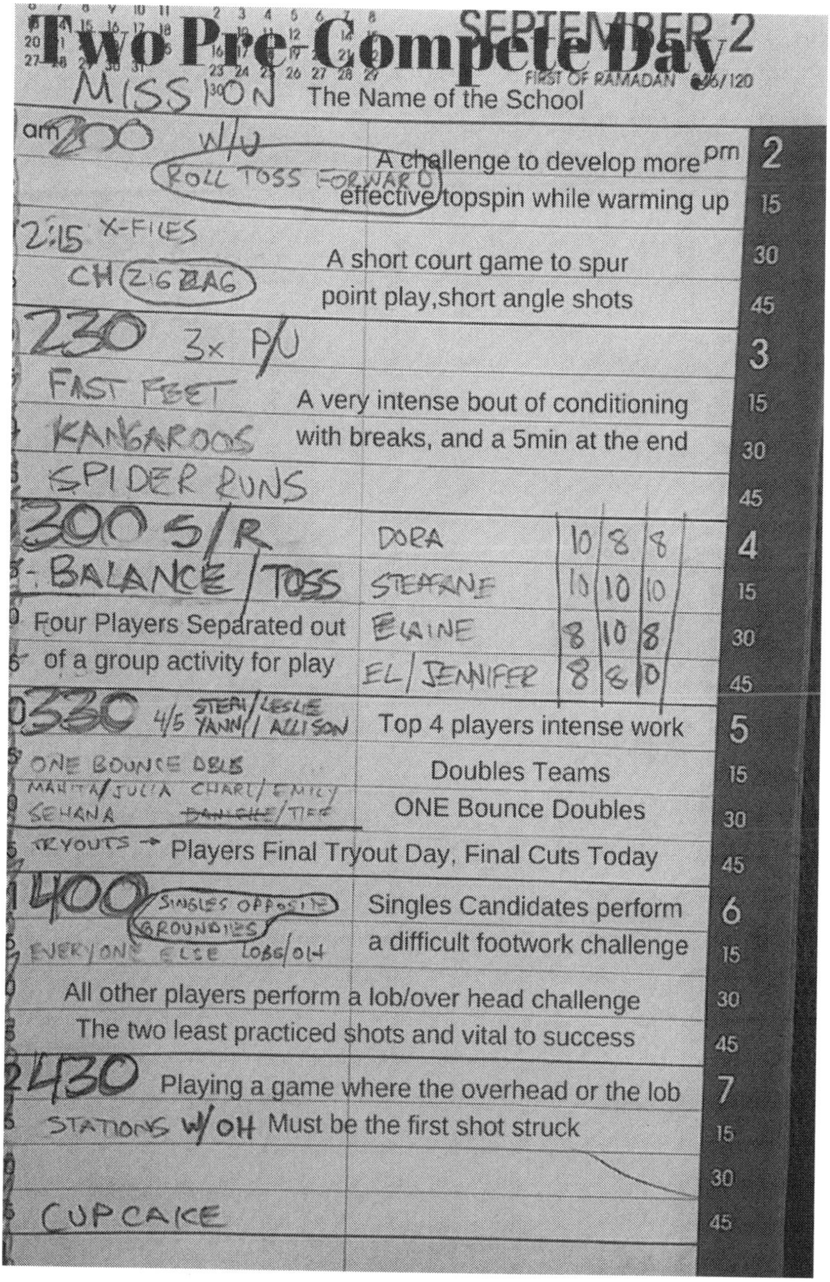

Two Pre Compete Day
SEPTEMBER 2
MISSION The Name of the School
FIRST OF RAMADAN 246/120

Handwritten	Printed	pm
am **800** W/U	A challenge to develop more effective topspin while warming up	2
ROLL TOSS FORWARD		15
2:15 X-FILES	A short court game to spur point play, short angle shots	30
CH (ZIG ZAG)		45
230 3x P/U	A very intense bout of conditioning with breaks, and a 5min at the end	3
FAST FEET		15
KANGAROOS		30
SPIDER RUNS		45

300 S/R	DORA	10	8	8	4
- BALANCE / TOSS	STEARNE	10	10	10	15
Four Players Separated out	ELAINE	8	10	8	30
of a group activity for play	EL / JENNIFER	8	8	10	45

		pm
330 4/5 STEA/LESLIE YANN// ALLISON	Top 4 players intense work	5
ONE BOUNCE DBLS MARTA/JULIA CHARL/EMILY SEHANA DANELLE/TIFF	Doubles Teams	15
	ONE Bounce Doubles	30
TRYOUTS →	Players Final Tryout Day, Final Cuts Today	45
400 SINGLES OPPOSITE GROUNDIES EVERYONE ELSE LOBS/OH	Singles Candidates perform a difficult footwork challenge	6
		15
	All other players perform a lob/over head challenge	30
	The two least practiced shots and vital to success	45
430	Playing a game where the overhead or the lob Must be the first shot struck	7
STATIONS W/OH		15
		30
CUPCAKE		45

Example Three - *Rainy Day Plan*

Indoor sport coaches don't have to worry about this, but for outdoor coaches, It's great if you can secure a classroom or some gym space. If you can play in the gym, I have a lot of fun ideas. If you can't get into a basketball gym, maybe you can get into a classroom to do a light warm-up and some stretching. Maybe there is enough room to throw some medicine balls around and do some fast feet or other explosive burst training. If not, having a fun discussion of strategy starting with having players summarize what they know about strategy for singles and doubles. When you can then ask a question that they don't know the answer to, then you can work with the players' natural curiosity to deepen their understanding.

Creating games by choosing teams and having a great quiz show makes for a really fun experience. You can give prizes like overgrips or a pre-approved energy bar, but make sure players don't have allergies to any of the ingredients. A great thing to do is to split strategy into two categories, one for singles and one for doubles.

Rainy Day Plan

RAIN

On a Rainy Day, some stretching and some fitness can occur, medicine balls are a great resource.

A lecture/discussion on strategy and tactics using a white board can be a revelation to players who may understand for the first time.

INDOOR
STRETCHING

3:45 FAST FEET

MED BALL THROWS

4:00 LECTURE
ON STRATEGY/TACTICS

4:30 TEAM
JEOPARDY

3 TEAMS

5 CATEGORIES

Players who know a game is coming while pay attention to the lecture better

A. STRATEGY AND TACT

B. TEAM HISTORY

C. STUFF COACH SEZ

D. MENTAL GAME

E. STRANGE BEHAVIOR

Example Four *An Active Rest Day*

A day like this is VITAL to the success of your team. Players get very stressed out after a very tough competitive phase against top competition and league rivals. Give them a day to rest, recuperate, and be together having fun no matter if they win or lose. Let the players choose the games and play them in reverse order. I have had players say they want to skip the practice because they don't feel like it's a valuable experience. Sadly, some players have been programmed not to have fun. I find this to be a vital time of team bonding and enjoyment that leads to a lot of great morale so that when the chips are down, the players realize that it's really supposed to be a fun time. A couple times during my career players have asked if we could have a normal practice because we did not play well enough in our competition phase, we did not have much hope of going to the post season, and they wanted to perform better in the final round of competitive phase. Only once did I grant this wish completely.

3:30pm 15 minute dynamic warm up.
3:45pm a quick recap of the competitive phase, successes and lessons learned
3:55pm Vote for games to play
4:00pm Game #4 Player's Choice
4:15pm Water Break Jokes, Grunting Contest
4:20pm Game #3 Players Choice
4:40pm Water Break Story Telling
4:45pm Game #2 Players Choice
5:05pm Game #1
5:30pm Practice Ends.

Three Examples from Styrling Strother

Pre-Competitive Practice 1		Cary Academy Tennis 2016			
		Varsity HS Girls			
Date:	8.4.2016		Skill	daily focus	
Coach:	S.Strother		Drill	practice skill	
Surface:	Hard		Thrill	competition	
Goals:	Technical	Proper Contact Point / Spacing			
	Tactical	Depth / Tempo / On the Rise			
	Physical	Balance while hitting / Reset court position			
	Mental	Decision Making			
Challenge 1:	Dynamic streching: Relay race (speed/balance/agility)				
5:00pm-5:15	Warm-up: Pro Volley / slice2slice (short court)				
Challenge 2:	Slice to Slice (Xcourt/DTL) 2 sets X 10 each way				
5:20-5:30	Rally Half Ct. (Speed 1/2) through cones (placed 10 ft. apart @service line)				
	Pyramid: set of 10, set of 15, set of 20, set of 15, set of 10				
Challenge 3:	Xcourt rally cone to cone - 4 ft. of net clearance - 4.5 min. - 150 goal				
5:30-5:40	in 3 minutes - Xcourt Deuce and Xcourt AD				
	Break				
Challenge 4:	Coach Racquet Feed · Opportunity Ball: FH xcourt/BH DTL Finishing shot				
5:40-6:00	Approach shot FH DTL/FH insidein : Finishing Volley				
	Break				
Challenge 5:	Bucket game: Coach Racquet feed				
6:00-6:10	2 baseline players / 2 net players - coach feeds from "T" where ball cart				
	is place (bucket) - baseline players are trying to hit "bucket" to win the				
	game or simply win the point - regular scoring (NO AD) - 2 net teams				
	are the Champions - rotate if win, baseline team wins become Champs				
Challenge 6:	Serve +1 / Return +1				
6:10-6:25	Players get 1 point for completing set - players must finish with 5 points				
	from Deuce and AD each				
Challenge 7:	First Strike Points - Tiebreakers to 7 points (Up/Down Court)				

1

Pre-Competitive Practice 2		Cary Academy Tennis 2016	
		Varsity HS Girls	
Date:	8.5.2016	Skill	daily focus
Coach:	S.Strother	Drill	practice skill
Surface:	Hard	Thrill	competition
Goals:	Technical	Proper Contact Point / Spacing	
	Tactical	Depth / Tempo / On the Rise	
	Physical	Balance while hitting / Reset court position	
	Mental	Decision Making	
Challenge 1:	Dynamic streching: Relay race (speed/balance/agility)		
5:00pm-5:15	Warm-up: Pro Volley / slice2slice (short court)		
Challenge 2:	Slice to Slice (Xcourt/DTL) 2 sets X 10 each way		
5:20-5:30	Groundstrokes - Rally tempo Med/High		
	Each player has to make 15 shots (if player nets - start back at 0)		
Challenge 3:	Pressure Points - Entire Team Play (1 on 1) - team bets on each player		
5:30-5:40	Player that loses point, teammates who bet on them and player run		
	1 up&down (doubles line to doubles line) - endurance/team bonding		
Challenge 4:	Coach Hand Feed - + and X movement patterns - 4 balls each		
5:40-6:00	Coach Racquet Feed - 2 ball passing challenge		
	Hill Runs (7 min) or 12-15 reps - Break		
Challenge 5:	Stinger Challenge Doubles play - Player 2nd Serve or Coach Racquet Feed		
6:00-6:10	Simulate 2nd second return and sting Xcourt w/ approach		
	Receiving team practicing pressuring Serving team		
Challenge 6:	Serve +1 / Return +1		
6:10-6:25	Players get 1 point for completing set - players must finish with 5 points		
	from Deuce and AD sides		
Challenge 7:	First Strike Points - Tiebreakers to 7 points (Up/Down Court)		

1

After seeing these, your reactions may run the gamut. Some of you are loving my chicken scratch because you, like I, am tired of coaches who are so anal retentive all the time. Let me reassure you that just because the writing is sloppy doesn't mean I don't run an airtight practice, but also one that has space for fun and getting to know each other. Some of you may have lost respect for me and are now loving Styrling's approach, so be it. There have to be some people in the middle. What you can see here though are two distinctly different styles of presentation on paper, but the same amount of organization, although with different amounts of time allotted to each item.

It is important to be detailed in your approach. Players might glance at my plan which is written down to the minute, commenting 'It says 4:30, but it's 4:37', to which I respond, 'If everything went according to plan, there would no need for leadership.'

My Take Away: Action Item(s):

CHAPTER FIFTY-EIGHT

Step Away From Glory

**It's never been my goal to be king of the prom.
It's been my goal to do the right thing and get the job done.**

~Gregg Popovich

A really good rule of thumb for victory and defeat, is to move toward players who have lost, and move away from players who have won. An athlete centered coach discovers the general way that their players handle winning and losing, but are always ready for out of character behavior. Be ready to give your presence, support, encouragement, empathy, or maybe more importantly SPACE, to those who are disappointed. For winning give a place for celebration and building independence in success for those who succeed. It's an amazing and humbling feeling to see the athletes you work with succeed at a high level, celebrating an enormous achievement, then realize that you or I did not actually compete, they did, and they came through. Moving along in coaching maturity means focusing more on the athletes outcomes than our own wins and losses. It's a tremendous privilege to facilitate the success of others, but being a glory hound is a bit unappealing. I have heard whispers that former athletes felt like I took too much credit for their success. That stings a bit, and so I have learned to focus much more on what they did that helped them succeed, and rarely tell my involvement, only as necessary. My hope is as you read this you can see how influential coaches can be, but at the same time cut the cord of ego connection to the success of the athletes. It's not easy to do.

Bursting Emotional Comfort Zones

I have seen some very low key competitors burst out into tears, sobbing uncontrollably because they felt their poor performance was the reason the team lost on the day. As it turns out, he was becoming a much more engaged competitor, and this was the first outward sign that he had a strong desire to win for the team. Acknowledging that, and simply being with him, briefly placing my hand on his back to give reassurance helped him make the transition to becoming a stronger competitor, and he later won the most pivotal match of the next season. I have seen joyous celebrations of players in total triumph, as they won what seemed unwinnable. I have also seen players win and lose while not fully engaged in the competition. The timing to address each of these moments can only be known by you. You as the coach must walk your own path, but it's far better to wait and think than it is to rush in and regret it later. Athletes can be very sensitive to being approached at the wrong time in these moments. Conversely, not engaging with a player who desperately wants it can be a danger.

Think of each of these moments as a chance to be a greater support to your players or not. The end of each contest shows whether you value the person over the competitor. Paradoxically, valuing the person more seems to be they way to aid in higher levels of performance. This is where love of the game and the people who play them comes into play.

Let Go of Your Ego

I see many many coaches who are overly ego involved in the coaching, and it actually works against them, because it creates more fear for the players. These 'mentors' seem to enjoy pronouncing judgement on performances, and the players for their own egotistical satisfaction. Every players win is their win, and every players loss is their loss, and they take it personally. Winners win and losers lose, so they will do their best to turn losers into winners, all the while gravitating more toward those that bring them glory while chiding or devaluing those that are less successful.

Ultimately the athletes are the heroes of their own stories, coaches can help offer suggestions in how they write it, or even draw a line in the sand writing their own story, but they can't make the player always choose to do it the coaches way. Our best decision will line up best with what our players want or need. Do they need our support or do they need space? Do they want to celebrate alone, or together with their coach? It's all about doing it at the best possible time.

My Take Away: Action Item(s):

CHAPTER FIFTY-NINE

Remembering What You Want

Discipline is Remembering What You Want.

~David Campbell

As you probably already know, discipline comes from the root 'disciple'. The focus of all discipline should be on learning and improving. Our teams need improvement and our players need learning. A portion of this discipline is done publicly, and another bit can be done very privately with individual players. 'Discipline is remembering what you want'. We owe it to our players to provide them with the transferable skills lessons that come from sports. In my life, it was the self-control I learned from sports that allowed me to finally become a good enough student to graduate from college and actually write a book. Teenagers are in a vulnerable stage in life where at times, they seem to be very mature and adult-like, but are still prone to childish behavior and magical thinking. They can also engage in adult behaviors that can get them in a tremendous amount of trouble, changing the course of their lives forever. My highest goal is to help mold the maturity, at least in the sporting arena, of a player so that by the end of their senior year, they are a fully an adult at least in the ways that will help them perform at their best and become a great teammate.

Encouraging Self-Discipline

A silver bullet question I use with players after a period of time, when I know they hear me and the words I say is: "Is it better to discipline yourself, or get disciplined by someone else?" When they hear this, sometimes you will see them in a state of reflection about a moment when they were in trouble, when they come back from that headspace, they will most all agree that self-discipline is better. I usually save this for a time when a group has been borderline out of control two or three times, and I have seen a habit of that.

We as the coaches need to have very clear expectations that do not waver, and we need to hold very closely to them, for every single player. When we allow some players to have different rules, it may affect the morale of the entire team. Some groups of more mature players may understand better the need to meet players where they are, other groups can have more rigid ways of thinking and need more iron clad standards. I took a workshop from a policeman about 'Gaining Voluntary Compliance". The course covered asking people to comply with the law, and when you pull them over, you ask easy customary requests like 'Sir, please remove your drivers license and show it to me', knowing full well that they weight of the law gives you authority to ask that. As coaches when we set up certain laws, then we can also ask for voluntary compliance and gain it more easily. So make sure that your rules are exactly that: enforceable laws. Taking the time to mindfully create those, reflecting on if they are actually being enforced by you or the team is a great way to test if they are really needed. Asking for voluntary compliance relies on self-discipline, when that breaks down, the the outside discipline begins.

Progressive Discipline

Molding the maturity of players is not an easy task and we as coaches need a full toolbox. From my time as a classroom teacher, I learned how to use 'progressive discipline', until I had created the best possible learning environment. Progressive here means increasing, not futuristic and experimental. One factor in student's or player's behavior that we don't often take into account is that they want attention. Some players will do almost anything for attention, and sadly over time a small percentage of kids learned to get negative attention from their peers and from adults.

Progressive discipline might look like this on a team: If a player is doing something distracting or off-task, and I call their name or get their attention in another way. They look at me. I make a non-verbal motion to stop that behavior, either a waving of the hand, a finger to the lips, and X with my arms, or a head shake. They stop. I say "Thank you". At the end of that transaction, the player got positive attention for stopping a behavior and the other players heard them being thanked. So, there isn't a negative outcome, or negative attention generated.

If that behavior were repeated and/or another one were to pop up with the same player, then I would take that player aside and quietly talk with them. "For practice to go well, we need you to stop these behaviors. I trust that you will." If I make this public, then they get attention to a greater degree for bad behavior. The quiet talk with me, however, is something they don't usually want. I find that these two steps solve at least 80% of all off-track behavior.

If there were another episode with that player, I would then pull them out of the activity they are doing and make them sit out. That will enter us into the negative attention sphere. A timeout becomes a very strong deterrent because the other players can see the childish consequence for the childish behavior. Very rarely do any further behaviors happen after a timeout, but if they do, it signals a fairly significant behavioral issue in the player. The after practice follow up is vital if they have a third infraction on a day or during a week. I would then hold them after practice for a full discussion of: What are your goals? What do you hope to accomplish? Do these behaviors fit with that? Can you save these behaviors for an appropriate time? Should I call your parents to gain insight, or do I trust you to do your best here on the team? I have called parents a handful of times for valuable insight into what makes the player tick. This might be the most frightening question you can ask them, which leads to immediate compliance. If the practice disrupter is not bothered by referencing their parents, then you might want to call ASAP to discuss and find out what is going on at home.

My Take Way: Action Item(s):

PART FIVE
THE ATHLETE'S WORK

Athletes play the main role in their history.

~ (Carless,Douglas:2013)

CHAPTER SIXTY

Square Pegs, Round Holes

**Herb Brooks, God rest his soul, wasn't coaching a Dream Team.
He was coaching a team full of dreamers.**

~ Jim Craig

Honestly, sometimes a player does not fit in the program. Sometimes there is no space in the program for more players, even though they might contribute, or add an asset on paper. While it seems not to fit the athlete centered coaching model, we frequently as coaches are in positions where we have to trust that a player's path is going to work out well, because its their pathway to manage, not ours. I have cut players from a high school team as a junior, only to find that they made their college team in future years. In reality that speaks to the relative abilities of those teams. It's not unlikely that the high school team I was coaching could beat some college teams, simply on depth of lineup, but that kind of imbalance is rare. Because I cut him, younger more talented players lower in the lineup gained valuable experience.

Coaches Are Not Therapists

While it behooves us as coaches to discover and work with players and their personal issues, some players have issues that would mean disaster for a team if they were included. Handling that situation with the utmost skill can help all parties to grow into the best possible future outcomes, although in the short term it might feel like failure. My heart goes out to many coaches who live in very difficult areas with a higher propensity for psychological issues amongst your players. My hope for coaches in those arenas, would help players get the what they need to be fully mentally well.

The Needs Of The Group v. The Freedom of The One

Part of the philosophical underpinnings behind the creation of the most vital documents in the United States can be traced back to the works of two British philosophers. John Locke and Thomas Hobbes argued back and forth about the rights of individuals and the rights of society to be protected from individuals.

In a team setting, every athlete will necessarily sacrifice some of their personal rights for the good of the rest of the team. Some will sacrifice more than others, based on their life circumstances, the demands of the position they play or other reasons.

Realistically, there will never be a time when there is an opportunity for everyone on every team, or in every league. There is a finite amount of space available. Also, there will be teams and leagues that are not suited to the individual and can't meet their needs, or further them along their path. Rather than try to fit a square peg in a round hole, its far better for the square peg to search for a place of good fit.

How Many Things Can Go Wrong?

My good friend Dennis Fogg who recently passed, loved to talk about all the factors that play into becoming a world class athlete. We would talk for hours on end about how easily things can go wrong for someone who aspires to be very good. One major factor is training environment. While no world class athlete had a perfect transition from one level of training to the next all the way through, early adversities, or dramatically limited access to adequate training can make the ascension to world class status much more difficult.

On the other hand, the difference between the treatment of the U.S. Women's Soccer team and the Men's U.S. Soccer team is striking, and so is the difference in the results. The women suffer from much less funding, far fewer amenities, but even with that impediment, they still have succeeded in dominating fashion for years. They have at least all they need, and who is to say maybe the men are spoiled by relative opulence. Bottom line, the minimal amount of training facilities and team environment are necessary. Because of the relative overall strength of the unit, absorbing one well known difficult personality was possible, but that is not always the case.

In some areas this access is lacking for those who need accommodations, and sadly not every team or program can wisely make accommodations for one player when doing so compromises the experience for the whole team. I have seen programs ruined, or take a very large step backwards when they entertain a player who is a major distraction. When I have a player in my program that creates a distraction in any way from the training, I deal with it immediately, and begin to manage the behavior. If that behavior becomes unmanageable and is enough of a distraction for the team that our performance is hindered, or the behavior spreads, then I will consider removing that player from the team.

Balance, No Off Balance

Different settings allow for differing levels of tolerance for outlier behaviors. At the beginning through the recreational levels of sport, you get what you get, and a person would be hard pressed to remove a player from the team except in an extreme case, like starting fights, and creating major disruptions by not following simple directions. As you go through to the highest levels of training, the 'machine' becomes more highly tuned, than smaller and smaller factors combine as the value of winning goes up, and the value of simple participation is largely reduced.

Finding an ideal balance between serving each person as equally as possible, while serving the needs of the group is not an easy thing to do. In general, team sports should be all about the team, and one of the major objectives is to teach team work. In individual sports, the focus is more on the individual, but there may also be a strong sense of teamwork between players and coaches and other support staff who work with the individual player. Players in individual sports are much more likely to have a customized program that meets most every accommodation possible.

Team Selection Criteria

When I was a young brand new coach, my selection criteria was quite simple. I wanted the best players who I thought could win, and with the nicest looking technique. Essentially, I had no criteria. Early in my career I was burned by this when I accepted a girl onto the team who would be quite disruptive, compared to the earnest hard working, as it turned out much more motivated player she replaced, her game was just a bit more polished early on, but the other girl had a much brighter future ahead of her. So I learned from this and I now use criteria like this for team selection:

Factors to Consider:

* Playing Ability
* Results of Intra Team Competition
* Attitude
* Teachability
* Team First Mentality
* Raw Athletic Ability
* Balance of Graduating Classes
* Opportunity at the Position
* Flexibility to Learn New Position

Your sport, your setting, your organization should set up what you think are the ideal criteria for team selection. Famously, Herb Brooks ignored the organization's idea of team selection, he did it himself and the results were amazing. You will find your way on this!

My Take Away: Action Item(s):

CHAPTER SIXTY-ONE

Teenagers and Brain Growth

Give me six hours to chop down a tree,
and I will spend the first four sharpening the axe.

~ Abraham Lincoln

A teenager's brain is not fully developed. According to some experts, there is one prime time of life to maximize brain development and those are the adolescent years. Many people never fully develop their ability to think things through, because they did not take advantage of every opportunity to do so at the prime time of synaptic development. One of the best possible athlete centered outcomes is that all coaches along the players timeline allow space for them to become better thinkers. Our own processing skills need to be refined constantly. One of the Seven Habits of Highly Effective People is that of 'Sharpening the Saw', which is partly about taking time for self-development, but also rest relaxation and exercise.

A sport psychologist friend, Jeff Greenwald, who does an amazing job working with teenage athletes gives an amazing presentation of some findings that have a major bearing on how we approach player development. In non-technical terms teenagers have a fully developed ability to detect a threat, so they can hear a sound or see what represents a visual threat to them. They also have a fully developed ability in the maturity of their brain to respond to threats fully. What they lack is a fully developed ability to regulate the magnitude of their response. The regulation occurs in the left parietal lobe in the prefrontal cortex. This is where great coaches come in, because sports allows for regular threats to be a part of the player's life, and we have an opportunity to help players make the connections in their cortex to allow them to regulate responses. We know that they will under react and over react, so a large part of our job is to help them understand what to do moving forward, when they see that same is similar danger again.

My Take Away: Action Item(s):

CHAPTER SIXTY-TWO
Team Leaders: Selection and Training

**Interdependent people combine their own efforts,
with the efforts of others to achieve their greatest success.**

~ Stephen Covey

On my teams, we hold an election for the leadership group. We end up with three captains, who then form a committee, so that they can vote on issues that dramatically effect the team. From that trio, I will begin to interview the three that were selected, and the top vote getter will unofficially be the main captain. As long as everything goes well with the first captain, I continue with them, but If I am having trouble communicating with that captain, or I don't think we are liked-minded as to the direction of the team, then I will move on to another captain. I still want a dissenting voice on the committee and I would never remove someone from the leadership group, unless there was some major problem involving discipline.

I make this all explicit to the team, that they will vote on the leadership committee, but I will pick the captain that I will communicate with.

Teenage Leadership Tendencies

Some teenagers very quickly shift into totalitarian dictators, I try to discourage that. Most though don't realize that if they are confident, and simply make requests, that the team will follow their lead easily. It's good to give some basic tasks for captains to lead. Having captains run the warm up, can give you an inside look at their mindset when it comes to quality control. Warming up well, can set the tone for a great day not one the field, yet many young leaders let things slip, they allow for less than stellar warm up time, leading to an ill prepared group when its go time. Helping players find the right balance, while working from their areas of strength is a great way to start, then helping them work on one area of weakness. More introverted soft spoken leaders may have a harder time being vocal. Highly confidence and gregarious leaders may be over bearing.

Using Empathy

Perhaps the most important ingredient for the team captain is that they have empathy for their teammates. That empathy can create a much better conduit for conversation, so that players will be able to share their true thoughts and feelings with their leader. Many times I get a good sense of having my finger on the pulse of the team, when I have a wise captain who can suss these things to full understanding. It's amusing also to me, when captains tell me later about their efforts at quelling team drama. 'Coach, you don't know how many headaches we saved you this season' is music to my ears. How much do I really need to know as long as these problems are getting solved by smart leadership? A word of advice in this regard: You may feel tempted to want to know everything about everyone on your team. Instead I highly recommend taking it on a 'need to know' basis. Respect players privacy, and only delve into items that you need to know because they directly affect the team, or have a bearing on the outcomes of that player.   I have heard so many rumors about players, and had suspicions about bad behaviors that were not really necessary for me to follow up on. Captains may know much more about the personal details of the players that you ever will. Great captains free you up to do the big picture stuff of leading the team.

My Take Away: Action Item(s):

CHAPTER SIXTY-THREE
Program Authenticity and Buy In

The [best] coaches... know that the job is to win...
know that they must be decisive, that they must phase people
through their organizations, and at the same time they are sensitive
to the feelings, loyalties, and emotions that people have toward one
another. If you don't have these feelings, I do not know how
you can lead anyone. I have spent many sleepless nights
trying to figure out how I was going to phase out certain players for
whom I had strong feelings, but that was my job.
I wasn't hired to do anything but win.

~Bill Walsh

In a team context, the first thing that needs to happen is for the group to decide exactly what the mission looks like, or if they are going to work with the coach's definition of the mission. Often a coach influences that mission in the largest way, but as athletes mature the responsibility shifts to them to express how high of a goal to pursue. Any coach can easily create challenging goals for themselves, but does the team buy into that? We all have had a range of teams that are motivated to simply improve and not be so easy to beat, to try to win one match, teams that want to rise in the standings, elite groups that want to win championships, and those that want to win prestigious titles. Many more teams are full of players who just want to have fun. What do you do in that case? Your coaching philosophy will guide you there, but without one, then you or I would be rudderless, directionless, unable to steer those players. I have already shared the pillars of my coaching philosophy.

Now that I have developed my philosophy, I have something authentic to offer my players. Authority and authenticity come from authoring the basic principles that are uniquely you as a coach and a program. Authentic people are attracted to other authentic people and they don't always have to agree, but it sure helps when everyone agrees on the fundamentals of an athlete-centered program. Without authenticity, then there is confusion about the issues. People might not know that they are in conflict if they are not dealing with someone on a strong level of honesty and transparency.

Establishing Player's Authority Over Their Game

From the beginning of my relationship with any individual player, I offer them this question: There ar three kinds of of people; parents, coach, and player, who is the decision-maker? Almost always, the youngster answers that the parent or coach is the decision-maker. They gues wrongly, and I answer no, they guess wrongly again and I answer no again. When by process of elimination they discover that they, the player, are the decision maker, they often get a look of wonder and empowerment on their face. It truly is amazing that 99% of the time, players guess wrong on this. **Allowing the player to be the decision-maker represents a paradigm shift in coaching.** In a recent discussion with Izabela Lundberg, who does coaching and consulting around the world, she found that the vast majority of athletes are dissatisfied with their training conditions. I would venture that one major piece of that is the relationship and power structure of the coaching. What is the coach's ideal role?

The Power To Guide

The next question I ask the player is: Who is the expert consultant? The player almost immediately says, 'You!', and I smile a knowing smile and say, 'That was quick!'

Final Approval

The amusing part now comes, when I ask the player, 'Who gives the final approval?' Many times say 'Me', then 'You', then they give a look of dread, reluctant acceptance, being caught, or the small shame of not knowing that their parents really give final approval. I say, 'If they don't approve of what is happening here, then it's over! So, whatever we do here better be worthwhile.' But what happens next is what determines if we even have a chance to develop a balanced relationship.

The Follow Up With Parents

After this first lesson, we go to the parents and I tell them what we talked about, that the player is the decision-maker. Then I study the face of the parent. The reactions range from total affirmation, surprise, reluctant acceptance, to disapproval. When I share that the player decided that I am the expert consultant, the same range of emotions can be seen in the parent. When I share with them that they, the parents, give final approval, the same range of emotions are present, but for some there is relief that they still have a measure of control.

What I find shocking is that for some parents, this conversation is not acceptable. Some parents want to play two, or even all three of those roles, and they don't want their child to be empowered to be a decision-maker. They also sometimes don't want the coach to be empowered as the expert consultant. So with those families, I usually never see them again. Good riddance, or maybe 'good luck finding a better fit', as trying to get anything done with them would be a waste of time. Which, of course, does not bode well for the time when these players will join a team because they are not team players, as taught by their parents.

With Whom Are You Working?

The above background can be quite helpful to a coach who can start to see more about the ongoing battle of having their players participate in a cohesive group. Truly winning the battle of hearts and minds is a big part of that.

To make this more applicable to high school coaching, it's good also to find an entry point to develop a trusting relationship with players. Early in a season, I may discuss with my players the general stages in the motivational development of a teenager and a fully mature adult. Ultimately, I want my players to be motivated to play and compete for their own enjoyment. In fact, just today a player said, 'I just want to have fun', to which I responded, 'Yes, I hear you and my job is to help you improve so much that you have even more fun playing the game, and I am never going to give up on that.' In contrast, many teenagers are still in a space of being extrinsically motivated. They find motivation in the approval of others and in gaining tangible rewards for a job well done. To these players, I make a blanket statement, while not specifically calling anyone to attention. I say to the group, 'If you want play to try to please me, you can, but know this: As long as you give 100% effort, I am always pleased. The rest you can learn.' Players will test this, they will try to find if they can disappoint me, and lose my approval. When I prove to them that they can't, then they normally stop trying to do that, moving in a more positive direction. When my players get to the place of playing for their own enjoyment and success, that's when they have achieved the height of the athlete-centered approach. Of course, all of this occurs within the principles and foundation set by my coaching philosophy because without that, there is nothing solid to build upon.

A large part of my coaching philosophy is that I treat my players as near equals, I treat them in the way I want them to be. A major part of treating my players with this respect is that I trust them to learn the lessons that come with being a smart tennis player. I can see that many of them appreciate that, while, of course, there are a few who don't reach that level quickly, or don't appreciate it. Even so, winning the hearts and minds of the majority of my players, so that they can play their own match, is very satisfying. One of the rewards is when the players get to a place where they play so well, you can simply watch them play. As John Wooden said, "If I have to coach them during the game, then I haven't done my job." That statement is one of the pinnacles of high-level coaching, which I have experienced only a few times in my career. One of those was in a match against a close and bitter rival team, where theoretically that team had a chance to beat my group. On that day, my players were so empowered to play their game and they played so well, I barely felt it necessary to talk with them as they dismantled the second-place team 7-0. Again, that would not have been possible without first having a well-developed coaching philosophy, teaching it to my players, then freeing them up to play as they wish within those parameters. It's my greatest joy in coaching, I hope you experience it.

My Take Away: Action Item(s):

CHAPTER SIXTY-FOUR
Talent Grit Code System

There is nothing new under the sun.

~ King Solomon

There are many popular and trendy books that come out, and they all have their value. The risk, especially for newer coaches to adopt a global acceptance of new and challenging principles. Slow down a bit, think, consider unintended consequences. A smart guy I like Scott Adams, who does political analysis says 'It was a failure of imagination', when people didn't really think far enough ahead about what would happen if they chose a certain course of action. Consider how all the dominos are going to fall when you introduce a concept to certain person. How well do you know that player, or team? How do they respond to new information? Some of my players trust me implicitly, and we have developed a short hand of communication, and a new concept can be absorbed and understood quickly. Other players and teams are more resistant, have a fixed mindset, and every new learning experience seems to come with consider work and salesmanship. How do your players interpret new information? Some of them will assume that new information means that they are not good enough. Others hunger for new knowledge to become better.

I know I have been subject to the fantasy of creating a buzzword that creates a ripple in the sea of coaching philosophy. Athlete Centered Coaching is not a buzzword, nor is it my invention, but it's a great phrase, and I hope this work helps further people along to put out their own entries, and I'm eager to receive the feedback and more contributions by guest authors.

Repackaging Timeless Concepts with Science

You may be quite surprised to discover that many of the so called new concepts that are being taught now, were actually used two or three generations ago, forgotten, then dusted off and presented as new. When you go about to read these books on myelin formation, practice, mindset, mental toughness, and any of the new fangled jargon, be sure to read the 1 and 2 star reviews. One of my favorite one star reviews is a scathing indictment into the pseudo science of a particularly popular best seller. I read what turned out to be an essay about how the book was wrong in many regards, exposing it's main premise. You may learn just as much from the reviews as you do from the book. Be a very strong consumer of knowledge and do your shopping. For that reason, I don't attempt to make very many conclusive statements in this work, because my primary objective is to spur your own thinking. Much of them are simply my informed opinions from having been in the trenches for 30 years In the final analysis it's what you own, that will be your take away. Yesterday I was on the phone with a legendary college coach, and we had a laugh about how many athletes we ruined along the way because we wish we knew then, what we know now. If you have been coaching over 10 years, honing your craft, you know exactly what I mean.

In a healthy way, deeply question what you are learning, and don't immediately trust this book, or any other. As I was working on a masters degree in education, I had the distinct pleasure of learning from from long time teachers and principals of schools. Some would be called innovative influences in highly innovative educational settings, but what they were teaching us was that there are many fads that come and go in education. The same is true in coaching. There are macro trends the people don't see that occur on a generational level. People actually retry methods that had been used 40, 60, 80 years ago and failed, which gave rise to another way, which in time seemed to fail, giving rise to another method. In the final analysis, what are the tried and tested timeless principles of coaching? That is for you to decide. But I caution you against being taken in with a fad. Making the most of every moment, that will get you far.

My Take Away: Action Item(s):

CHAPTER SIXTY-FIVE
Balanced Lifestyle Issues

There is no other place I would rather be, than here, right now.

~ Unknown

Today in the age of Fear of Missing Out, FOMO for short, coaxing players into a balanced lifestyle seems to be more and more difficult. It's unrealistic for us to think that we are going to reach every player, every parent with a message of proper dedication to gain the most value from the experience, but it's always worth a try. If we break the families into groups, we can strategize how to deal with them. Perhaps this is too simplistic, but I look forward to your comments, and that may guide future editions of this work. We can call on our athletes to live a balanced lifestyle, and in so doing, potentially have a positive impact on the whole family. I know for a fact that my communications with parents has lead to a realignment of their mindset toward sports, and in some ways have lead to my being fired.

1. Full Buy-In

If there are no families that are fully bought into the program, then the first question is why not? The obvious first goal would be to create at least one fully engaged family with their player(s). These people are committed to all practices, games, and communicate quickly and completely about any difficulties. This group treats you like and equal, and gives you the respect of being the leader of the program. It's important to show gratitude to this group, empowering them to be influential on the others.

2. Wait and See

Many people these days wait to see what they think the quality of the experience is going to be before they make a full commitment. If they find something lacking in the program or the people, then they have no issue with not giving their full commitment. Proving yourself, without feeling like you have to prove yourself, or letting them know that you are willing to prove yourself to them scores a lot of points and allows you to add to group #1. It's good to be aware of who these people are. When they make a commitment, its great to acknowledge that!

3. Actively Skeptical

Teams, clubs, programs have been burned before. The previous coach might have taken the money and run. Bless you for getting in there, plowing the fallow ground, and planting the seeds of trust. It may take a while to harvest, but when you show up every morning to do your chores, you can win these people over. The future of your sport probably depends on this group more than any other. Wounded families and players who can be restored are won into the sports world, and that's a great thing for your community and beyond.

4. Commitment Challenged

This is a group that seems to be growing, as many parents seem not to want to 'deprive' their children of experiences, even when it runs counter to established programs that have the potential to be much more valuable to their child's education down the road. Finding some balance here is important, because there are sometimes once in a lifetime opportunities that you would not want to miss for the sake of ONE practice.

5. The Dysfunctional

Show me the perfect family, and I will ask you to wait a little longer. Every family has some measure of dysfunction, even the ones that seem so great on the outside. Many dysfunctional families work so hard at denial that creating an image is very important in perpetuating that. Other families are acting out in such a way, that their problems are quite obvious. This can be a minefield for a coach. Be very careful in how you approach this. Remember, as a coach you a designated reporter, and that you have a responsibility to contact authorities if you believe that child abuse is taking place.

6. The Over the Top

The dad asks, "What else can be done?". When he asks that, he does not acknowledge that your program may provide almost all of the needs of the player. This dad does NOT want to hear that he can play catch with his son, or kick the soccer ball around with his daughter. He wants to be super dad, high performance parent who pushes his little superstar into the stratosphere. The message is, it always has to be MORE.

In all of the above, focus on the athlete, the needs and wants of the athlete, and that alone is your stake to have influence in any other area of the above. The above groups may have completely different ideas about what constitutes enough rest and recovery, what kind of diet a player has, how much and what type of training is appropriate, and how many different kinds of activities can be pursued while also striving for competency or excellence in any one of them. How much are they willing to sacrifice to pursue excellence?

7. Low Vision / Low Standards

These parents just want their children to have fun, and show almost no concern about the quality of the experience or learning how to compete. Good luck with this group, as they place a very low priority on showing up, or maintaining team discipline. Similar to the 'friend' parent.

8. Parent Friend

More common in this day and age is the parent who treats their child as though they are a mini-me friend. Everything is about being buddies. These parents have a hard time disciplining their children, and take a relational approach on most things. Many of the standards and actions of the family come down to negotiations.

My Take Away: Action Item(s):

CHAPTER SIXTY-SIX

Pursuing Excellence Over Outcomes

Excellence is doing ordinary things extraordinarily well.

~ John W. Gardner

Pursuing excellence is the ultimate conclusion to this work. In my entire life, one of the most critical pieces of advice I have ever received was stated very simply by Geoff Fong, Geometry Teacher, a mentor of mine when I was teaching public school, who said, "Teach to the top kids, keep them challenged. The next level of student's will also be challenged. There is a pretty large group of students that won't be challenged no matter what you do, but if you let the top students become bored, then they will lose interest quickly and then it's all over for you." This was counterintuitive in the time when 'No Child Left Behind' was coming into effect nationwide. Of course, any good teacher is going to do everything they can to reach out and help the students who are not doing so well, but when they actively choose not to do well or have a deeply disturbing track record of failing and almost no self-belief, not all of them can be won immediately. Let's now apply this to coaching.

Prepare the Challenge

It's vital to prepare activities that keep top players engaged in every practice. On the other hand, we as coaches are not going to cater every moment of practice to our top players, but enough to keep them challenged most of the time. Helping our top players strive for a new level of excellence can have a teamwide effect. When the #2 player sees the #1 player improving, they then realize they must do more if they ever want to take that position. When the #2 player takes that challenge, then it falls to the #3 player and so on, down the line. We want as many of our players as possible to buy in and strive for excellence. This is perhaps the greatest life skill for our players.

Overlooking Aaron

Aaron was one of my all-time favorite players for a few different reasons. He was one of the nicest young people I have ever met. When he was first on the team, he was so quiet that I overlooked him. When I finally discovered how smart he was on court, I wished I had spent more time developing him earlier. This is part of the challenge of coaching a very large team. We had 42 players and me. As is my custom, I spent of lot of the early practices focusing on the varsity team. Then once they got settled into a routine, I began to work more with the junior varsity, and finally what we call 'exhibition' players because their matches fall outside the Varsity/JV structure. Aaron was a JV player in his sophomore year and had just picked up a racquet. I finally saw him play a full match late in the season. He was not at all flashy, and his strokes were a little stiff and mechanical, but he could place the ball where he wanted, and he had an uncanny ability to create shot combinations. I later found out that he was a point guard on a basketball team, so he knew about misdirection and creating openings in a defense, while looking for weaknesses in an opponent.

Aaron Emerges

Aaron then came to summer time training and worked on his game a lot. As a junior, he ascended to varsity, in what was a pretty large jump up the ladder, and did a good job as a part of our #2 doubles team. Aaron started to show some great enthusiasm for the sport. That summer, I was hosting two 18/under USTA Team Tennis Teams. The A team was a sort of 'all-star' team made up of #1 and #2 players from our league, and we did quite well in the summer. The other team was made up of everyone else. I challenged Aaron to play on the B team. I told him "You are going to get beat a lot, but I want you to do it so you can improve a lot this summer, never give up on anything." So he played.

Aaron Hones His Skills

As far as his game, I noticed that Aaron was not shy about getting to the net, but his volley skills were not great. If he only had to play one volley, he could win a lot of points, but if he had to volley twice, then his win % went down considerably, more than most players. We focused on his approach shot. Aaron spent hours working on hitting an approach shot in a 9' by 9' box in the backhand corner, so that he could get an easy volley and have the opponent out of position. If you don't coach tennis, then you might not know that it's a pretty large target area, but very effective in high school play. Aaron improved dramatically in his ability to come to the net and knock off one volley for a winner.

Number Two Doubles to Number Two Singles!

That improvement meant that he would ascend to the #2 position behind only a player who had many years of USTA Tournament Play behind him. In an amazing surge, not only did Aaron play #2, but he went 15-1 and was voted first team all-league, because he also had wins at the #1 position. This kind of achievement is fairly rare in high school play. Aaron was also the main team captain because he was such a great example of hard work, diplomacy, and he was a kind-hearted individual. It didn't hurt that he and I got along so well. Aaron was one of the most important factors on court through his leadership and other intangibles for a championship season.

Zero Star Aaron Plays College Tennis

During that season, it occurred to me that Aaron was improving so fast that even though a year ago I would have said he had little chance of playing college tennis, he had a real shot of playing JUCO tennis at least.

He and I discussed this and I challenged him to consider it. We talked about what he needed in his game. Aaron's groundstrokes were not going to be offensive weapons because he never quite loosened up all the way, so it was imperative to make his net game better. So I challenged him with an approach shot target area that was 5' by 5', which is about one-fourth the size of the high school target. We also spent a lot of hours working on hitting two volleys, and making a great decision on the first volley whether to go for a winner, or set up the next volley. By the end of the season, he was ready for college tennis. His approach shots were like laser-guided missiles and if someone did manage to make him volley twice, he could make them pay. His teammates saw his willingness to work on a strength and make it more excellent and to develop what was a relative weakness.

What he did was contagious with the team. So in the space of less than three years, Aaron went from an undiscovered sophomore to a college tennis player. Of course he had some athletic talent to work with, but his work showed that it's clearly possible. Aaron was a zero star recruit.

Unlocking The More Difficult Players

It all sounds so easy, right? Aaron made it easy.

When we deal with more difficult players who don't cooperate in the same way, it's important to break down barriers and try to understand why a player is not pursuing excellence or cooperating in the process. We won't win everyone, but we can try!

Let's go back to the Inner Success formula:

$$Performance = Potential - Interference$$

The natural starting point in developing more excellent performance is to reduce interference and I am not going to explain it, because we know it when we see it. But then we can ask, why is their interference? Knowing that answer can be a huge key in creating the solution. Also, we can build up our player's potential in a holistic way by helping a player find an area of strength and building upon that. Conversely, finding a player's area of weakness that can be addressed in a season can help improve their potential by a larger margin.

Coaches Pursuing Excellence Engender Players Who Do

Great coaches pursue excellence in their own coaching, reflecting on what they do have an influence on players. Asking themselves, parents, and players, 'How can this be better?'. I often ask my team captains, 'How are you? How is the team feeling? Is everyone having fun? Are they feeling challenged enough? Is there something that needs to be different?' Each team has its own personality and each captain has their own style and that makes coaching different every season as we navigate helping players pursue excellence in a fairly wide variety of means.

My Take Away: Action Item(s):

CHAPTER SIXTY-SEVEN

Trust Engenders Overcoming

**I want my team to be more detached from the wins and losses
and be more focused on doing the little things well.
When you focus on getting the win, it can suffocate you,
especially during the playoffs when the pressure gets thick.**

~ Sue Enquist

What you will see here are some outcomes of the creation of an atmosphere where players can rise to the occasion. You will see that there was history between player and coach. Trust had been established. A mutual problem solving approach based in a collaborative relationship was key, leading to the empowerment of the player. At its root was a growth mentality, a process orientation toward success. Enjoy.

Preston Was Tight, Did He Rise Up?

Preston was tight. In fact, he was nearly incapacitated. The moment had gotten to him and he was nearly frozen on the court. He was a team captain and he cared a lot about our match as a #9 seed going up against the #1 seed. Preston was not rising to the occasion. He and his doubles partner lost their first set. Varun was playing a bit better than he normally does. On a changeover, we discussed that I did not expect Preston to play a lot better, but any shot he hits should be to a certain location to allow more balls for Varun and to try to set Varun up as much as possible. "Now Varun, feel free to go completely nuts, you get to carry Preston today." Varun stepped into that space and it happened. What transpired was inspiring. Varun, for the first time in his high school career, played to his full potential. He had almost always held back, but now he knew he needed to play his best for the team. This team of two juniors was playing a very experienced team of two seniors who had an amazing record over a couple years, no one would have bet on Varun and Preston, especially with Preston playing so tightly. There was very little in the way of coaching from then on because Varun stole the show, and the match, as they won 7-5 in the third set. I had a nice talk with Varun, as I admired how well he had played. A lot of work had gone into creating this atmosphere and I can assure you it never happens in one day, it takes many weeks for teenagers to learn to trust an adult in a way that will allow them to let loose with their full powers. The following season, in the sectional championship match, Preston's partner froze up and he was the one who rose to the occasion in the pivotal bout that won the match, equivalent to a state championship in many states.

From Styrling:

Chloe Trusts Styrling

Chloe was engaged in a single's battle to clinch the Conference Championship, but after winning the first set 6-4, her opponent began to hit moon balls big time. Chloe went down 0-3 in the second. Coming to the fence to chat, I asked her if she was willing to come to the net more and she agreed. So I asked her to look to play a two-shot sequence, a high moon ball approach to her opponent's backhand and then rush the net in a controlled way as to look for a lob or high loop ball to come back. At first, Chloe struggled a bit to find her rhythm and timing, down 1-4 on the changeover, she seemed a bit hesitant. I encouraged her and said, "You are starting to find your timing, your opponent is very nervous about you doing this because she knows her lobs and loops are too short, you just need to take your time at the net." Chloe smiled and said, "I can do this!"

Chloe Overcomes Fear, and Rises!

Chloe went out and won the next 4 games in a row, making it 5-4. After a battle back and forth 5-5, 6-5, 6-6, they go into a tiebreaker set. Chloe maintained her cool demeanor and won 7-4 in the tiebreaker, clinching the Conference Championship. This story is about Chloe being able to overcome her fears and believe in the game plan that would work against this game style. She had the tools and just needed to believe in herself to face the adversity of executing in that moment. As coaches, if we can give calm and clear suggestions and advise in these times of great adversity and pressure facing our players, it goes a long way to teaching them that overcoming their fears raises them to higher levels of play.

Dean Used Practical Mental Skills to Overcome!

Dean was facing a tough opponent, he knew he had to stick to his game plan no matter what happened on his opponent's side of the court. He had struggled in the past with giving up when he began missing shots, plagued by thoughts of 'it's not my day today'. I had been encouraging him to push through the adversity and pressure, to find a way to play the ball with more spin on his serve and groundstrokes instead of just 'hitting' the ball with little intention other than trying to blast it past his opponent's racquet. That day would be different had Dean collected himself, remembered his training of playing the ball with more intention, setting up his patterns to force his opponent into difficult and defensive positions. As Dean began to execute his strategy, he saw his opponent begin to weaken in confidence. His opponent also seemed to be a little shocked at how Dean was not losing his temper as in the past when he missed shots. We had been working together on keeping his cool and rituals of breathing between points, taking a little extra time to collect his thoughts and execute the next pattern. So the training with practical actions helped him manage his own internal struggle. Dean succeeded that day in winning against an opponent he'd not beaten before. This was a great confidence booster for him in knowing that pushing through the pressure, following his plan and executing fearlessly throughout the entire match.

My Take Away: Action Item(s):

CHAPTER SIXTY-EIGHT
How Athletes Might Use Defense Mechanisms

There is another side [to ego] that can wreck a team or an organization. That is being distracted by your own importance. It can come from your insecurity in working with others. It can be the need to draw attention to yourself in the public arena. It can be a feeling that others are a threat to your own territory. These are all negative manifestations of ego, and if you are not alert to them, you get diverted and your work becomes diffused. Ego in these cases makes people insensitive to how they work with others and it ends up interfering with the real goal of any group efforts.

~ Bill Walsh

In some areas of psychology (especially in psychodynamic theory), psychologists talk about 'defense mechanisms', ways in which we behave or think to better protect or defend ourselves. Defense mechanisms are one way of looking at how people distance themselves from a full awareness of unpleasant thoughts, feelings and behaviors.

Psychologists have categorized defense mechanisms based upon how primitive they are. The more primitive a defense mechanism, the less effective it works for a person over the long-term. However, more primitive defense mechanisms are usually very effective short-term, and hence are favored by many people and children especially (when such primitive defense mechanisms are first learned). Adults who don't learn better ways of coping with stress or traumatic events in their lives will often resort to such primitive defense mechanisms as well.

Most defense mechanisms are fairly unconscious – that means most of us don't realize we're using them in the moment. Some types of psychotherapy can help a person become aware of what defense mechanisms they are using, how effective they are, and how to use less primitive and more effective mechanisms in the future. Coaches must be mindful of these, and when athletes also learn to become more sophisticated in the use of these mechanisms and begin to see the processes by which they are not needed any more, then they can achieve more and more.

Primitive Defense Mechanisms

1. Denial

Denial is the refusal to accept reality or fact, acting as if a painful event, thought or feeling did not exist. It is considered one of the most primitive of the defense mechanisms because it is characteristic of early childhood development. Many people use denial in their everyday lives to avoid dealing with painful feelings or areas of their life they don't wish to admit. For instance, a person who is a functioning alcoholic will often simply deny they have a drinking problem, pointing to how well they function in their job and relationships. Athletes sometimes go into denial using excuses to somehow make it seem like they should have won.

2. Regression

Regression is the reversion to an earlier stage of development in the face of unacceptable thoughts or impulses. For an example an adolescent who is overwhelmed with fear, anger and growing sexual impulses might become clingy and start exhibiting earlier childhood behaviors he has long since overcome, such as bedwetting. An adult may regress when under a great deal of stress, refusing to leave their bed and engage in normal, everyday activities. Athletes can move to a lower level of technique when feeling extreme stress from the fear of competition, especially when they fear losing. When players regress in using their skills to try to win, then it's a great idea to step back and regress their training to build up the fundamental that they should have been using.

3. Acting Out

Acting Out is performing an extreme behavior in order to express thoughts or feelings the person feels incapable of otherwise expressing. Instead of saying, 'I'm angry with you', a person who acts out may instead throw a book at the person, or punch a hole through a wall. When a person acts out, it can act as a pressure release, and often helps the individual feel calmer and peaceful once again. For instance, a child's temper tantrum is a form of acting out when he or she doesn't get his or her way with a parent. Self-injury may also be a form of acting-out, expressing in physical pain what one cannot stand to feel emotionally. We see this in throwing bats, gloves, racquets, and throwing objects to the ground. Some acting out in a sporting event is normal and healthy, much more so that doing it at home when something could be broken. Of course, when acting out puts others in harms way, then it has gone too far.

4. Dissociation

Dissociation is when a person loses track of time and/or person, and instead finds another representation of their self in order to continue in the moment. A person who dissociates often loses track of time or themselves and their usual thought processes and memories. People who have a history of any kind of childhood abuse often suffer from some form of dissociation. In extreme cases, dissociation can lead to a person believing they have multiple selves. People who use dissociation often have a disconnected view of themselves in their world. Time and their own self-image may not flow continuously, as it does for most people. In this manner, a person who dissociates can 'disconnect' from the real world for a time, and live in a different world that is not cluttered with thoughts, feelings or memories that are unbearable. I have seen this a few times in my career where a player seemingly can't handle the anxiety brought on by competition, and they float through it, not at all engaged, while the other player seizes control of the game. When another team mounts an amazing comeback, and there is a disbelief that a team that was down four touchdowns is now only down a few points or tied, then multiple players may dissociate, and thus open the door for the complete turnaround.

5. Compartmentalization

Compartmentalization is a lesser form of dissociation, wherein parts of oneself are separated from awareness of other parts and behaving as if one had separate sets of values. An example might be an honest person who cheats on their income tax return and keeps their two value systems distinct and un-integrated while remaining unconscious of the cognitive dissonance. I have seen this with parents who don't recognize that their children are cheating at sports, or are bullies on the field. Players who have high ethical values may compartmentalize their bad behavior to sports, but somehow they are able to contain it inside the lines. I know that my behavior is different when I compete, as opposed to my every day life. People who are low-key, may exhibit a highly agitated presence while competing.

6. Projection

Projection is the misattribution of a person's undesired thoughts, feelings or impulses onto another person who does not have those thoughts, feelings or impulses. Projection is used especially when the thoughts are considered unacceptable for the person to express, or they feel completely ill at ease with having them. For example, a spouse may be angry at their significant other for not listening, when in fact it is the angry spouse who does not listen. Projection is often the result of a lack of insight and acknowledgement of one's own motivations and feelings. Athletes may blame teammates for making errors, but not recognize that they make just as many or more errors themselves. Helping players to learn to reflect on their own play, and to realize that projecting can be a negative from a team chemistry stand point can help them learn to identify their own projection.

7. Reaction Formation

Reaction Formation is the converting of unwanted or dangerous thoughts, feelings or impulses into their opposites. For instance, a woman who is very angry with her boss and would like to quit her job may instead be overly kind and generous toward her boss and express a desire to keep working there forever. She is incapable of expressing the negative emotions of anger and unhappiness with her job, and instead becomes overly kind to publicly demonstrate her lack of anger and unhappiness. I know that fairly immature players may actually go into the tank in the competition, essentially handing the competition to their opponent, rather than maintain a high level of determination in a tough competition make more difficult by the opponent's poor sportsmanship.

My Take Away: Action Item(s):

CHAPTER SIXTY-NINE
More Mature Defense Mechanisms

Less primitive defense mechanisms are a step up from the primitive defense mechanisms in the previous section. Many people employ these defenses as adults, and while they work okay for many, they are not ideal ways of dealing with our feelings, stress and anxiety. If you recognize yourself using a few of these, don't feel bad – everybody does. Consider how at the right time, we can move away from these. Our athletes can also learn to be more mature competitors, by taking things a step further beyond defense mechanisms.

8. Repression

Repression is the unconscious blocking of unacceptable thoughts, feelings and impulses. The key to repression is that people do it unconsciously, so they often have very little control over it. 'Repressed memories' are memories that have been unconsciously blocked from access or view. But because memory is very malleable and ever-changing, it is not like playing back a DVD of your life. The DVD has been filtered and even altered by your life experiences, even by what you've read or viewed. Some high level athletes are adamant about not wanting to see video of themselves performing poorly. There is a case to be made for only looking at the best performances in similar situations, but some level of constructive criticism is very healthy. It's amazing that some athletes can perform at a very high level, while also engaging in high level repression. It's not uncommon for me to try to ask a player about a certain sequence in their match, and they seem not to remember. I can't fault them for that, but I can help them learn to be more reflective.

9. Displacement

Displacement is the redirecting of thoughts feelings and impulses directed at one person or object, but taken out upon another person or object. People often use displacement when they cannot express their feelings in a safe manner to the person they are directed at. The classic example is the man who gets angry at his boss, but can't express his anger to his boss for fear of being fired. He instead comes home and kicks the dog or starts an argument with his wife. The man is redirecting his anger from his boss to his dog or wife. Naturally, this is a pretty ineffective defense mechanism, because while the anger finds a route for expression, it's misapplication to other harmless people or objects will cause additional problems for most people. Sports is a great place for a healthy outlet for displacement. The sublimation of violence in sport is a great way to get this all out. Again, when other players or spectators are in harms way because of over the top displacement, then there has to be some type of intervention. Sometimes I see great performances from players who are displacing anger from other circumstances, channeling that energy into great focus and effort.

10. Intellectualization

Intellectualization is the overemphasis on thinking when confronted with an unacceptable impulse, situation or behavior without employing any emotions whatsoever to help mediate and place the thoughts into an emotional, human context. Rather than deal with the painful associated emotions, a person might employ intellectualization to distance themselves from the impulse, event or behavior. For instance, a person who has just been given a terminal medical diagnosis, instead of expressing their sadness and grief, focuses instead on the details of all possible fruitless medical procedures. Players may obsess about minute details of technique, instead of understanding that their mental approach to the game was off target. They might find other factors to explain a loss, rather than deal with the reality of a lack of fundamental play.

11. Rationalization

Rationalization is putting something into a different light or offering a different explanation for one's perceptions or behaviors in the face of a changing reality. For instance, a woman who starts dating a man she really, really likes and thinks the world of is suddenly dumped by the man for no reason. She reframes the situation in her mind with, 'I suspected he was a loser all along.' Sour grapes or sweet lemons are a problem in sports, and sometimes people like to say, 'I could have beaten you if I had tried', is a rationalization for the loss, meaning that they just didn't feel like winning that time. One of my least favorite parroted phrases in sports is 'Sometimes you win, sometimes you learn', meaning that when you lost you gain something, and when you win you proved something. Well, that creates a strange rationalization for not winning. How will you learn to win, by losing? Also, even when you win, you can learn something from the less than ideal aspects of the performance. Never ever accept losing as a lesson, when learning to win is a possibility.

12. Undoing

Undoing is the attempt to take back an unconscious behavior or thought that is unacceptable or hurtful. For instance, after realizing you just insulted your significant other unintentionally, you might spend then next hour praising their beauty, charm and intellect. By 'undoing' the previous action, the person is attempting to counteract the damage done by the original comment, hoping the two will balance one another out. The concept of redemption in sports is an undoing of sorts. It's amazing how a player who has made a pivotal mistake can sometimes come up big in later situations. Ultimately, the cliche of 'the next play is the most important play' holds true. We can't undo what we did, but we can try to leave that behind and rise to the occasion.

When players can learn to accept that perfect or even nearly perfect performances do not happen very often at all, then they can learn to avoid using defense mechanisms. A coach identifying which defense mechanisms their player naturally falls into, can learn to accept that player's failing in that regard, while also helping them to discover strategies to move past the problem and move forward in their performance. More mature responses can be found in the next chapter.

CHAPTER SEVENTY
Strategic Defense Mechanisms

Mature defense mechanisms are often the most constructive and helpful to most adults, but may require practice and effort to put into daily use. It's probably best to use the word strategies now, since there is something more constructive in place, a way to win the mental battle. A mindful coach or athlete can work to capture their thoughts moment to moment and redirect them to more effective ones. While primitive defense mechanisms do little to try and resolve underlying issues or problems, mature defenses are more focused on helping a person be a more constructive component of their environment, a higher performer, a better collaborator and teammate. People with more mature defenses tend to be more at peace with themselves and those around them, and can more readily achieve their highest potential.

13. Sublimation

Sublimation is simply the channeling of unacceptable impulses, thoughts and emotions into more acceptable ones. For instance, when a person has sexual impulses they would like not to act upon, they may instead focus on rigorous exercise. Refocusing such unacceptable or harmful impulses into productive use helps a person channel energy that otherwise would be lost or used in a manner that might cause the person more anxiety. This is one reason that sports can be a highly redemptive activity in someone's life. Taking energy that could lead to self destructive behavior, using it for something that can lead to many more positive outcomes is a far more preferable course to take.

Sublimation can also be done with humor or fantasy. Humor, when used as a defense mechanism, is the channeling of unacceptable impulses or thoughts into a light-hearted story or joke. Humor reduces the intensity of a situation, and places a cushion of laughter between the person and the impulses. Fantasy, when used as a defense mechanism, is the channeling of unacceptable or unattainable desires into imagination. For example, imagining one's ultimate career goals can be helpful when one experiences temporary setbacks in academic achievement. Both can help a person look at a situation in a different way, or focus on aspects of the situation not previously explored.

The fascination that many people have with who will become a world class athlete can be channelled into humor and/or fantasy. Sometimes that imagination of achieving great things can be the conduit to high levels of motivation. You might even call fantasy: Visualization. Allowing for the creation of strong dreams to achieve in young athletes is not only healthy, but it is far preferable to being pessimistic. In fact some great research exists that shows children ages 4-10 who have dreams of being the greatest in the world at something are far more mentally healthy than those who have a realistic view of the world and what they can do in it.

14. Compensation

Compensation is a process of psychologically counterbalancing perceived weaknesses by emphasizing strength in other arenas. By emphasizing and focusing on one's strengths, a person is recognizing they cannot be strong at all things and in all areas in their lives. For instance, when a person says, 'I may not know how to cook, but I can sure do the dishes!,' they're trying to compensate for their lack of cooking skills by emphasizing their cleaning skills instead. When done appropriately and not in an attempt to over-compensate, compensation is defense mechanism that helps reinforce a person's self-esteem and self-image.

Compensation is a great thing when applied to a team. When a balance of traits among players allows them to make a unique contribution to the mix of the group. When I teach team unity, I list twelve things that players do to positively or negatively affect everyone. I ask them to pick two things that they are great at and do those things. I also point out two aspects of relative weakness, reminding them to try to mitigate those behaviors that would have a destructive influence on the team.

15. Assertiveness

Assertiveness is the emphasis of a person's needs or thoughts in a manner that is respectful, direct and firm. Communication styles exist on a continuum, ranging from passive to aggressive, with assertiveness falling neatly inbetween. People who are passive and communicate in a passive manner tend to be good listeners, but rarely speak up for themselves or their own needs in a relationship. People who are aggressive and communicate in an aggressive manner tend to be good leaders, but often at the expense of being able to listen empathetically to others and their ideas and needs. People who are assertive strike a balance where they speak up for themselves, express their opinions or needs in a respectful yet firm manner, and listen when they are being spoken to. Becoming more assertive is one of the most desired communication skills and helpful defense mechanisms most people want to learn, and would benefit in doing so.

One of our chief goals in coaching in developing a collaborative atmosphere where everyone happens according the to the best possible timing requires that everyone involved is assertive. The greater the level of assertive communication skills by all parties, the more can be achieved. All the issues that need to be addressed can be met with action when they are expressed in an appropriate context.

It's obvious that coaches of very young athletes will have to say things like 'use your words', while at each new level we can see more and more mature behavior with those who we want to work to develop the highest levels of performance. Whichever stage our athletes are at, we can strive to take them to the next level.

My Take Away: Action Item(s):

PART SIX

TEACHING AND COACHING

The best time to plant a tree is 20 years ago,
the next best time is today.

~ Confucius

CHAPTER SEVENTY-ONE

Know the Essentials of Training in Your Sport

I won't accept anything less than the best
a player's capable of doing, and he has the right
to expect the best that I can do for him and the team!

~ Lou Holtz

The best case scenario is that we are expert coaches, or moving toward becoming an expert coach at a speedy rate. One of the earmarks of someone who has coaching mastery is that they have a well-developed, concise coaching philosophy that translates into action. For coaches who are most influential their philosophical foundation is grounded in the enduring values of the coach. Now, let's take a look at the application of these goals for the actual coaching job. We want to do our best at all times. Giving our best does not always look the same for everyone.

When we apply these principles, we can start to take a look at how we apply them on a team level, with individual players, and as a coach in the league or region. We can give our best by being active, and we can give our best by being very passive, even though that might seem strange at first.

Think Time

Let's start with the team. In order for coaches to give 100% effort, then we need at least a penciled-in plan for the season. When we don't take a look at the bigger picture of the full season, we may suffer from a missed opportunity to develop our players. Putting the puzzle pieces of the season together, and anticipating potential problems before they arise is paramount to getting the most out of time together. Once we have an idea of what we want to accomplish in the season, then we need to look at how many practice days we have. Asking yourself how much time realistically can be devoted to what you want to achieve helps eliminate unrealistic expectations. From there, we develop daily plans. Like a sea captain who must change course when a huge storm comes along, we must be ready to make changes to our plan and maybe abandon some of the less precious cargo in our schedule to make the schedule lighter in rough seas.

When making changes, it's important not to remove indispensable parts of the plan. Two essential aspects of a team's training that should never be jettisoned are fitness training, or the fun portion of practice, which on my teams amounts to the 15-20 minute time of large group games at the end of practice. Those two things are the lynchpins of success for the team player. Why? Training players for improved strength, speed and muscular endurance is normally the most important factor in young athletes success. Developing a fun team atmosphere is important, creating a strong sense of morale between teammates, only helps keep players loose prior to competitions. Don't sacrifice either of those aspects, but do have a plan on a daily basis that fits the phase of training you are in. Of course, there are mitigating circumstances that might mean cancelling   the fun stuff for a day. The late Al Bowlin who was a top flight basketball coach said often, "Piss Poor Planning Prevents Performance."

Spreading Attention

If we zoom in a bit, and look at the coach's interactions with each player, let's examine how well the coach divides their time. Ideally, the coach could have a stop watch to help them give exactly the same amount of time to each player. This is not at all realistic, but if we take a mindful approach, we can identify players who don't need as much attention and players who need a bit more. Some players have a very low tolerance for receiving a lot of information at one time, while others want very detailed explanations, and some players can seek too much attention from the coach. Balancing all the needs, wants and predispositions of players giving them what they need makes for a more efficient environment, where players learn to plug into   right amount of coach interaction.

In the early in the season, I spend more time with my very best players to make sure they are getting dialed in fast with good timing, playing at near midseason form. I then work my way through the lineup in ensuing days. In some team sports the opposite approach may be more effective, as some players may need to be made fundamentally sound in order to help the whole team run better. I make every effort to be sure I have at least one contact with every player on the team each day, but it doesn't always happen. After working closely with my top 4, I would move into working with the next 6-8 players who comprise our doubles teams for a day or two, then move down the ladder until I have had some concentrated time with every player on the team in a smaller group setting. When a particular player is having a problem with a particular shot, scheduling a time to work with them when the whole team is working on that shot is ideal because it maintains the flow of practice. Bottom line: be mindful of communicating to players, "I tried to give as close to an equal amount of time to each of you as needed, but if you are feeling neglected, let me know and I will address that." No matter what happens, it's likely that some players will feel like they are being ignored, or getting more attention than they want.

Work it out!

My Take Away: Action Item(s):

CHAPTER SEVENTY-TWO
The Fall Line

The athlete centered coach creates an atmosphere where those who love the sport can improve close to the maximum of what is possible. Those who don't love the game, can learn to love it, or make better decisions. The coach is mindful moment to moment as to how best to spend time, very little time is ever wasted, although sometimes being still and quiet for a moment might seem like a waste. Resting, talking, having some fun moments that have nothing to do with the sport can be the most important morale boosters that create more energy for the ultimate in effort.

A great coach I know likens their approach to a skier. Skiers have to approach the fall line without falling, veering off the fall line creates wasted milliseconds, cutting turns precisely gives the closest to the fast time possible. There will always be wasted time, but minimizing it in the effort of putting more time into the task with the greatest efficiency to gain the greatest outcomes teaches one of the greatest lessons in life, the value of time.

My Take Away: Action Item:

CHAPTER SEVENTY-THREE

Start Where You Are: Observation, Understanding, Communication

Everything in coaching hinges on listening because what we are listening for affects where we are speaking from and unfolds how we are being with and for each other.

~Marilyn Atkinson; Rae Chois

Where am I? Where are we? Where is that player? At the present moment, what is our current situation? It's easy to get impatient, going ahead in time. Try too hard to make the future come more quickly. It can be difficult to escape from what weighs down on us from the past, but we can let those things go to move forward. We always begin with knowing where we are. In order to get where you are going, how can your find your way, if you don't know what is the starting point of your journey? It's possible, but much more difficult to plot a course. Once we know where to begin place, we can being to plan where we want to go, and finally the path to arrive where we want to go. As we work with groups of players, start with where your group is, observe carefully and try to understand what the experience looks like for the players.

Stop, Look and Listen

One great aspect of working with smaller groups of players at one time is that it facilitates observing closely what is happening. Stopping to pay attention and devote the necessary attention to what is going on around us runs counter to the constant business of our live. One of the more passive aspects of coaching is taking in the sights and sounds of what the players are doing. You may notice that they are not performing a certain action the way it was taught. This is a great time to check for understanding of the skill development that had gone on before. In contrast, often our educational system resembles people using power tools. The teacher seemingly attempts to drill a hole in the student's head, uses a funnel, and pours the information into the students head and using a rag to control spills. Really the opposite is much more engaging.

Socratic Method/Zone of Proximal Development/Prior Knowledge

We can start most lessons by asking the student what they know already. Like Socrates, we can use questions as a way to educate, to get players to think. Using prior knowledge eliminates the endless repitition of instruction by the coach. The zone of proximal development theory by Lev Vygotsky states that people learn more quickly from those who are very fresh from having learned the same thing, facing similar struggles. Using a few moments to cement the lessons of the past pays dividends, especially when driven by the players. Let the team do the teaching, allow leaders and conscientious students show what they know. Checking for prior knowledge and understanding is vitally important to doing our best job. When our loyal subjects gain affirmation for rightly giving good information it's a morale boost for them, and potentially for the team.

Conversely, imagine how it feels to be told something you already know. If you are like me, and many of the people I know, you don't enjoy too much repetition from the same source. It can be a waste of time and create needless frustration. So, when you are planning educational experiences, always be on the lookout for fresh talent, voices that have not been heard before. When the same speakers repeat the same things it feels like being stuck in the past. In some cases it can have you wondering if the person talking to you thinks you are stupid. The hidden cost of repeating that same instruction over and over is that players may tune out on you. Now turn that around. Do you want your players to show their smarts, save time and be empowered? Yes! So ask them, 'What do you know about (objective, strategy, tactic, technique, etc)?' When they give their answers, they teach the less experience players, they become experts, you save time and energy, and you can refine their thinking on the topic at hand. You develop a more collaborative culture on your team. Continue to ask questions until they prove to have a thorough enough understanding and stop when they have no answer. Start with some easy questions, work your way up to more difficult ones, that players still have answers for, and then, then you ask a question that the players do not know the answer to, you tap into their curiosity. Not knowing naturally creates a natural hunger in their minds. That desire to be filled brings us fully into the present moment with baited breath. So, instead of simply lecturing work up to a point where the team doesn't know enough about a certain topic, and you will have more interested learners on a new topic, or you can give them another lecture. Good luck with getting engagement on that!

How Deeply Do We Pay Attention?

Another aspect of our coaching is the level of engagement we bring to it. When we are having a conversation with a player are we mainly focused on listening to them and ready to respond, or do we maintain an internal dialogue thinking of what we are going to say next? Moment to moment, when we fully engage, our players appreciate that. We draw them out with real listening because it's becoming more scarce in this age of competition for our attention.

It's also important to be kind and firm about times that we are not available. We need to set some limits. Sometimes teenagers want to conduct a difficult conversation at the worst possible time. As gracefully as we can, we need to put a time on it, and allow our players to know that we want to hear them, but this moment is not the best time for that conversation. Still other moments require stopping on a dime, all activity will cease, and a team meeting called because of something said or done. Using your best judgement as to when to bring everything to a halt takes experience. It could be a safety issue, it could be a conflict between teammates, or something destructive or very informative that was said. Sometimes there is a major positive breakthrough that warrants a quick meeting. When we seize on the opportunities to engage with a problem even when it breaks up our routines, we communicate that we are athlete-focused. So when we give 100% effort to our players, sometimes that means more in the quality and wisdom of how we approach it, rather than the volume or amount of time or rigid regimented time structures.

Be Rock Solid

Consider that teenagers can be fairly impulsive. They come and go from the present moment, to the past, into the far future, and many other places in time. Being fully present with them can be a challenge when they are not. Quite often, they may have a thought that they have been suppressing for a long time, and finally the day comes that they are thinking about it while they are present with you the coach. Some teenagers have no filter in the way they express themselves, while others may have no one that really listens to them, so they act out because of that. Of course, they will feel an urge to act on it right now because they have forgotten so many times in the past. We can facilitate communication by consistently proving that we are listening and available to our players at the appropriate times. At times it may be necessary to manage players in how they communicate. Keeping all the talk at the appropriate time and in the best way, sometimes calling a parent for some insight on what works at home with a problem player can be the solution. At other times that phone call leads to the discovery that the parent is having a hard time with their little darling. In that case, you have a rare opportunity to collaborate with the parent to be influential in that kid's life. Another benefit of calling to talk to parents is building a collaborative culture on the team. You can expect word to get out among the players, 'Coach called my house', and the resulting accountability that comes with that. In order to give 100% effort we should exhaust every avenue to work with our players and build the lines of communication.

My Take Away: Action Item(s):

CHAPTER SEVENTY-FOUR

Major in the Majors

Facing life each day, we all make this mistake. We spend time on the wrong stuff. Priorities get mixed up. Big things get forgotten or set aside while little things get all our attention; both emotional and physical. We major on the minors and minor on the majors.

~Doug Thorpe

Maybe you have heard the phrase 'Major in the Majors, and Minor in the Minors'. The majors will have the most long term benefits, working on the big things, the foundational pieces will help players to build and progress, instead of break down and regress. Making the greatest use of time for maximum achievements with your players, consider carefully the main objective for your athletes. I'm surprised how often in my first year in a new location how often I need to teach fundamentals that were not taught by the previous regime. In many sports, coaches and players get seduced by the special skills, the flashy stuff, and yet mastery of the very basics can be lacking. A good friend of mine played in the NFL, having been a very good defensive lineman at University of California. He was not a flashy, and did not have impressive statistics, but his fundamentals were amazing, he was never out of position, always on balance, and ready to set his teammates up for a stop. He is a perfect example of someone who achieved a higher level than he could have without having someone investing time into him teaching those vital basic skills. How to maintain possession of the ball, position yourself on defense, how to make yourself available to a teammate on offense, moving without the ball, great passing skills, and knowing the fundamentals of strategy are so vital to future success.

Build Up On Fundamentals

In other cases the opposite is true, the kids have been so bludgeoned by the fundamentals well beyond mastery, that no intermediate or advanced skills were developed. I'm appalled in my sport at how little in the way of strategy is taught to young athletes, so they only see the sport as a physical contest. One our our major objectives is to build into our on field decision makers enough X's an O's, that they have the information to make the best move at the right time. Every week at the Division 1 and even the NFL level a player makes a fundamental strategic mistake, that to many of us who grew up knowing the rules and strategy for the sport see as simple. An athlete centered coach, knows his players and team well enough to know what is the next logical step in the players understanding of how to win the game.

Balanced Work and Fun Load

Plan the work and work the plan! Finding the best balance between teaching (which can be boring), coaching (to many players is annoying), and free play (the fun they want) can be the largest factor in an athlete's experience. In one season, if each of your players can mitigate their biggest weakness, using a balanced approach between those three things, will have a lot more confidence and less fear of making the crucial mistake. I remember a boy on my son's little league team who played right field and caught less than 100% of the fly balls that came his way. He dropped quite a few in practice and in games. I didn't see the coaches working with him on technique or building his confidence. After one particular bad drop which lead to a few runs scoring, the sons of the coaches began giving that player a hard time. I could easily see that he was on the verge of quitting the team, as he had also missed practices. When I am not the coach, I try hard not to be the nosy parent, but I go the two coaches aside and told them what I saw, and that they were on the verge of losing that kid. Later in the season with bases loaded that kid made the catch that sealed the inning and the win, which I assume had to be one of the best moments of his 10 year old life.

Keeping It Simple

We can also capitalize, teaching players a new way to use their biggest strength. In one season, working on one strength and one weakness with each player that can go a long way toward massive improvement on your team. It's also very manageable, and not hard to stay fully present and engaged with the task. Our minds however may want to get busy with other things, but we can remember what our main objectives are.

When in our minds we jump around to every possible weakness trying to solve them all, instead of staying fully present with the major goals for each player, that's when we get wrapped up in the minors. Coaches and players gravitate toward perfectionism, but if we take time to stop and think, to closely observe the commonalities of what a team needs, we can refocus on what's most important.

Give Mental Game Enough Time

Every sport has a mental and emotional component that needs work, but almost every study shows that coaches spend far less time on the job of building these skills, than the value they reportedly place on developing them. I have done a lot of low level psychological testing with my teams, having them take inventory tests to find out their collective strengths and weaknesses mentally. The amazing similarities between most boys taken together, and most girls helps a coach see how to coach the overall team. But, the other discovery is the outliers who defy the stereotypical range of answers. So, while as a team I will address the top two negative outcomes, and praise wildly the two positive results, when there is time, I will get one of my outliers aside to talk about their particular issues.

General Gender Differences In Mental Game

In general, boy's are strong in the ability to see themselves succeeding, and regulating their effort level. Girl's rate much higher in positive energy, and team chemistry issues. Boy's struggle in controlling negative energy, and girls with the ability to see themselves being successful. We call that ability, visualization. So, I spend much more time with boys on developing positive energy, and with girls on visualizing success. Perhaps the greatest story of my coaching career came when after two full years of helping my boy's develop this positive energy, and my girls to plan to do the work so they could succeed, but won sectional titles one after the other, and after having those each tested to the maximum. It was extremely satisfying to see these players manifest the characteristics into which we had invested so much time.

Global Team Skills First

When there is a global skill that your team needs to develop, like blocking in football or volleyball, or passing in many sports, first we need to make an assessment of how good they are already. When I want to help my team globally on a specific ability, first I need to identify the levels of my players. If you want to get somewhere, first you have to know where you are, then where you want to go, before you can plot a course. As a tennis coach, building in the ability to go to the net to finish points is a major advantage over players and teams that do not feel comfortable doing that. First, I like to sort out my players between those who can move comfortably forward to make a decent approach shot and a decent volley, and those who can't. On one of the earliest day of practices, I will run the drill of having players simply come forward to approach on a short ball and make one volley. If I am going to build this thing into their games, we have to start almost immediately in the earliest part of practices. I can then see the number of players who can perform, making a realistic goal of increasing that number. I then know who does not need to be taught the very basics of that move. We lose a lot of morale, and bore a lot of kids when we presume that they don't know how to do something, and begin to teach them what they already know. Far better to test them, and if they pass the test, move on, but don't make your test 100% pass/fail, because then a 95% success rate is not honored. In tennis we can actually tolerate lower success rates, because our game is so full of errors. As we go, we can strive for higher and higher levels of mastery. Once I get my fairly competent group feeling confident coming forward to net, I can do some instruction to the group of players that are not as comfortable moving forward to the net. That group most likely will need some fundamental instruction, which I am sparing the upper group. I can have another relatively self guided activity ready for the players who are fairly confident, one they can do independently or with the help of an assistant coach. After working with the group that needed some basic instruction, I would identify an aspect of the performance of the top group that was a common issue and have those players work on that.

Keep Instruction Concise

After a short period of instruction, less than 5 minutes if possible, I would have the players play some type of point play situation where one player must come to the net. It can't be emphasized enough the value of keeping instruction brief, before letting players perform the bit. When the players begin playing points, they can be tallied or not. It's more important to look for players who are getting closer to achieving the objective than it is to criticize those that don't. If you must call out a negative, its best not to use the person's name with it, and keeping at least a 3:1 ratio of positive praise, to corrective comments is good. Sometimes we need to take a player aside to check understanding. Some research indicates that players perceive technical advice on how to perform as an affirmation that you believe they can do it, while criticism is seen as a personal attack. Praising players only on their effort can be perceived as meaning, 'you don't think I can do it, so you only praise my effort.' My experience on court bears this out.

Use Generous Praise

People are so hungry for attention, they will gravitate toward that which gets them praise. I created a video course on getting to the net, which has a fun anecdote. During the filming of a task, I asked the group, 'who will be the first one to perform excellently'. Immediately one of the female coaches got a very determined look on her face, she self selected, it was as though in her mind she said, 'I am going to be the one'. In fact, she was the first to perform well. Look for that in your team, give them opportunities to show you how they rise to the top. Depending on the dynamic of your group, you may even want to hold one player up as an example for the others to follow on any particular objective. Some players may really dislike being placed on a pedestal, or given too much attention, so you may want to ask their permission. From point play situations that you place players in, it's vital to observe carefully what seems to be more effective for certain players and what are the top one or two items that cause them to lose the points. When you bring the players together, ask them what they thought was effective and ineffective, and see how their answers differ from you answers. Consider those differences.

Realize that they way you assess your team, might differ from how others outside, or near the program assess your team. Many people have opinions that they like to share with the coach.

My Take Away: Action Item(s):

CHAPTER SEVENTY-FIVE

Where is The Sports Experience?

Why is success so ephemeral? Ego shortens it. Whether a collapse is dramatic or a slow erosion, it's always possible and often unnecessary. We stop learning, we stop listening, and we lose our grasp on what matters. We become victims of ourselves and the competition. Sobriety, open-mindedness, organization, and purpose – these are the great stabilizers. They balance out the ego and pride that comes with achievement and recognition.

~ Ryan Holiday

What is more important to your players? Is it more important that they understand *your* experience of their play, or is it more important that they understand *their* own experience of their play? What is more important for you? I hope you said 'their experience, because that's athlete centered. After they have shared their experiences, you may or may not need to share what you thought. How magical is it when the players have all the best answers and they don't require the opinion of the coach? Then you can praise them for being smart players. It's awesome when the coach says "I agree with you", or "I agree with you up to a point, but I want to clarify something…". The player-centered coach builds much more empowered, mindful players whose sport becomes a form of self-expression. The more we can avoid being an imposing force, the better. Ultimately, the players will either own the objective or they won't, and their level of ownership of it has a large bearing in how well they do under pressure.

Urging Them Onward

I had a girls team that was quite talented, but they were underachieving before I arrived at the school. They seemed very content to win their league and then lose in the first round of the playoffs every year. With my doubles teams, our one objective was to control the center of the court, and it was not an easy thing to accomplish with those girls. The level of buy-in was not 100%, but when they were winning more and easier, then the percentage rose.

Even so, in a tense playoff upset win, I had to urge my players to continue to be aggressive in their movement at net. After winning that our first round as a 10th seed against a 7th seed matchup, the same thing happened when we took on the #2 seeds. The girls wanted to shrink back from being aggressive. We won two of the three doubles matches and the decisive match was at #2 doubles, where I reminded the players on every changeover what we had worked on all season. They won that match in a third set tiebreaker and the team went crazy. Had I not been extremely determined as a coach to teach, coach, encourage, remind, and urge my team onward, then that victory would not have been theirs. So, even though they owned the strategy, under the feelings of pressure, they were tempted to move away from what had succeeded all season. Their issue was not of ego, but more a lack of full self-confidence.

Ego Check

This next story is about keeping my own ego in check, and I can only wonder what was going on in my player's mind. I saw this player getting better at the net and also experimenting with a one handed backhand groundstroke. I suggested that he consider switching to a one-handed backhand because it would help him be even better at the net. He resisted, we talked about it a few times, and he did not switch. I gave up on it. A couple weeks later, he was hitting nothing but one-handed backhands. I teased him, 'I see you took my advice!' Nonplussed, he gave a disassociated answer, 'I don't know what you are talking about.' Pow, smack, kabam, it was like an Batman comic book! That was a bit of a slap to my ego, but I let it go.

After his net game became appreciably better, I suggested to him that he consider using the strategy of serve and volley, where you serve, moving right in for a volley. He tried it a few times, failed, and seemed to blame me for some lost points in practice matches. Again, I stopped pushing him in this way. A few weeks later, after winning our league tournament, he stately boldly. 'Coach, I have decided to become a full time serve and volley player.' I was so pleased and said, 'Wow, that's great we talked about that a few weeks ago, I'm glad you are ready.' He looked at me like I had lost my mind. He did not remember our conversation. I smiled inside because it didn't matter if I got any credit as a coach, what mattered was that he had made the change. The awesome part of the story is that he far exceeded expectations, made the semi-finals and would play a future #1 USTA Sectional Player for third place, losing a thrilling three hour, three set match 7-5 in the third, coming to the net 114 times and winning 71 points. If he had won three more points he likely would have won the match, that was a great accomplishment for a #62 ranked player.

Conclusion

So, what was important to the players took on different looks. They all want to win, and they might need a little push, but sometimes they need to have nearly complete autonomy for whatever reason. Getting ego involved in the process may lead to disappointment for everyone.

My Take Away: Action Item(s):

CHAPTER SEVENTY-SIX
Facilitation

To a man who only has a hammer, everything looks like a nail.

~ Mark Twain

We want our players to have as complete a set of tools that we can possibly help them assemble. Helping them gain mastery over the tools takes time and patience. It's almost guaranteed that when you put players in their first competitive situation of the year against another team, using a new skill, the combination of nerves and newness will make performing difficult. I can't think of a time when players shined in that first match playing competitively while using a new skill or strategy. Depending on what happens in that first match up, there are decisions to be made. It's best to start with the positives, even if that is only in making an attempt. When players do not attempt the new skill, then the obvious question is why not? Praising players for going out of their comfort zone trying to make a new strategy work is important. Having them identify which aspects need work, is a better way to draw them out, than immediately critiquing their performance. Again, ask the players, don't tell them. Ask them where they did well, and what the breakdowns were. If you agree, discuss that. If you don't agree, try to understand why the players think that was where the breakdown came. "I kept missing my approach shots." Their perception and reality may be far removed from one another, so it's vital to understand their perception for that reason, so as to reconcile the difference, enhancing players critical thinking skills. Sometimes it means that they missed the first approach and the third approach, and after that it was fine, but that's what they remember from the match. They may have been extremely effective, but often they will remember their mistakes more. If we reinforce the criticism over mistakes, we make it very difficult for players to appreciate their successes no matter how subtle or great. Many times, I saw. "I know you feel that way, and you remember X, but I really saw Y. What do you think of that?" Asking players what they think will be the next step in development for the new tactic creates even more ownership of the overall plan.

When To Progress, or Regress

After they have played, you might decide that they don't need much more training because you were very pleased with their progress. My experience shows that it's a little too easy to believe that one good performance means mastery. A second match up might not be as favorable, and the strategy may be exposed, schedule in one or two refreshers into the practice schedule. If they struggle, build them up with two or three more practice sessions targeted at their specific issues. If you don't intervene, you run the risk of a significant group of players not achieving your major objective. Generally, by the second match you should see a big improvement, but players may still not feel fully confident. They will most likely need more encouragement and some fine-tuning of smaller issues that reduce their effectiveness. So, while most of the work gets done early on, the job of coaching it up in players continues all season.

Listen To Player's Thoughts On Transition

All along the way, be a great listener to how your players are feeling and what they are thinking about the objective. Do they understand why it's important? Observe closely, not only their technique, but their body language. Do they look confident or at least competent when they perform? Or do they look scared, shaky, or undertrained? Ask them about it and don't always trust your eyes because sometimes, players may feel very confident, but it doesn't always show on the outside. As the season progresses, you can remind players of things previously learned, spur them on as they gain greater confidence, console and encourage them if they have a bad performance. It's how you finish the season that matters most and I find that if the work of teaching and coaching is done in the early going, then the free play will be the laboratory where the player finds their own way.

Teamwide Objectives May Take Multiple Seasons

As for the team I mentioned at the beginning whose leadership struggled with 'negative energy', they learned that lesson over two full seasons, and when presented with a very strong negative circumstance, they were able to maintain positivity and it lead to a very fulfilling finish to the season. Instilling that principle took a lot of time, mindfulness, and repetition.

My Take Away: Action Item(s):

CHAPTER SEVENTY-SEVEN

Developing Full Engagement

**A common mistake among those who work in sport
is spending a disproportional amount of time on X's and O's,
as compared to time spent learning about people.**

~ Mike Krzyzewski

Creating engagement requires mental and emotional capital with youngsters. The dwell time in winning their hearts and minds has no short cut. Let's start with creating a better conduit for communication. Managing our own expectations for the level of interest our players show in the lesson is also part of the equation. We can do our part, but there is a finite amount of brain energy that can be directed at the task. When do people engage? Is there a formula for engagement? Will everyone engage equally? How do we create and capitalize on engagement? Did those questions engage you? If so, then part of the equation is your curiosity. Asking open end questions and then listening on purpose, is a large part of the engagement solution.

Remember Being A Kid

Go back in your mind to the days of being a teenager or younger and the feelings of being thrown into that what might have felt like prison to you where teachers, using a drill, a funnel, and a large amount of mostly useless information tried to pour it into your head. Later, they tested you on your ability to remember and interpret it. Overall, it's a pretty dull experience for the vast majority of our high school kids. Although, around 20% or maybe more of high school teachers, really know how to engage students and draw out the students' learning.

As coaches, our teams will do much better if we become masterful educators. The word 'education' comes from the root word educos which means to 'draw from within'. But what do we draw out?

8 Reasons To Let Them Start The Teaching

Engaging players mainly starts with mining their prior knowledge. For example, if I am starting a new year of coaching a team, I may ask all my doubles player candidates, "What do you know about doubles positions and/or strategy?" The players then share their ideas, which accomplishes a few different objectives: 1. Players who have good knowledge get to share and contribute. 2. Players are sometimes more interested in learning from their peers. 3. Players are promoted as leaders and teachers. 4. The 'zone of proximal development' means that sometimes peers explain in terms that their age group understands more easily. 5. The coach saves energy. 6. Players get to teach what they already know, instead of being taught what they already know. 7. The coach can praise, affirm, redirect, clarify, and debunk the notions taught. 8. When the player's knowledge runs out, the coach can ask more questions about the missing essential information. When players don't know the answers, then you have achieved... curiosity. Curiosity causes engagement.

The Sound Of Our Own Voices?

Unless a coach is really in love with the sound of their own voice, they really should love to have players in a curious state of mind after their prior knowledge has played out. When players share out what they know, a best practice is for the coach to praise players who give exceptionally clear and concise answers. Players readily accept a little redirection if they missed the mark by a bit and will accept being told they're wrong if the coach says, "I'm not sure I agree, but we can discuss it." There is bound to be something that needs clarification. When a coach proves to be a skillful listener, and not an overly critical corrector, players really blossom in their ability to give great answers.

Paring Short Talks With Immediate Action

Another way to engage players is to give them a short lecture on a topic, then challenge them with an activity that uses a skill in that range. While performing a challenge, take a break to ask a question that requires critical thinking. Today, I taught my girls for about three minutes on the concept of Stretch, Cage, Run, which is what we want the other players to do. I asked them what do those things mean on a tennis court. After we discussed for another couple minutes I asked them which one they wanted to work on first? Most girls agreed on 'Caging' the other player, which essentially means restrict their freedom on court so that they can't move. While working on hitting a deep drive up the middle of the court, I stopped the drill. "If you are playing someone and you are running them, and they are running you, and you are losing, what are you going to do?" No one had the answer. This is quite common. But I allowed them a period of NOT knowing, I let them struggle. The context was confusing because we weren't performing a 'Run' challenge. Helping them think out of context was critical. There was silence as they thought. Don't be afraid of a little silence! I asked them to think harder. Then, I asked the question again and a little more slowly. More silence. I asked, "Do you need a hint?" They said yes. But before I could give a hint, one player said, "Cage them?" I said yes, cage them, because if you are losing to someone who is moving better than you or moves you better, take the movement away. They got it! I ask these questions when the answer converges with we are currently practicing, this enhances their value of the drill. The team is one it's way to globally owning a tactical solution to a losing match. I also sometimes like to teach the girls to give an answer that is NOT in the form of question, so they can learn to give confident answers, an important life skill. I am now fairly certain that if I ask them tomorrow what to do when they are losing a match with lots of running, they will know the answer. At the end of the day that's what we want, to make sure that each day they take away one very good lesson.

My Take Away: Action Item(s):

CHAPTER SEVENTY-EIGHT
The Space Between The Ears

Baseball is 90% mental, the other half is physical.

~ Yogi Berra

Tennis and Golf are intensely mental games, largely because of the relatively long periods of time between plays. Every sport though seems to have a respite, and how good your mental game is in those moments can be a key factor for success. Here I will share one of the iconic strategies from Tennis and one of the great sport psychologists in the history of sport. You can use this template to create similar strategies for your athletes.

The 16 Second Cure

Jim Loehr, also developed the template called The 16 Second Cure. During the 16 seconds, which is a bit of a misnomer because it's not a finite amount of time, there are four stages and you might not need to go through all four stages between each point. With my most competitive players, I urge them to use each of the four stages in any key sequence in a match or if they are going through a tough or nervous stretch in a match.

First, is the **Decisive Stage**, where for a moment, (2 seconds?) a player physically and mentally puts closure on the point before. Great athletes can put closure on a play, placing it firmly in the past. As they say of great cornerbacks in football, 'they have to have a short memory', so they can forget what happened in the past, staying present with what they are doing now. On a great play a quick celebration is fine, players can pump their fist if it was a great shot, but they should turn their back on the point. Why? It's over, that point is complete and can't bother me. That point is decided, and nothing can be done about it now.

Next is the **Relaxation Stage** (could be 5 or more seconds), where a player checks to see if they have tension, might take a deep breath, shake out their arms, do the limp legged 'Federer Walk', and simply let go physically for a moment. The eyes can also 'rest' on an inanimate object, like a tennis racquet for a moment.

The Third Stage **Preparation Stage**, which sometimes can be the longest stage in terms of time, where a player might quickly recap what happened in the previous point, and give themselves a quick 'do that again', or 'change that', and move on to planning the next point. Taking a moment for a mental note to program your mind for what you want to happen in the future is a great strategy. Internally it can be, "The next time I see that, I am going to do this." As a server, the kind of point you want to play, the corresponding serve type, and +1 contingency can be planned, thus increasing the chance of a performing well on the +1 ball (which will be explained in depth in a future post). As a returner, reflecting on the serving tendencies of the opponent, along with the strategy for mitigating their strength, in addition to what kind of +1 ball you want to make, if you get a chance, also increases the chance of a better performance. For intermediate players, it can be as simple as 'serve wide and keep the ball cross court'. For a recreational soccer team, it can be on defense keep them to the outside, on offense attack down the middle. For more advanced and specialized style players, it gets much more complicated.

After the planning is done, it's time for the final stage, The **Ritual Stage**, which should only take a few seconds, where you do your ball bounces or your special rocking motion that prepares you to return. A volleyball player may have a special run up to serve, and the returners a certain movement that they perform just prior to the serve. Baseball pitchers have maybe the most divergent rituals preparing for the same thing as any athlete in sports. As fans, its comforting to take one look at the preparation for the play, and knowing 'oh, that's ____' from recognizing their ritual. There is a wild set of idiosyncrasies that accompany the rituals, so keep it simple and enjoy them, we can't discuss them here. The rituals are an important part of coping for players, as it gives them some 'sameness', familiarity with something in a match that is so unpredictable.

Emotion As A Major Factor

One of the key pieces in helping develop champion players is helping them to become mentally and emotionally stronger and more flexible. Many times, we leave out the emotional part of sports. For some reason, in the realm of what passes for mental training, the most common approach is to try to mitigate emotion in the player. It seems to be clean and nice to try work with our players to be only rational, logical players, but when we do that we lose out on a powerful force for inspired play. Look at a player like Draymond Green from the Golden State Warriors an his ability to change the course of a game on a dime, with one intense outburst of emotion. Some of the most inspiring performances I have seen in my players were fraught with emotion. Desire, Passion, Anger, Fear, Vengeance, Grieving, and Humorous behavior and much more has been evident in some of the greatest wins, and fantastic moments on my teams, but only when managed well by the player. Pete Sampras pulled off one of his most amazing comebacks in a match, when a fan from the crowd yelled, 'Do it for your coach Pete.' Referencing his ailing coach who would succumb in brain cancer. I was beaten by something similar when a casual bystander referenced that I would win my match soon and easily when up a set and one service break in the second set. My opponent heard that comment, used it as motivation, and became unbeatable to me for the rest of that match. He beat me on emotion. Each new team, each player has its own personality, it's up to you as a coach to find the group's strengths and relative weaknesses, then devise a way to bolster them, helping players find strategies that work. The 16 second cure is one way for a player to check in with their responses and give themselves a pep talk during the preparation stage about managing their weakness and/or capitalizing on their strength as a player.

My Take Away: Action Item(s):

CHAPTER SEVENTY-NINE
Relative Mental Strengths and Weaknesses

The energy of the mind is the essence of life.

~ Aristotle

The process of discovering what the mental and emotional strengths and weaknesses of athletes in performance, requires a period time, and a fully developed relationship. Athletes may not allow you to understand them immediately, as people are naturally guarded about revealing their true selves. Putting the long term holistic development of the person who is your athlete ahead of any of their performance outcomes is not an automatic mindset. In occasional pangs of weakness, I have been tempted to, and have actually sometimes placed the health and longterm development of the person behind the outcome of today's match. Not often, but often enough. Even when making tough decisions to pull a player from a contest the inner convulsion that comes from 'now we don't have as good a chance at winning', is palpable. As competitors do we ever fully get over that? The name of the game is to win, that's why we play. Making those decisions has become easier, and I now do not hesitate to remove an injured player who could continue to play, if there is a risk of further injury. I am fine with disciplining a player, even if in the short term, it may affect their performance or that of their teammates.

Getting Started Is The Toughest Moment

What are the reasons we neglect working on the mental and emotional foundations of our player's games? For one, it can feel like a 'spooky', 'woo-woo' thing. For concrete thinkers, we run into 'Why does this matter?', as an objection. For others, working on their thoughts and feelings can be an intrusion on their private world. At the outset, we may need to work on our own mental and emotional game as a coach. Modeling what we want to see in our players is huge. If we are throwing tantrums, how can we expect emotional control from our players? If we are blaming players for mistakes and losses, how can we expect teammates not to point the finger at each other. If we place too high a value on the final outcome of the competition, how can we think that players will keep sports in perspective?

If we are truly honest with ourselves, we will notice that at times we can be disconnected from the principles of our own program. First, reconnect.

Some great tools for identifying relative mental strengths in ourselves and others as it pertains to sports come from Jim Loehr. Jim is one of the most influential Sport Psychologists in the world. Dr. Loehr's *Mental Toughness Training for Sports* has two editions, and each one has a different test in it, each test has its own merits, I particularly like the first one. Players self report by answering different questions that measure different capacities of the mental and emotional game. Once they get done, you can go over the questions with your player(s) to check that they fully understood the directions, and you can also better interpret the results.

General Observations From Three Years of Testing

For a number of years, I gave my players these tests and I got some interesting results. Boys tested *high* in **Intensity**, and **Ability to Visualize Success**, but they tested *low* in **Negative Energy Management**, and **Attentional Control**. So, they played hard most all the time, and could see themselves being successful, but could sometimes be very negative with themselves and have a harder time paying attention, or concentrating. Girls tested *high* in **Positive Energy Management**, and **Attentional Control**, but tested *poorly* in **Intensity**, and **Ability to Visualize Success**. You can count on girls to keep the atmosphere fun in general, and they pay attention much more than you might realize, and the can surprise you with remembering something you said a month ago, but managing their own effort level can be tough, and they don't have an automatic feeling that they will win. So really, we need to coach boys and girls differently. Year to year the numbers would vary slightly, but the gross outcomes were the same. It's very important to realize that each team has outliers in the various capacities, and that we can't ignore them or try to force them into a stereotypical gender box. Nonetheless, coaching boys on having positive energy and concentration will help most players. Coaching girls on visualization and maintaining high intensity will also help most players. I use some spare moments with players who are outliers to discuss with them their individual areas for improvement, identifying two areas of strength to operate out of, and two areas of relative weakness to work on.

Fire Them Up!

I was recently talking to a coach whose players are already two weeks into their season and were facing a dip in intensity, so he really lit into them to get them fired up. We discussed the different approaches to boys and girls. Boys generally have an expectation that training is going to be tough and more readily sign up for the 'torture' of high intensity fitness, almost taking it as a badge of honor. The girls have a tendency to avoid high-intensity exercise in general, but the most competitive ones will embrace it. What can be done? I like to call it, 'cooking frogs'. I hear that if you put a frog into boiling water, it will jump right out, but if you put a frog into lukewarm water, it will be quite content, and if you slowly increase the temperature, since they are cold blooded creatures, they will stay in the pot until fully cooked. So when teaching our players who struggle with intensity, we can start at the level where they are, and gently apply a bit more heat and increase slowly the intensity, until they are at a level that will lead to their best possible success. When we push them a little harder and ask that they do things faster, you can reach a point where they discover that in the past they were holding back on effort.

The Pain Is Forgotten When The Benefits Are Received

All along the way, you can begin to ask them questions about what they need in their physical performance to have a better chance of winning. As we have discussed in building a coach philosophy, the #1 capacity is giving full effort. You may also have to reconcile the 110% effort notion that someone instilled in the player. In my experience the majority of young athletes don't even understand how to fully give 100% of themselves to the task. The same girls who really dreaded a particular agility drill that I run, wondering how I could be so cruel, then sing its praises a few weeks later when they are winning matches they used to lose. When they make the connection that they have to feel bad now, in order to feel better later, then I get more buy in from them.

Redirecting Negative Energy

For those who suffer from negative energy problems, it's good to start with questions. Why do we do express that? Does it help you play better? How does it affect your energy in the competition? Are there players who can play very angry and play well? Do they play well match after match and for long periods of time? One short burst of anger can be helpful in a match, but only if well-directed and then followed up with positive energy, 'can do' energy. Helping negative energy challenged players to discover the moment when they reacted with unproductive anger, disappointment, confusion, self-blame, self-pity or their negative emotion of choice, can help them to discover the turning point in what might have been a winnable competition, that suddenly took a turn for the worse when they were triggered. When they can identify the moment, that they go down that wrong emotional road, then in future situations, they will have greater awareness and can make a better choice, staying on track. From there, developing a strategy to track the thought life, and the emotional states can be an essential part of a performers checklist. Every sport has different amounts of down time, and requirements for mental and emotional management in the moment.

My Take Away: Action Item(s):

CHAPTER EIGHTY

In Game Relationship

Good teams become great ones when the members trust each other enough to surrender the 'me' for the 'we'.

~ Phil Jackson

Quite a while ago I read an amazing article that I will try to recreate. I am unable to locate it, and maybe you can help me find it. The subject was guageing the relationship between a head basketball coach and his point guard at the moment the coach calls time out. There are different levels and different reactions.

1. Anger and Disgust - The point guard immediately shows a moment of anger because he is not in alignment with the coach on whether a time out is necessary at that time. This is an obvious rift between the two. You may see the player delay in getting to the huddle thus sabotaging some of the time in the time out. If a coach has to urge his PG to come to him, then there is a serious problem that needs to be worked out for the sake of the rest of the team. When and why to call time out should be something that the player can at least accept. It could be the coach's fault that they are not a good time manager, or they don't understand their team. Maybe the coach lacks patience in allowing previous instructions to work their way out through the team. There are so many different things that can go wrong.

2. Tolerance - The point guard knows that he could get in trouble with the coach if he shows anger or disgust at the whistle. So, they will dutifully move toward the coach, but it will look a little robotic. So he learns to tolerate the time, and the lack of enthusiasm for stopping to talk is noticeable, but there is no mutiny. It's just nowhere close to where it could be. Some coaches wrongly think that this is O.K. It's not really acceptable, because you are nowhere near developing the most vital relationship for your team to succeed. Often players come away from a time-out, confer with the point guard about what they really are going to do, rather than what the coach told them.

3. Professionalism - The player may turn quickly to the coach, saving the most time for the time out to have the greatest impact, but their is a noticeable lack of enthusiasm. This is an improvement, and while the relationship is not great, at least both parties are doing their best to get the job done. They can put any personality issues aside for the sake of winning a basketball game. They may even have some point counter point. The coach and PG actually listen to each other. The team is less likely to be confused by mixed messages from coach and point guard.

4. Collaboration - When the player and coach reach this level, there is more enthusiasm, and now the PG may actually begin to rally his or her teammates to the huddle more quickly. There is more often than not hope that something good is going to come out of this break, and the team will get something that unifies them to some degree to work through the next phase of the game to build a lead, shrink a deficit or continue to battle in a tight game.

5. Tight Knit - The player instantly seems happy, and can't wait to talk with his best friend the head coach. Together they will solve the problem. The PG knows that the coach trusts him or her to give details about how things are going on court. The player is empowered to show leadership, make suggestions or changes in the huddle, asking tough questions. There may also be a time when the coach can ask that his plan be carried out exactly the way it was drawn up on the white board. The point guard will do their level best to lead that charge. This type of relationship requires a very high level of maturity from both entities, and does not come easy, many battles must be fought together to get to this level.

My Take Away: Action Item(s)

PART SEVEN

LISTENING AND OBSERVING

What makes a good coach?
Complete dedication.

~ George Halas

CHAPTER EIGHTY-ONE

Counterintuitive 100% Effort: Doing Nothing

**Probably my best quality as a coach is that I ask a lot of
challenging questions and let the person come up with the answer.**

~ Phil Dixon

Giving 100% effort can also run counterintuitively. It can be that the moments you do or say nothing can be the most important. The effort goes into biting our tongues, and quieting our minds. There are times the players are building their own relationships, proactively and independently from the coach. We may need to wait for a better time to interact with a player or parent on something we are seeing now. Sometimes players long for negative attention, and they will do whatever they can to get a rise out of us. A healthy amount of ignoring can help squelch that desire. In many other instances, there are situations where a certain flow or student centered problem solving effort is taking place. Players can be allowed to really struggle through their own solutions. The coach engaging with these situations can work to mitigate the initiative of players, can give the wrong kind of attention, or simply break up the flow of problem solving among the players or the whole team.

Now Is Not Always The Best Time For Action

Sometimes giving 100% effort is holding back from addressing something and waiting for a better time. One of the most pivotal moments in my team coach career came when I was coaching a team that had a few players that were out of control. A few of the girls would come late or skip practice, they would make up stories about why they had to miss a practice, and generally did not give a full effort on court. After numerous interventions without a dramatic improvement, I asked the team captains if they could handle the situation. I had reached the point where I allowed the girls to prove that they were going to continue in their behavior, befor having asking for this meeting. These two captains proved to be among the very best that I have ever had working with me. 'Ask them if they want to win and be champions at a higher level, if they do, then act like it. If they don't, it's ok, I will back off from expecting so much, but I don't think a lot of you will like how that looks.' Charlene and Mahita seized on the opportunity to run a team only meeting, for which I was not present.

The Process And The Outcome

The story goes that numerous teammates expressed how disappointed they were in the undisciplined girls and that they really wanted to win. There was crying, forgiveness, and a renewed commitment to excellence. From that point on, every player was all in. That team really came together and as a #10 seed in sectional playoffs, won a hard-fought upset of the #7 seeded team. This for the right to play the #2 seeds. The #2 seeds had beaten us routinely in the regular season, and many of their players simply looked too strong for our girls. The improvement that came from renewed and improved trust in each other resulted in a unity that allowed the team to come together, pulling strongly for each other, as we beat that #2 seeded team with the final match coming down to a third set tiebreaker. Perhaps I could have been more ego involved as a coach if I made that happen by running that meeting. I seriously doubt that I would have had much impact on the poor teammates if I had. It would have been easy to become more and more impatient with the team members that were not fully committed, but trusting and waiting were the order of the day. I am actually more satisfied and happy to have suggested and allowed the meeting to take place without me. The next year, the girls won the sectional title without me as their coach. The head coach of that team reached out saying, 'The girls wanted to express their gratitude to you for teaching them the work ethic that set the tone for winning NCS (a collection of 145 schools in Northern California, which is a bit more significant than simply winning a 7 team league).'

So, 100% effort is mostly about full engagement, but it's also about giving full effort to disengaging when the time is right to allow players to step up and take control of their own destiny.

My Take Away: Action Item(s):

CHAPTER EIGHTY-TWO

Ego Boundaries and Communication Styles

What you do speaks so loudly that I cannot hear what you say.

~ Ralph Waldo Emerson

We encounter players or parents who want to do us 'favors', but then it's quite clear that there is some kind of catch. Be careful to clear up any potential expectations. I often like to joke, 'This is really wonderful what you are doing, but I think your daughter is still going to have to compete for her spot on the ladder. Haha, just so we are clear.' 'Wow, these things you do for the program are awesome, it would be tempting to show some kind of favoritism, but that would be wrong.' 'I owe you a really big thank you at the end of the season, because I think that's the only way I would ever be able to repay you.' I know that coaches get caught in this bind often, and the higher the level of play with the greater level of financial contributions offered, the more the strings start to look like ropes or nooses. Every coach has an obligation to consider how beholden they want to become in returning favors to those who give to the program.

Be Open To ALL Communication

It's always great to listen and acknowledge those who offer suggestions, feedback, and information while expecting nothing in return. These are the kind of people that we really want to reward, because those are the ones for whom the work is all worthwhile. I once met a parent, who came to visit one of our matches, and he was asking me hypothetical questions about what it would be like, for a player to play in our program. The next year, his son transferred from a private school, that played in another league into our program, which was completely legal and not at all solicited by me. Did I recruit him? No! Now I had to be quite clear with that parent that where he and his son decide to go to school has no bearing on how this program is run. Setting that expectation turned out to be quite helpful. In recent years, the rules have changed in my area, and that conversation with that parent would be considered recruitment. The parent in question, who was friends with the superintendent of the school district, brought him by to see the deplorable, unsafe conditions of our courts, which led to the district promptly putting up the money for our courts to be resurfaced. At the conclusion of pulling major strings for the good of the program, that parent stayed quietly in the background, never looking for any kind of payback. His son was a bit of a thorn in my side, but even though he was rambunctious, he brought a certain bravado that was the missing ingredient that helped boost the team to its first championship in 26 years.

Show Some Acceptance Of All Efforts

When dealing with players, it's almost universal that a teenager is not going to be very happy if their idea is not accepted. Adults might be slightly better at accepting this. No matter who we are listening to, whether or not we accept and put their idea into play immediately, it's almost always a great idea to follow up with a conversation later that says, 'I did hear you and I am considering what you said.' When kids answer questions, and they are off track, simply saying 'interesting', is a much better thing to say than, 'wrong'. That kind of listening is so rare, you and I can gain a considerable amount of relationship capital when we do this. When people prove themselves to be unreasonable, or to be carrying a personal agenda that would override the mission of our program, it can act as a litmus test for the future of that relationship.

Talk Is Cheap

Players may make commitments to accomplish tasks, but then their actions may tell a completely different story. This brings us back to 'all behavior is purposeful'. 'What you are doing talks so loud, I can't hear what you are saying'. I had a team that was not only a last place team, but in the years prior to my taking over the program, they had not won a league match in 6 years. We would talk about commitment, being present every day, and working hard to improve, but there always seemed to be a player or two who had an excuse for missing practice. We would talk about it, players would commit, and the same thing would happen. One day, over half the team was missing. I asked my captain, 'Where is my team?' 'The chemistry teacher said there was a special lab to help with the upcoming test, they are all there.' So I made my way to the chemistry lab. After the lab, the girls saw me coming toward them and they were scared and caught, before they could go home. I asked them, 'What does this do to our relationship? Do you know how it feels when I am here to help you and you don't even show the courtesy of letting me know where you are?' Hearing that I seemingly cared so much about the relationship had them near tears. I asked them if they would recommit to being at practice. I knew that I was manipulating them, but at that moment, I had to do something to meet them where they were. Their actions were speaking so loudly, I had to listen to what they were telling me so that I could address it. In a few weeks' time, that team won their first match, breaking a 71-match losing streak, and our team captains and myself were interviewed on local TV. It was quite a thrill.

Moments, Hours, Days, Weeks, Months and Years

While these kinds of exciting moments are not happening every week, month or year, it's the daily work of communication that has a long lasting effect on our players. There are factors in people's personalities, and the way they choose to communicate that can help guide you as a coach on how to deal with them. People can be aggressive, assertive, passive-aggressive, passive, or a mix of different styles in the way they communicate. Sometimes this has to do with their ego-boundaries.

Ego Boundaries And Communication

The word ego is a good one, and I want to be sure that we use the psychological definition, as the most modern urban dictionary definition holds ego as a negative connotation. Ego simply means, your sense of who you are, your identity.

People with normal healthy ego boundaries are generally assertive, but sometimes can be passive in their communication. They won't stand to be abused by aggressive communicators forever, and they will call someone on their passive-aggressive communication. When you have a healthy ego, you realize that being passive may make sense sometimes, because a short period of putting up with a bit of bad behavior is better than starting a full-blown conflict. At other times, the conflict must be taken head-on.

Aggressive And Passive-Aggressive Styles

People with oversized ego boundaries tend not to understand where they stop and other people begin. These people can be aggressive, but they also can be passive-aggressive. The aggressive communicator many times is giving orders, sharing opinions, and placing expectations on then people around them.   Players or parents with oversized egos may think they are always right, and/or everyone should see it their way and follow their edicts. People with weak ego boundaries tend to be passive-aggressive communicators and can express some hostility, resistance, or rebellion in their actions, but in their speech they feign passivity. Interestingly enough, aggressive people with overly large egos tend to be found with passive people with very little ego strength, as the one serves to have enough ego for the two of them. Weak ego boundary people are many times attracted to much stronger egos, so as to be almost absorbed into a symbiotic relationship, where one is a parasite of the other. Passive-aggressive people drive me nuts because it's so difficult to really talk about what is happening, as many times they will deny having any negative experiences or feeling any conflict.

What Is The Purpose Behind The Words?

Whichever style you are dealing with, consider again, 'All behavior is purposeful'. Why are they acting in this manner? What do they hope to achieve? Can we help them to really ask for what they want and otherwise express that in a clear, concise, and respectful way? What I have found to be most empowering and to ease the communication with any group is to praise those who make attempts at proactive, assertive communication and sometimes make it a lesson for the other players on how this is done. It could be a major mistake to attempt to turn an interaction with a parent into a lesson.

We may need to place limits on the behaviors of those with oversized egos, including our own, while drawing out the passive ones, helping them learn to be a bit more assertive with their communication. When we listen to our players, parents, and coaches, it's wise to consider these factors in how they communicate and what it says about their style. There can be ways to manage people according to their style, but I strongly encourage teaching the players to have an appropriate amount of ego strength, and to be assertive communicators at the right time.

My Take Away: Action Item(s):

CHAPTER EIGHTY-THREE
The Power of Story

The role of the storyteller is to awaken the storyteller in others.

~ Jack Zipes

What is your story? This currently is one of my favorite questions, but it wasn't always. Its a hard question to ask, and when I first heard it, I didn't like it, because it conjured up images of 'the story of my life' in a negative way. It brought my failures to light. I didn't have a story that I wanted to tell. Later, when I felt I had a story to tell, I wasn't sure if it was one that people wanted to hear. As I get further along in life, I feel very blessed to have been confronted by this question. It challenged me, it taught me, it opened me up to learning and engagement. What is your story? Think about it, you are in the middle of a story. The story of your life, the story of your coaching, playing, growth as a person. Our stories can be rewritten, and written freshly starting now. Presumably, I could move forward from this moment living a perfect life. Of course, I won't live a mistake free life, but I can try to mitigate those, and fix errors quickly.

Generally, we have an idea of how we want our stories to end. Figuring out how to get from where we started to where we are now can be an instructive pursuit. When it turns into excessive psychoanalysis, and/or 'navel gazing', it's not as helpful and empowering. More importantly, it's figuring out the next steps, from where we are at the moment, where we want to go, that is the story we want to write. It starts with a question. What is my story? Sometimes you hear people say in a sad way, 'that's the story of my life', as though hardships follow them more than anyone else. We have the power to write a new story!

Disconnect: Story, Coaching and Learning

While we have become so plugged into technology, we have become more disengaged with people around us. The time-tested method of teaching throughout the centuries was that a master would take on a small cadre, or maybe only one apprentice, to show them the ropes of how to work at a vocation. I was recently in Bethlehem, Israel where the story goes, that the art of carving olive wood will most likely die with the last remaining carver of such wood in a certain style. Reportedly, there is one last master craftsman in that specialty and the art will die with him because none of the younger generation is willing to learn the trade. Is that true, or just really good marketing? I don't know, but we face real challenges in coaching, as many long-time coaches retire and die off from the generation of baby boomers. Part of the great handoff that will have a tremendous impact on future generations will be captured in great storytelling, and younger coaches sitting at their feet will be engaged in that learning. Our stories will also need to transcend and engage the new technological culture and generations X, Y, Z and beyond.

How did we get here? Where we currently are is in a space where coaches gather on a court or in a room and hear a lecture, having no further contact with the instructor, left alone to interpret and synthesize the knowledge for themselves. I want to work mainly in the mentorship space. We listen to your story and we share our own when it's appropriate to help with the lesson of overcoming a challenge. We want to know your story. And we put our story out on every major social media channel.

Stories Engage Real People

Coaches as storytellers have a much deeper impact on the lives of players than those who simply give out information, commands, and instructions, as though we could drill a hole in someone's head, insert a funnel, and pour the information into them. A story told by Steve Chandler, one of the great life coaches, who worked with Lute Olson, one of the greatest college basketball coaches of all time, highlighted how this works. The story goes something like this: Lute was running practice and something was going wrong on the court, a player made a bad decision. Lute did not yell at the player like many coaches do when players make mistakes. He blew the whistle, asking players to freeze. Everyone stopped, and there was a pregnant pause. He then asked a question, "Jason, what do you see?" Jason paused, looked around, and responded, 'I see that I had an opportunity to make a pass to a player who had an open shot.' Lute agreed, blew the whistle, and play resumed.

What does that story mean to you? Stop, and write yourself a note about what you see in that very short story from a masterful coach. How is your story similar or different as a coach? Take note of the fact, that I am not telling you the point of the story, I simply told it, and then ask you what you got from it, then you own the information better. See how that works?

Tell Your Players Stories From Your Point Of View

I tell my players stories about how other players were successful or had failed. I then ask them what they learned from the story. They might miss the point, but I can fill in later. Sometimes they pick up a nuance that I had never thought about. When I coach, I ask them 'What do you see is happening here', in the competition. They tell their brief story and I listen. I'm not the one running out there. I don't feel what they feel. I'm not pressured by what they are pressured by in the competition. I may ask them, "Do you see how...?", helping them to recognize an important aspect of the competition. We don't have time to argue, either they see it or they don't. Perhaps, given a few minutes to process the thought about the story of the competition, they come to a realization, or maybe their interpretation is different. I have had players come back to me with a different idea as to how to attack the situation, or seeing a more subtle but important advantage to be gained, we write the story in a way that will work for them. When they are honest with me about a relative lack of confidence in performing a certain game plan, we save ourselves a lot of agony, because they are not afraid to tell it from their view point. Honestly, I do ask them fairly often to go outside their comfort zone a bit, but when everything is on the line, I want them playing from a place of full confidence in the game plan and themselves.

When I coach a team, the most engaging stories for my players are hearing about people they know, current players, recently graduated players, and players from the school who have gone on to a measure of fame. The subconscious message that comes across during the telling of these stories is that stories could be told about them later. This is a sidebar motivator that they can become a part of the annals of sports legends.

When I taught high school, quite often in class, and almost every class, I would tell a story about people succeeding, or perhaps cautionary tales for my high school students. The amazing reactions from students and their perceptions of what was actually happening were quite odd. Even though I was well-known, and hated by some, for using the entire classroom period with very little dead time, students' memory of my classes were quite different from reality. The rumor that was told was that 'Mr. Patton is ALWAYS talking about himself' 'He talks about stuff that isn't math, the whole period long', 'He wastes a lot of time with his stories'. Which is amusing, but also many more students remember lessons I give in the telling with a lot of appreciation for making class fun and meaningful. Over the years I run into numerous students from that high school around town, and when they want to talk with me, it's usually because they enjoyed my class. When I ask them what they remember, you know what they say: the lessons from real life people made it fun and inspiring. I would tell them about my own life and it would give the students who cared and wanted that a better connection because of the transparency and authenticity.

So, the challenge is this: be a storyteller, be a better storyteller. Listen to other people's stories, help them write better ones. Each competition is a story, and each interaction, each bit of dialogue develops the plot and can change the direction of the outcome when told well.

My Take Away: Action Item(s):

CHAPTER EIGHTY-FOUR
Athletes Sports Stories

*Telling someone about your experience breathes new life into it,
moving it out of the inchoate swirl of unconsciousness into reality.
It takes on form and allows us to examine it from all angles.*

~ Mandy Aftel

How can we understand players if we don't know their stories? Do you want to know their reality? What's past is prologue, and if we are to help a player write the next chapter in their sporting life, then we need to know something about their history. Being intentional about developing as complete an understanding about our players as is practical, lends itself to working with the player to develop them further. Beyond listening to players and parents in the here and now, we begin to look for themes that run in the players personal history. When we listen to our player's stories about their play, we do well to discover the player's narrative. A recent case study of elite athletes (Carless,Douglas:2013) showed differences in the way elite athletes present their personal histories. They propose that athletes stories are manipulated by the sociocultural context of elite sport. We as the culture makers force athletes into these stories, but the final story is one not captured in the study. Researchers found three main narratives by which athletes tell their stories, and as coaches, we are wiser when we seek them out. Building on that research, I will offer a fourth alternative.

First, let's differentiate between elite athletes, who are competing at a national or international level, from more recreational or hobby level players, who might be playing college, high school or club sports, but are more concerned with academics and career success than they are the outcomes on the field. It's fine to accept the athlete for living the role they are playing, but we can also aid in helping them step out of that, into one that may work better for them.

Living The Part of Athlete

Among high level athletes, the dominant feature in the narratives of athlete's stories are that they are 'Living the Part of Athlete'. When an athlete's complete identity is wrapped up in their performance of the sport, then they are really living it. When using the word 'part', the idea is that of playing a role in a theatre of the story. Of course, there are negative ramifications of this identity. As we saw with olympic swimmer Michael Phelps, who must be one of the ultimate examples of the performance narrative, he had to deal with some very difficult issues when he came out of the training bubble. In recent years he has acknowledged that for a time he was dealing with mental illness. Likewise, some of the behaviors of the US Olympic swimmers in Brazil clearly showed a lack of propriety, if not even criminal behavior.

Many times, these extremely elite athletes with a performance narrative assume entitlement that society is happy to hoist upon them, at least until it becomes embarrassing. Once embarrassed the media community enjoys putting them back in their place, especially after previously placing them on a pedestal. Wise coaches can prepare these vulnerable athletes for their certainty. Relationships and some social environments are set aside for the sole purpose of allowing for best performances. Character issues may go ignored because the athlete is seen as very talented and a contributor to the overall mission success. Associations, federations, governing bodies, coaches and even parents will often sabotage efforts to work on character issues, if it's seen as a threat even to short term performance. Almost every childhood sports movie seems to depict those players as the antagonists. Players may later reflect on the damage being done to relationships and choose a different narrative. Examples of players who continue to tour and/or train with their team even while family members suffer a tragedy bring this narrative to light. In contrast, the next two narratives may provide more balance, but the narrative I want to advance was not mentioned in the study.

Resisting the Part of Athlete

Resisting athletes have classic examples in Serena Williams for the positive and Johnny Manziel for the negative. Each of these athletes has drawn way outside the lines, but Serena doing so while still marshaling her resources. In Serena's case, since the early days as a professional, she told a story of a multidimensional experience as a person and has resisted the conventional labels thrust upon her. Serena's most recent controversy at the U.S. Open brought many other issues to light, and further underline her resisting the part of athlete in an effort to be something more. Resisting the performance narrative that society attempts to place on athletes casts them in more of a role of rebel. Williams track record of great success creates a very strong contrast to Manziel, not only in that she plays an individual sport, but she has made it work for her. Football has among the most rigid social norms of any professional sport. This can create a love/hate relationship with the athlete, but also make them more interesting to the general public, as the athlete attempts to do all the extracurricular activity that is frowned upon by teams. Athletes in this category seem to have PR directors whose job it is to keep them in the news. As both the Williams sisters have had a major impact on the WTA, more and more women's tennis players, and female athletes in general, have become far more entrepreneurial. By far the most entrepreneurial female athlete is Maria Sharapova, and she herself has become a lightning rod for controversy.

For most elite athletes who do not live life in the spotlight, resisting the part of athlete simply means playing by their own rules. They may have certain non-negotiable requirements regarding where they live, when and how long they train, and how much they have access to the comforts particular to them. An example being a multiple gold medal-winning para-Olympic swimmer who chooses to live in a part of the city that created a difficult commute to his place of training. He resists training at the national center that is foreign to him and isolates him in another town away from his comfort zone.

Playing The Part of Athlete

Our third studied narrative is about those who "Play the Part of Athlete". In 30 years of coaching, I have coached far more players who play the part of athlete rather than living the part of athlete. This happens even among some very gifted championship-level players. Those who play the part of athlete make sure they do the right things that will get them noticed and recognized as being serious. They may do a certain workout, because they know that players who do gain favor with the coach, even if they don't find much value in the workout. The organization or coach sets up a 'game', and they play it to win.

Great coaches are cognizant of how the structures they create for players may lead to playing a game of how to gain favor. From the study, one such athlete was being passed over for playing time and there was a passive-aggressive communication style being perpetuated by the coaching and fitness staff with the performer. When this player found out that the trainer perceived him as not dedicated enough, and passed that along to the coach, he then decided to attend an 8 am workout, which he felt did not help him much at all. This act gained him favor with the coaching staff, which subsequently rewarded 'his improved attitude'. The fitness trainer then approved him to the coach saying, 'he is much more fit', even without a whit of data to support that notion. This does not seem to indicate an athlete centered approach, in fact, quite the opposite. Let's avoid creating false hoops for players to jump through, instead focusing on the reality of what is effective with the player. When our every activity does, in fact, move the dial forward for the vast majority of players, then playing at being an athlete can be diminished. At the very least, being up front and honest with players about expectations, perceptions, and consequence is far more honest.

My Piece: Loving the Part of Athlete

The study above was conducted through candid interviews. This is instructive, because we can operative similarly. We can discover a lot about our player's stories by interviewing them, not formally, but probing, asking questions, and observing behavior. Actions speak louder than words, so really observing our players as objectively as possible to find out which is their chief narrative is very important. Is it just me, or does it seem like an ideal narrative is missing? The study also shared that each of the 21 athletes had found a great level of success, so the way they present the stories of their lives did not inhibit their outcomes.

I would suggest the following: 'Loving the Part of Athlete'. When players bring love and appreciation to their sport and also maintain balance in their personal lives, then optimal outcomes of satisfaction occur. We can play a role in helping athletes love as many aspects of the sport at possible. I believe that players who love their sport play from a greater place of authenticity and self expression, rather than reacting to outside forces.

Roger Federer is the most sought after athlete at the Olympics, many of the world's top performers get a thrill from meeting the man who best embodies love of the sport, and is not only the best ambassador the sport of tennis has ever known, but sport in general. Mia Hamm represents this same level of representative joy in soccer, especially in the U.S. The Golden State Warriors embody a love of the game, team, and exhibit an amazing level of unselfish play, and people gravitate to Steph Curry for the same reason. Even though some people are offended, they are not shy about showing their joy in the experience of playing together. We can point to these athletes who really show their love of sport.

My Take Away: Action Item(s):

CHAPTER EIGHTY-FIVE
Cultural Issues In Sport

Everyone is influenced by their culture, but no one is bound by it.

~ From a Masters Degree Text in Education

Culture Shock - The disorientation that people experience when they come in contact with a fundamentally different culture and can no longer depend on their taken-for-granted assumptions about life.

The cultural setting in which you work, is different than another organization. One team to another, one league, one sport, city or state has a different culture than the next. Even greater is the shift for someone who has traveled halfway across the world to what may seem like a polar opposite culture, and there will be plenty of cognitive dissonance. In education, experts used to espouse the 'melting pot' as the great goal of assimilating everyone into the dominant culture, at no time was that ever fully true. Nowadays, the 'salad bowl' is probably more accurate. All the ingredients of a salad, and the dressing, mix together and the flavors rub off on one another.

Your Unique Salad

We as coaches have widely varied cultural settings in which we work. These differences in the backgrounds of civilization are a major part of the stories of our players lives. Understanding the socioeconomic conditions, diversity, race, sex, sexual orientation, school culture, and regional societal norms, all play a major part in how we serve our players in the best possible way. In preparing for this chapter, I read a lengthy essay by a feminist basketball coach, who endeavored to create a feminist coaching philosophy and pedagogy. I will go into more detail on that, but the coach discovered something about the lines of propriety in the culture of her team.

There Are No Cookie Cutter Solutions

Since I don't know your situation, I certainly can't tell you exactly how to proceed. But we can discuss some issues and possible solutions. Some questions are necessary to answer prior to creating a coaching pillar in your area.

To what extent is it appropriate for players to fully express their private lives on the team? I was at a team tournament and I overheard a conversation from a group of players from an exclusive private Catholic high school discussing their favorite porn stars, with graphic descriptions. I don't think the coach was very far away when this conversation was taking place. Unwittingly, this group has brought some embarrassment to their school, and they may not be aware of it. Of course, a coach can never fully know everything their players do in secret, but at a public event, it would stand to reason that they could provide adequate supervision so that their players would not speak out loud on that topic. For me, the number one mission of school sports is to be an ambassador for the sport, representing the school in such a way as to bring honor to the competition, and the relationship with the organizing body. So my first guideline in considering any behavior is: Does it fulfill the mission of representation?

Word Choice As A Reflection Of Bully Culture

Another example is the use of the word 'gay' in a derogatory fashion that can easily seen as bullying. Homosexuality and the move to mainstream it into American society is still a controversial topic. Some in more liberal areas of the country might scoff at that last sentence, but that's exactly why I am writing this chapter in more of an open discussion and creating guidelines, rather than delivering advice with moral absolutes. Our feminist author mentioned above, wanted to create a culture of near full disclosure, because she felt that keeping these secrets did not advance the overall team culture. She wanted players to disclose their sexual orientation to one another. While she worked to advance that idea, her players did not buy into it. While it's hard to conclude anything absolutely, I would advise that it's not a great idea to force maximum transparency on your players. These kinds of disclosures only happen in a very trusting setting, as a result of an incredible relationship, and not from an edict by an administrator. It's not athlete centered to impolitely extract

319

information from people who don't want to, or are not ready to share. What I would recommend is that everyone be treated with respect, and that the use of the word 'gay' in a bullying tone, would be outside of that rule of respect. I am certain that I have had players who had a homosexual lifestyle who have played on my teams, but this was never explored, identified, or considered, although some where open about it in their daily school life, we simply did not discuss it on the team. I simply let everyone know that it's not appropriate for the discussion of sexuality on a team, how does that further our mission? In unifying a group, it's a far better and much more helpful to celebrate that which unifies the group, rather than that which divides it into different sub groups.

Race And Culture

When it comes to race, over almost 30 years of coaching, I have seen dramatically diminished racial tension in sports. This is one of our society's greatest achievements. However, in the early days, I would hear derogatory comments about those of Asian, African, and Latin descent. Some regions of the country still have battle lines, and the right and wrong side of the tracks. As coaches, we can find our way in diplomacy to break down these barriers. Locally, there was a great story of two basketball teams: one from the inner city, and one from one an extremely affluent area. The inner city team defeated the affluent team to win the Northern California Title. Somehow, the losing team became aware that between the school and the parents, getting to the State Championship playoffs was going to be a financial hardship for some of the families on that team. Some parents could not afford to take time off work or were not working at all. They could not afford hotel rooms, meals, gas and other expenses of the road trip. The affluent school became aware of this, and amongst their group, raised money together to fund the trip. This from a mostly white and Asian community to a mostly African-American community. These kinds of stories are what can inspire us to further break down barriers along racial divides.

Daily Acts Of Respect And Kindness

You as a coach, your parents and players don't have to spend money to break down this issue. Sometimes the simplest act of kindness, friendship, and respect can go a long way to furthering racial harmony in this country. Please don't discount the effect of a friendly greeting, curiosity about a person, and respect during and after competition. No matter a person's culture, a sincere interest in who they are, coupled with the respect of their silence on any matter is a good guiding principle. Any behaviors that create an atmosphere of bullying in any regard to any aspect of a player's being, should not be tolerated. I challenge everyone to make a once and for all commitment to understanding their players and teams.

My Take Away: Action Item(s):

CHAPTER EIGHTY-SIX
Accounting for Cultural Bias

Determine what behaviors and beliefs you value as a company, and have everyone live true to them. These behaviors and beliefs should be so essential to your core, that you don't even think of it as culture.

~ Brittany Forsyth, VP of Human Relations, Shopify

Sports around the world are becoming more and more a multicultural experience. I remember a time when the world came together for sports only every four years for the Olympics and other rare events. Since that time more and more athletes are moving from one land to another. They bring with them a different culture. One of the hot topics in many countries around the world is the issue of assimilation of new people into the mainstream culture of their new home. You will need an ethic in regard to your dealings with players who bring dramatically different underpinnings to their lifestyle, some of which may be diametrically opposed and even longstanding enemies of one another. In this way a coach can be a mediator for world peace. Think globally, act locally.

You should know that I have a bias toward national sovereignty and the preservation of native culture. It's an amazing thing when people are transformed generationally so as to be fully included and functioning positively in a new society. Unfortunately, you may meet those who have plan, wish or desire to assimilate into their new home, instead they will want the new nation to bend to them, and it can manifest itself on your team. Your program needs to have clear guidelines established to assure that everyone is on the same page as to how they plug into it. Your training environment necessarily has to be a safe place where everyone understands the limits of their own behavior for the greater good of the making it a place of development.

Example: U.S. Assimilation

Some cultures are promoted more easily in the dominant society of the United States, and some less so. The reasons that I discovered had more to do with a lack of understanding than really good decision-making. I discovered in writing my Master's Thesis, that African-Americans and Hispanic-Americans are selected into fewer academic programs at an incredibly disproportionate rate that cannot only be explained by socioeconomic status.

The interest in my research came from my experience teaching in a low-income school. I was amazed and frustrated at how many African-American and Hispano-American students were being placed in classes that were not on college track for mathematics. When interviewed, the most common sentiment from the counselor to the student was 'Take this (lower level) class so you can get a good grade'. In essence, these students were essentially docked a year of progress, by not making progress toward college because of a bias the counselor had toward them. What little did the students or parents know that part of the so called magic of public school administration is simply trying to balance out classroom sizes to meet budgets. The best interests of the students do not always come to the fore. The most important factor I saw was that schools that are predominantly run by those in the mainstream culture, do not read the cues from other cultures well. For example a latino boy who lowers his head and averts his gaze is seen as being disengaged from learning, when in reality in his culture he is showing the respect of 'Don't speak until spoken to'. I could go on with other cues from various cultures, but that's a safe one for me. Use your imagination, and learn to discover the cultural norms of those you are working with, and you can help bridge the gap.

Account For Your Own Perspective

Additionally, the main discovery of my research showed that dominant culture themes rule the outcomes of minority cultures especially in the interpretation of their behavior. Specifically, African-Americans are perceived to be lacking discipline and intelligence based on a strong cultural trait of exhibiting demonstrative behavior, and not wanting to sit for long periods of time. Why should they want to sit for long periods of time? Hispanic-Americans, by virtue of their deferential behavior in averting their gaze as a sign of respect are seen to be disinterested. The societal reverence for 'El Profesor' works against them, because the dominant society has an expectation of eye contact and engagement. When I explained to parents of Hispanic children that they need to advocate for their kids, and that 'El Maestro' of the school district is more concerned with butts in seats than they are in making sure your child has the best possible opportunity, then the light goes on for them.

These same sorts of issues can translate onto the sporting field.

Additionally, consider for a moment the people we don't understand well from a cultural perspective. No one person will we ever fully know, but we can stop, look, and listen. We and try to understand the background of each and every program participant to word toward empathy. This may also be something to consider when someone has moved to a different state, from the city to the country or vice versa, there is a culture shock that takes place. I had great fun with a bit of a statistical anomaly in my coaching. When teaching tennis in an area with a significant east Indian population, one class in particular, was made up completely of Indian-American boys ages 11-15. What ensued was quite entertaining, as they were very comfortable mocking their own parent culture, and we would laugh a lot. Then they also taught me a lot about India and it's diverse cultures. They seemed to really enjoy Apu from the Simpsons, even though nearly all of them had aspirations to be much more than a mini-mart owner. I felt compelled to read the entire Wikipedia entry for India. I learned quite a bit, which gave me a lot to engage with my students on. I would share with them what I learned. They appreciated this effort, and things only got better until there was a problem.

A Blind Man Felt The Elephant's Trunk, Calling It A Snake

Someone observing from the outside, not understanding the culture of that group wrote a fairly extensive complaint letter about me to my direct supervisor. I was then in the hot seat. My supervisor had never once taken the time to actually watch what I do, so it was hard to explain how positive the experience really was in the face of the complaint letter. The complaints mainly centered around accusations that I had made disparaging remarks about the boys, and that I was 'racist'. Some things were taken out of context, and others were bald faced lies, that put words in my mouth that I would never say. So, the risk we run when we go out of our way to work with our players in the place where they are, is that others observing from the outside might not understand. After a few meetings, and doing his research, my supervisor began to understand, and I was cleared of any wrong doing.

Speak Their Language

Language and culture are inextricably linked. The two go hand in hand. There is amazing power in affirming someone by making the effor to learn a few phrases in their native tongue. If you can learn a few phrases from someones home language, they will really love hearing you speak that. Speaking a little Spanish, Tagalog, or Mandarin has helped open doors with my players. It has also lead to some embarassment from mispronounced words, idioms and other stuff. One student however became offended by my request to learn a few words in the hold language that was not to be taught to outsiders like myself. I was taken aback, so be careful, it's important to approach this with the utmost respect.

My Take Away: Action Item(s):

CHAPTER EIGHTY-SEVEN

Caring Enough to Listen and Say No

**No problem was every solved by using
the same level of thinking that created it.**

~ Albert Einstein

How we say no is also important. We say no, because we have to reject the former way of thinking. When you come to a situation where there are many problems, saying no to the conventional wisdom that has prevailed is the top task of the new leader, but people don't care how much you know until they know how much you care. They probably also don't admire your discipline very much if you don't show that you are interested in what's best for them and the team. It's not a good idea to be the coach who automatically says no without listening or thinking. Be fully present, and when appropriate try not to cut the player off, even when what they are asking should be obvious. If you have time to calmly explain exactly why we are saying no, players seem accept that much easier, even if they don't show it immediately. We want to encourage our players to have voice and choice in how they are to train. Shutting them down, putting up a wall between you and your players can harm their morale, when they feel as though they are not being heard.

Account For Culture Shift Year To Year

Even choosing fun things to do can be source of conflict. I find it amazing that the sequence and enjoyment of certain games or drills changes every year. Every team, every group, and every group minus one player can have a completely different list of preference for games. And it is funny how one player can extremely vocal, about 'I hate this game!', so we play it anyway, but maybe a bit more and longer when they are not around. Some of my teams love 'Torpedo' to the point of addiction, while others take a while to warm up to it before beginning to enjoy it. Other teams love 'Attack!' and would play it until the cows come home, others think it's silly, and still other teams love 'Stations' the best. When we have a menu of a wide variety of games from which the players can choose, they have the freedom to say no. Now and then, I may open it up and ask "Did anyone learn a game since last season that you want to teach us?" At that time I am saying no to my own desire to be completely in control, except that if I find little value for teaching in the game, we won't play it again.

Stop Practicing

When something serious happens, everything might stop. Sometimes players can treat each other very poorly in a way that is completely unacceptable to a team, or really any group of civil people. A major safety issue that could lead to injury and liability can arise, and it must stop immediately. When a coach can be called grossly negligent for not addressing major issues, they can lose their job, come under legal scrutiny, or even be arrested. That's when a loud 'NO!' is very important, along with a meeting that goes like this: "No, No, No, No!". There was a coach in my area whose team created vile nicknames for each other that were overtly sexual and perverse. It was quite disturbing and very embarrassing for their opponents, when they shared the nicknames in the introductions prior to a sectional playoff match. Somehow that team, and it's coach did not feel any shame. My athletic director was present and I asked him to follow up with that school's athletic director. That coach was fired by the school, and later they no longer fielded a team. Recently, a friend of mine has begun coaching at the school and has re-instituted the team in a more sporting manner, without the disgusting names. Every team at all times should keep in mind their ambassadorship for their school.

So No To Bad Ambassadors

I had a team captain who was amongst the worst team captains I have ever dealt with, who threatened a player loudly as a match progressed. She threatened physical harm to the other player. I immediately suspended her from the team, she lost her captaincy, and was only allowed back into competition after her apology was accepted by the other school and the player in question. Unfortunately, the athletic director at that private school was not very supportive as I tried to create a real team out of a collection of very self absorbed, cliquey in individuals, there was one conflict after another, and I only coached there for one year. It's a much longer story of how my time ended there, but if you contact me, I will tell it.

Say No To Humiliating Opponents

We can be on the other side of what might embarrass others, so having rules that govern these things is important to preserving the dignity of the opponent. I have a fun game that I play with my teams that helps them learn to be good frontrunners and save time and energy during the season. Many times, high school tennis players race out to a big lead, then become bored, and their play can go down to the level of the opponent. To combat that, I give a reward to the first player who comes off the court winning at least one set 6-0. If a player takes a bit longer but wins 6-0, 6-0 they can trump the player who finished first, but had only one 'bagel' set. This is a lot of internal fun for my team. They can win an energy bar or a grip re-wrap to freshen it up. But now, here is what I say no to:

* Don't rub it in the opponents face.
* Learn not to rush so fast that you make mistakes.
* The opponent must not know about our secret game.
* You must not tell anyone outside the team about our game.

Invariably, there is a player who talks loud, brags, or makes it obvious what is happening. They are stripped of their prize. Early on, the players rush too fast, becoming sloppy in their play until they discover an ideal pace of play for front-running. If players do brag or expose the game after one initial slip up, it stops at that point. I won't continue that practice, if their is potential for them to embarrass their foes. If the coach of the other team becomes aware of it, I apologize and explain why we do it and explain that it's nothing against their team. One time, my players came to me to say 'The other guys on that team have a money bet going about who will beat our guys faster.' We used that as motivation to beat them, which we did in a semi-final playoff on our way to the championship. Similar behaviors go on in teams all across the U.S., let's say no to that for the sake of respect, or at least find a healthy outlet.

In conclusion, the best way to say yes to all the great things we want to do and experience, is to say no to anything that would confuse, ruin, compete, or otherwise interfere with moving in the direction we want to go with our teams.

My Take Away: Action Item(s):

CHAPTER EIGHTY-EIGHT

Listening On Purpose

All behavior is purposeful.

~ Dr. William Glasser

When people do things, they might know the reason or they might not, but in the vast majority of cases, it's not hard to trace the purpose of someone's behavior. When you can find the meaning behind why someone performs an action or says a certain thing, then you can begin to understand them better.

I have a tremendous amount of respect for Coach E, as she played a crucial role in some amazing successes, especially looking out for my blind spot. Coach E had a purpose. Her purpose was two-fold. She wanted to do what was best for the team, and she wanted to do what was best for her son, who was on the team, for which she was an assistant coach. How can we measure the ratio between her interest in the team's outcomes and those of her son? We can't. She is also an assertive communicator without a huge ego. She also was the one who recruited me to be the head coach of the team. She asked if she could remain on as assistant coach. Given the depth of involvement from Coach E in years past, far be it from me to deny her the opportunity to stay involved, even though I really prefer to coach on my own. The previous head coach had cautioned me about E, that she would be 'watching'. I took that as a moment of sour grapes from a coach who had been asked to step aside.

The First Conflict

My first year at the school Coach E's son, K, had struggled with injury, and his attempts to challenge for a more prominent role on the team were cut short. As a part of my coaching philosophy, I want players to know their role on the team fairly early in the season, so that they can cope with accepting their place in time to perform well. I also manage the challenge ladder (a lineup tool for high school tennis coaches), so that if a player has improved, they can have an opportunity to challenge. I would schedule any necessary challenges at a time that works within the overall plan of the season. Over time, coach, parent, and player came to an understanding that the best way to manage K's injury was for him to play almost exclusively in a lesser role, until he was fully healthy. He played hurt the entire season, which I managed to keep an eye on, and we were careful not to push him too hard. With the help of a dynamic partner, he was on the winning end and almost an automatic win in the lineup.

There was an interesting moment early in the following season, when Coach E made the assertion that K should be granted a full opportunity in the new year to challenge for that more prominent spot on the team. The way she framed it made it seem as though I had denied her son a chance to play a more prominent role. That's not how I remembered it, to me it seemed far more collaborative. At the beginning of a practice she brought this to me to advocate for her son, which was a little out of bounds, but I had already done my homework. I had asked K more than once if he wanted to challenge for singles spot, he went back and forth before deciding he was happy playing doubles. Oddly enough, when I did not acquiesce to Coach E's assertion, she became upset and spent most of the rest of practice as far from me as possible. I let her have some time away from me, as it would have done nothing good to try to confront her, argue you with her, or even have a discussion in the middle of practice when we are supposed to be focused on our players. In my denial of the assertion, I mentioned that K himself had said he wanted to play doubles. It didn't take long for everything to return to normal and there were not a lot of hurt feelings, but I can imagine that things may have been quite different if I had not been assertive myself. If I had been passive, then I would have had to take her assertion into close consideration, and most likely be obliged to offer a challenge match. Having the strength of character to be patient and allow short term conflicts to work themselves out, waiting, giving people time to process, rather than rushing to full resolution immediately helps keep your day on course. But the most important moments were when I allowed her over an hour of 'space' to process what had happened. She is a smart woman, and it did not take long.

Understanding Communication Styles

This first story serves to introduce the topic of communication styles, taking into account different states of people's ego boundaries to understand the complexity of how to best listen. In truly listening, we need to take into account our purposes, and the purposes of those we are talking with at any given time. I could count on Coach E to be sincere, and I don't know to what level she was self-aware of her strong advocacy for her son, or to what level she trusted me to do what was right, not only for the team, but for her son. Had I not allowed her to speak her mind, things would have been much more difficult. If I had not proactively addressed her son about the situation prior to this talk, I would not have been fore-armed to deal properly with the situation. The amount of listening and the value of the message and messenger should remain very high.

The amount of damage that can be done when coaches seem to rule with an iron fist and do not consider the feedback, suggestions, crazy ideas, and occasional complete trash that comes our way on a weekly basis is quite significant. At the right time, listen to everything. Real listening means trying to understand the words, working to discern the motives, finally to understand the people. As it turned out, Coach E who quite often had suggestions for lineup changes that were welcomed, but denied by me 98% of the time, made the suggestion ahead of tournament play that was a stroke of genius.

The Outcome Of Keeping Lines Of Communication Open

Her contribution lead to fairly miraculous sectional championship by our #3 seeded team that would need to beat #2 and #1 in the same day in 97-degree heat. Coach E, by virtue of her constant commitment to leave nothing on the table, and my commitment to listen to her, which allowed our collaboration lead to an experience for young people that they will never forget. The previous year, her advocacy for a certain player saw him gain varsity status and that player was pivotal in another upset of a #1 seeded team. It would have been a grave error on my part to completely shut her down. Additionally, influenced by her willingness to shuffle lineups, I was able to recognize an opportunity with our girl's team to have two different lineups that would create great matchups with different opponents. The work that went into this coaching relationship, helped that team win a sectional championship the next year after I was not at the school any longer, but the work had been done.

My Take Away: Action Item(s):

PART EIGHT
PROVING OPPORTUNITIES TO REFINE CHARACTER

For gold is tried in the fire and acceptable men in the
furnace of adversity.

~ George Santayana

CHAPTER EIGHTY-NINE

Serious Character Issues

**Sadly there are many coaches who do not belong working
with children. I am not saying that is the case here, but it is
the case in many places. Winning does not make for a great coach.
Being a great role model and leader for your young athletes,
teaching character and life lessons, caring about your athletes,
and coaching a child not a sport,
those things make for a great coach.**

~ John O'Sullivan - Changing the Game Project

For very few coaches, the need to intervene in very serious character issues is a common problem. In Tennis, I have had very few of those, and almost no violent players ever. I have had to deal with a few selfish players who will destroy team chemistry if I allowed them to do so.

It's hard for me to speak to those who regularly work with youngsters who have been raised in a violent area, and I admire and solute those who do. Don't get me wrong, I have spent plenty of time in the city, and mentored some kids that came from broken homes with drug addicted parents, but not as a regular coach building a program with those same kids. I welcome your feedback on this chapter for future editions.

Sexual Behavior Early In Life

This opens up a can of worms and the attempt in this chapter is not to preach to anyone, but to create an opportunity for reflection. When teenagers are in active rebellion to their parents, and beholden to the morals or lack of them within their group, a respected adult can be a great source of reality check for them. Very commonly coaches are rated as the most respected adults in the lives of young athletes. This presents us with a nearly constant opportunity and dare I say, responsibility. In some pockets of our society, it's expected that kids will become sexually active very young in life. There are differing stats for different groups, but generally speaking inner city youth become sexually active much younger than their suburban counterparts. Many children are active in their early teens, and some before their teenage years even commence at the beginning of puberty. A coach can possibly have some influence against the tidal wave of pressure from the culture in which that child is raised.

Consider Rape Culture

Lately in our society, there has been a proliferation in the use of the phrase 'rape culture', and it means more to some people than it does to others. I am not going to define it here.

In the Journal of Sports and Social Issues this is an important study, *The Role of High School Coaches in Helping Prevent Adolescent Sexual Aggression : Part of the Solution or Part of the Problem?* In this qualitative study, the researchers examined whether male high school coaches could effectively serve as advocates, or educators for male-focused programs to prevent sexual aggression. Open-ended key informant individual and focus group interviews were performed with high school coaches and administrators.

The five themes the authors identified suggest that coaches (a) believe they have influences over athletes, (b) lack education about sexual aggression, (c) endorse rape myths, (d) minimize the problem of sexual aggression, and (e) are resistant to being engaged in sexual aggression prevention. Our results reveal that coaches may need in-depth training on sexual aggression even if they do not want to engage in prevention efforts because they may be transmitting values and beliefs that support and condone sexual aggression of their athletes.

How can anyone in their right mind call themselves an athlete centered coach, if they stand silently by allowing a rape culture to perpetuate itself? The damage to everyone touched by this, including the perpetrator is nearly irreversible. Whether by ignorance, convenience, or fear we allow players to abuse or be abused, clearly we as mentors of life skills, this would indicate abject failure. Players whose major character flaws go unchecked may continue on toward lives of many other crimes, DUI, Assault, or Rape/Murder. We need to notice, be interested and respond to complaints! At a high school where I was coaching a sophomore football player dropped his pants in the direction of my girls tennis team. I left practice to find the nearest football coach, and immediately raised the issue. I followed up until I knew that the maximum amount of accountability was given, but I was still disappointed at the relative slap on the wrist he received. I can only hope that this young man was later taught about decent public behavior.

Consider Extreme Examples And Your Legacy

Imagine for a moment that you had encountered O.J. Simpson, or Aaron Hernandez two now infamous football players, during a time when they were clearly disturbed. In Hernandez' case, his violent problems were well known, and his personality issues are now finally being reported. Imagine having had the chance to intervene with a young man or woman like that, but instead passed that task off to someone else. Imagine then seeing the product years later. I applaud any coach who made their best efforts with each of those troubled men, and there are certainly many of those in the inner city. Those that chose short term success and the glory of winning with players who are deeply flawed have more than a tarnished legacy, theirs is one of destruction of lives for the sake of sport. It's a percentage game. A good friend of mine worked for years in the inner city, and many of his players got up and out of the ghetto. Some though succumbed to a life of crime or violence. There was a strange silence if I asked about the whereabouts of someone who was no longer around. It was an unspoken acknowledgement that the subject had met their end. Even so, soldier onward and keep working for those that will make it. If you are not an inner city coach, please consider doing something to encourage those coaches and players.

Fresh Red Meat

When coaches accept high dropout rates, violence, and poor citizenship in their players, how could they possibly say they are coaching the whole person for a life of success? If indeed they look the other way on character flaws, like a lack of sportsmanship, because the player is talented and seemingly should not face any setbacks of discipline, then the coach has failed, and is certainly not athlete-centered. If coaches accept a culture where cheating is normal, and 'Everyone is doing it so, why not me?', 'If you aren't cheating, you aren't trying hard enough.', then the future of that sport is in peril, and a culture that expels players of good character ensues. People of good character will many times choose to pursue other endeavors, rather than face routine cheating, cheat themselves, play against those who are doping, or dope themselves. When a sports culture rejects, or is rejected by players of good character, it's time to take a step back and evaluate. Coaches who are not fighting such a system cannot say they are for the best in athletes, when they perpetuate a system which is against the long term wellbeing of the athlete. Some coaches simply need to recruit some fresh red meat into the program as practice fodder for the stars on their team. They have no interest in the person.

Training A Killer, Not Training A Killer

In the case of Aaron Hernandez, how is it that through the many contacts with coaches, who really can know their athletes very well, the deep character issues were never addressed adequately? Pre-High School Football, High School, College and Professional Football, not one position coach, coordinator, head coach or any other interested mentor was effective in identifying that Aaron had a major problem? I find that hard to believe. If you are the coach who recognized Aaron's issues and tried to intervene, bless you! It's not a stretch to think that the majority of those people, if not every single one, knew he had issues, but his talent and the short term successes overrode the any desire to disrupt his path to the top with an intervention. For how many talented young athletes is this true, but to a lesser degree? The issues that these bullies hold inside went ignored, festered, and eventually peaked in great violence? One thing we know is that the majority of abusers have been abused, so if we treat them like victims, not only can we help them, but save those they would hurt.

What a tragedy as a coach to know that a player you worked with became a monster, was a monster during the time you worked with them, and could not get through. Even more tragic are those monsters who go completely unnoticed or even coddled because of their natural gifts and influence on a game. In lesser ways, we engage with those who will drop out of high school or college, nor never finish college. We work with those who will become addicted to pain killers, drugs, or alcohol and end up feeling, and causing, tremendous amount of pain. In nearby cities I see men on the street wearing authentic sports jerseys from the local university. It peaks my imagination, is this guy a former player, now cast out on the street? If as coaches we are not engaged, and working with our students, educating them also on being great citizens, then there is absolutely no way we can call ourselves athlete-centered.

Putting Character And Long Term Success First

In sharp contrast, look at a coach like Bobby Knight has been vilified by the press, and in some cases deservedly so, for his outbursts and physically threatening behavior with players his obvious and outward angry behavior captured so much attention that, he gets almost no affirmation for having had the highest graduation rate among his athletes. Why aren't all NCAA coaches graduating 80% or more of their athletes? In this way, Knight was among the paragons of being athlete-centered because he saw the player's long term success, the holistic approach to helping them prepare for life. What is interesting is that no one asks the question, 'Why did you agree to play at Indiana if you knew that Coach Knight was presumably so tough on his players?' Why does no one ask that question? It stands to reason that every one of those players knew that Bobby Knight was perhaps among toughest coaches physically, mentally, and emotionally, but that everything he did was based on a deep sense of caring for the preparation of young men in the world. When was the last time you heard of a former Indiana player under coach Knight who later became a criminal? I probably lost you right there and perhaps there are other better examples of caring coaches who teach the whole athlete, so I am open to suggestions. Geno Aurriema is a paragon, and his success has never come at the cost of absolving players of personal responsibility Some coaches are well-noted for their extremely low graduation rates, but for getting slightly more players ready for the NBA. But what of those who don't .make it and end up without a degree? Who cares, right? Just another slab of fresh red meat.

Collaborative Holistic Relationships With Players

Some coaches look at the players simply as pawns, a means to an end. A minimal amount of caring about other aspects of a player's life means that we can avoid trouble, and have a certain level of denial about what we are putting players through to meet our personal objectives. The story of Don Nelson and Chris Mullin comes to mind. Don noticed that Chris was drinking alcohol, and his weight was getting out of control. Instead of confronting him, he simply bet him that he couldn't go a week without drinking. Mullin lost the bet, and came to grips with his alcoholism, and the rest is history, as he became a hall of fame player. So, one player, rather than a wash out, became great largely because of one wise act of kindness. I have been in both places, that of being a blessing to players, and a curse at times. I'm not perfect. We can wax into some Sufi wisdom about what is a blessing and what is a curse, but for the most part, we as coaches err on the side of not caring, not knowing enough about our athlete's lives.

Conclusion

I am not advocating that we should be intrusive, and I know for a fact I don't want to know everything about every player, but I always want to be aware of the important factors. One example where I was shamed was when there was a sneaky player on the team who was doing mild hazing of the younger players on the team. All of this went unnoticed by me and unreported by players until the end of the season. So from that, I had to teach my players that if there is something they want me to deal with, they have to trust me with the information. If they aren't going to do that, then I won't be able to intervene in any realistic way.

My Take Away: Action Item(s):

CHAPTER NINETY
Empathy Isn't Always Non-Competitive

Empathy
1: the action of understanding, being aware of, being sensitive to,
and vicariously experiencing the feelings, thoughts, and experience
of another of either the past or present without having the feelings,
thoughts, and experience fully communicated in an objectively
explicit manner also : the capacity for this
2: the imaginative projection of a subjective state
into an object so that the object appears to be infused with it

~ Webster's Dictionary

Empathy is an important ingredient in athlete-centered coaching. Seeing through the eyes of another, walking in someone else's moccasins, going outside of our own preconceived ideas as to what the other might be thinking, takes time and effort, and there can be some unforgiving minutes in that pursuit. As coaches model empathy to their players, they then can teach better rapport of players one to another, and also incorporate an 'other-centeredness' into the competitive situation. Craig O'Shanessy of Brain Game Tennis, who consults with some of the very best tennis players in the world, says, 'You are the second most important player on the court. Your opponent is first. You need to know his or her relative strengths or weaknesses in order to create your game plan.' Understanding the the challenge you present to your opponent is maybe more vital than that of knowing what they present to you.

Experience From Their Point of View

Our working definition for the use of the word empathy is to be able to see things through the eyes of another. You can decide whether or not you want to include identifying with their thoughts and feelings. At times, using empathy with an opponent's feelings can have a negative effect on the competition. Helping players learn to compartmentalize aspects of the competition helps them gain the most value from the pursuit. But if they are going to let the opponent off the hook from a loss, in order to spare their feelings, then it's gone too far. In fact, beating another team or player puts them in a situation where they have an opportunity to address a weakness.

We can empathize in regards to issues of sportsmanship, but reverse that when we attack an opponent at their weakest point to win the game. Exposing an opponent's relative weakness has the effect of challenging them to become better, thus raising the level of competition for everyone. One of my players discovered a weakness in his opponent and in the first match up exploited it perfectly to beat him routinely. Heading into the second match up, we planned to exploit that same tactic again, only to discover too late, that he had worked very hard to not only shore up that defensive weakness, but had developed an offensive shot from it. As a coach, I had to take the blame for not having suggested moving away from turned out to be the losing game plan earlier. If I hadn't been so stubborn with the game plan, my player and I may have found another method of attack. In effect, my player helped that other player improve. In the third match up we picked on other relative weaknesses of that same opponent so that my player beat him in the league finals. This principle is generally true when teams or players match up directly and you and use your relative strengths against your opponent's relative weakness. Using empathy helps you understand that.

Empathy from Coach to Player

It's practically required that if we are to be athlete centered, then we must have the ability to have empathy for our players. How can we help them discover their ideal pathway, if we don't see the challenges they see, know the thoughts they have, or have an idea about the feelings they have about moving forward. This can be challenging when we are dealing with introverts, but we still have to make the effort. As leaders, we need to make a plan, and execute until we get some push back. When we are aware of changes in enthusiasm, effort, and other forms of engagement in our players, then we can wonder about the cause and effect. Fairly frequently, I go about executing a game or drill, but in short order I discover that the players look like they have a lack of intensity, engagement or concentration. At other times I may feel bored, and if I feel that way, then there is a good chance that some of my players are feeling the same. Boredom is not good from a high performance standpoint. So, I stop, and ask my players. 'Do you find this as boring as I do? Shall we continue, and if we do, why should we continue?' The answers get interesting, and sometimes a player offers a compelling reason why we should continue, even if only for a few more minutes. I love it when players say that we should continue simply for the discipline of it. Giving players their voice at these moments can help create a timeless bond of trust and understanding between players and coach, and between teammates with each other. Not noticing and/or pushing past it can have the opposite effect.

Knowing the fears a player brings to a competitive situation is also important. In order to help our players become better problem solvers in their own experience, we first need to help identify the problem they face. If the problem is not well identified, then solutions will miss the mark. To reference again the chapter on real listening, it should come from a place of real empathy. Empathy does not mean bending to the will of a tyrannical coach or player. Amazingly, there are programs, where coaches and players will actually cow tow to the whims of the star player. There are parents who give advice counter to the goals and mission of the team. Those types of activities need to be redirected. We can even be empathic with those who are short sighted in their approach. If we try to see things they way they see them, we can turn around to show them a wider view, and a larger vision of how things can be. We can open up a bigger world beyond their own self interest. I find it poignant and slightly amusing when I catch parents of players repeating back things I have said, as though they are trying to retrain their own mindset. Having an attitude of anything other than empathy will make that kind of intervention much more difficult.

Empathy With Outcomes

One of the most powerful acts in developing a strong bond with players is to have empathy with players who lose, and celebrate with players who win. You have to know your players, some may want you nearby when they win or lose, or far away. They might want the same thing all the time, or the opposite for each outcome. When my son loses, he doesn't want to talk about it for a while, but when he wins, he talks about it right away. Coaches who have lost touch with how it feels as a young athlete to lose, have a harder time being empathic. Very young athletes may cry, just as elite athletes who have seen the biggest prize slip away may cry the same bitter tears. I will never forget the day one particular player let the occasion get to him, and because of nerves he overplayed. He lost a match that turned out to be pivotal to the team, this after our team had dealt with a pretty strong measure of adversity. I had urged everyone on the team to simply do their very best, and he certainly took that too heart. Two of our top players had quit the team midseason for different reasons, something I will talk about in a future chapter. On that day though, this young man was crushed, and while he did not cry, his body language spoke for his utter disappointment in himself. I stayed with him for a while, and we did not talk a lot, but I did reassure him that I trusted he gave his all, and that the other team was just better than us on the day. I placed my hand on his shoulder for a long moment, and it seemed appropriate and he was reassured by it. If it felt at all uncomfortable, forced, or if he had given any sort of indication that I should not, I would have removed my hand instantly. When I left I said, 'All this will have happened for a good reason, I am sure of it.' It all turned out very well the next season.

Young Athletes Put Plent Of Pressure On Themselves

Young athletes already put a lot more pressure on themselves to win than we give them credit for. When we heap more pressure on players ahead of 'big' matches, or put them down after tough losses, those are not empathetic actions at all. What we really can do to help our players succeed is help them to eliminate feelings of pressure, or turn it more into a challenge, creating excitement around the game.

Empathy might not always mean having sympathy for the feelings of athletes, but more understanding the future regret players may experience from not putting in the best efforts now. As coaches we have usually have a stronger vision for what players can become, than they do, and if we betray this vision out of sympathy for the adversity they may face along the way, then we do them a disservice.

My Take Away: Action Item(s):

CHAPTER NINETY-ONE
Aircraft Carrier Course Correction

When you pull on that jersey, you represent yourself and your teammates, and the name on the front is a hell of a lot more important than the one on the back. Get that through your head!

~ Herb Brooks

When we take on the course correction of changing a team's culture, like turning an aircraft carrier, it will take time for the entire vessel to come about in a direction we want. The speed of the course correction depends on a few factors, like the overall culture of the organization that the team is connected with like a league, a school, a club or some other influence.

Find The Rudder

Sometimes working with one player to change their behavior can change the whole team. When you quickly identify the leadership of the team, and those that disrupt the team, you can influence the leadership collaborating with them to develop the new vision for how the team will operate. Also discovering who is least cooperative with the program in the past or in the new vision for how it will run, that player or players might need to be disciplined or let go in order to proceed. In one case, I took over a team that had a reputation for being entitled, underperforming in playoff action, and for bad sportsmanship in the form of cheating in competition. It would have been easy to trumpet my intentions to fix all of that. In fact, a rival coach mocked me for taking the job and wondered out loud, 'How are you going to handle that team?' I told him 'I feel a little uncomfortable with you rooting for me like that, since we are rivals.' To which he responded, 'O.K. then, bring it on, we are going to beat you.' It was on like Donkey Kong! That one moment helped motivate me to be patient with my team to bring about the change I desired.

So I set about working with my new group. The first thing that happened was that players would arrive late to practice. The former coach would wait until the players arrived to start, or would accept their lateness, allowing them to disrupt practice by entering immediately into drills, of course his players became accustomed to coming later and later. I started practice at the very second my clock said it was time. When players showed up late, I did not punish them. I simply asked them, 'Do you know when practice starts?' They would respond '3pm', and then I would ask rhetorically, 'Why did you come after that?'. Fewer players came late. After a few days, I would have those that came on time run laps, and anyone who came late ran extra laps, one extra for every minute they were late, and had to start the opening game on the lowest court. I would then praise them for spending time with the players lower on the ladder. Which didn't make them happy, but it helped me avoid giving them negative attention. Within a few more days, no one came late and many players would come running to be on site at least a minute early. After another week, a player came late and I made a really loud big deal about it, 'DO YOU STILL NOT KNOW WHEN PRACTICE STARTS?' It was fun for everyone but him. After a while, the discipline was good and players might still come late, but they would come with a reasonable excuse and know that they will start on the end court that day. I was happy with being 99% successful within a few weeks.

Heavy Hand Or Light Touch?

As for the cheating, I said on the day before our first match. 'I have seen some tight calls from this team, and I want you to know I take playing fairly very seriously because teams that cheat feel guilty, and then don't win big matches.' End of speech. During our first match, my number one player made a very suspect call. During a time out when players change sides of the court, matter of factly and nonchalantly I said, 'Oh, by the way you blew that call at 15-30, so be sure to play two 'out balls' until the opponent wins two points at your expense. And be sure to build your points crosscourt... blah blah blah.' He was stunned! No coach had ever told him that before. I can't remember whether he actually played an out ball, but this scenario repeated itself with various players over the course of the season. I don't even know for sure, but I assume that these players talked about this with each other. It all ended with me being very confident that my players would not embarrass themselves, our program and me with bad calls. Every once in a while, I would see a bad call and immediately approach my player, which was enough for them to play fair. I could have been very heavy-handed and punitive, but I simply took each player and gently corrected them. They also began to feel better about themselves. While I did not have 100% success at curing this team's propensity to cheat, instead of cheating at least once in every individual match, we reduced that by about 90%. When players accused my team of cheating, I did not get defensive, I simply reminded those players what their recourse was, and when they went through the procedure, I did not bat an eyelash. That may have sent an even stronger message to my team. Standing up for fairplay is a huge life lesson.

Training For Post Season Success

As for underachieving in the playoffs, we made sure everyone conditioned themselves properly and that we would build up our energy stores to peak at the best time. At the beginning of our conditioning, there seemed to be players who would take one repetition off, going on a mental vacation, not giving their best. I would call my attention first to everyone giving 100% and leave their name off the list, then look at them. If after a few days of that, there were still players taking a repetition off, then I would call them out, not by name, but by general location in the practice area, making a few players there wonder if I was talking about them. I let them know 'I have eyes in the back of my head'.

Along with the use of wonderful motivational phrases like 'Legs feed the wolf.' In time, nearly 100% of our repetitions were performed at 100% effort. After we were fully conditioned, we simply didn't lose many long matches. When we went to play our rival, the team whose coach made the mistake of issuing a challenge to me, the opposition brought 100 people out to watch and heckle my team. That's a huge number for a tennis match in California. High school tennis simply does not draw crowds that large. When the home team came out on fire and won four of the first seven sets out of the seven matches, it looked like we might be in trouble, as it put them on track to beat us. Our guys, due to their conditioning, and new found attitude about fairplay won two matches in three sets, and we won going away 5-2 from what might have been a 4-3 loss. In the next matchup, we beat that same team 7-0, routinely and never looked back. I did not breath a word to the rival coach, other than to thank him for the congratulations for winning the match, as the results spoke for themselves. I needed to model the kind of discipline I wanted to see in my team. There was no need for me to give him an 'in your face' moment. We carried that training into the post season that included an upset of the #1 seeds.

This Miracle Turnaround Is Not Normal

The culture of our program made about as speedy a turn as you can make in a few weeks. This was borderline miraculous, so you might not want to expect this to happen so quickly. The work continued for another 18 months before we were able to be champions in our section of 145 schools. Many times an entire season goes into affecting a cultural shift, and even then the reality of it won't hit until the next season or later. It all depends on how deep the cultural problems are, and how much buy in you get from the leadership of your current group.

My Take Away: Action Item(s):

CHAPTER NINETY-TWO

The Range of Understanding and Action

Seek first to understand, then to be understood.

~ Steven Covey

Sometimes our best efforts to discipline players or teams are not 100% successful. We need buy-in from our players in regard to the need for some discipline. When players have already been presented with the choice of self-discipline or discipline from others and they are still not focused enough on achieving our goals as a team, I started to feel a little desperate to get things under control. Perhaps most crucial to a team is the discipline shown by captains and the top few players on the team. The examples they give to other players serves as a model. My most difficult and frustrating years of coaching have been when captains or #1 players either don't give their best efforts or make excuses for not being fully committed to the team. Maybe three or four times in 28 seasons, I have more or less given up on my Seniors. When I say I give up on them, I don't mean that I quit working with them, but when I come to the realization that they are not willing to work on personal growth, then I shift my focus to younger players who do have a growth mindset. In turn, I begin quiet conversations with junior players who will become the leadership nucleus for the following year.

Take Things Slowly Step By Step

When one of these key players is not performing as a great example, it's best to start with a quiet talk off to the side. Prominent players might be sensitive to being called out in front of the team, having their status questioned. It can be a grave error to call out one of these players without understanding what is going on in their world. Especially when it's early in your career at a certain school, it's essential to give time and conversation to the gain full understanding about why this player or players is not showing the way. 20 years ago, I had a very talented number one player who often gave less than 100% effort early on, and the other players began to give less effort in following her example. After more than one private conversation about this with little permanent change, as she did not seem to see the need to do more and better, a change in leadership took place. It was time to talk with the other players to not look to her as a leader, I then called her out and the others for not giving their best efforts, while praising those who did. I redirected younger player's focus onto the good examples, and a talented freshman stepped up, becoming our top player in her sophomore year. There were other controversies of a personal nature, which showed that the girls were more concerned about petty grievances with each other, than they were about getting better as a team.

Almost 10 years later another girl's team, all the same issues were in play, with the main difference being that we had very strong captains. Even though they played lower in the ladder, they had the full respect of their teammates, and were very strong in the area of attitude and effort. I already told the story that they held a team only meeting I asked the captains if they would hold a team-only meeting, which they did. The result was amazing and it creates a great contrast with the previous team. Ultimately, knowing your team, it's make up, maturity, and how good are your captains and top players in terms of leading the way? Understanding the hand you are dealt will give you a lot of insight into playing the discipline hand.

When To Use A Short Burst Of Emotion

I have to admit, that at times I have made the choice to explode in anger with my teams, but in general I am against the practice and I will explain that. A word of caution, expressing anger should be pre-meditated, the coach should know exactly what they want to say and their motives should be to provide a wakeup call. Coaches who yell at their players more than one time run a serious risk of losing their team. It is far better if you can use all the tactics in previous chapters to full effect rather than yelling. Ironically, going silent, completely silent, and just looking at your team might be more scary for them. Each time I had an outburst, it was followed up with explaining how much I care. Getting angry with youngsters and leaving them with no explanation about why, and how much it shows your deep concern for them, is like sending them home with a ticking time bomb. There has to be time for them to process what is happening. I DID NOT YELL AT MY TEAM A SECOND TIME!

Avoid Multiple Outburts At All Costs

As we move forward, we certainly need some iron clad standards, but we ought not to try to rule with an iron fist. Taking the time to figure out our team, our players, and what are their issues helps facilitate the buy into the discipline. Most of the work of discipline should be easy and done quietly one player at a time. Sometimes drastic measures need to happen and it's best to ramp those up quickly, at the beginning of a season so that they can be solved with much more than half the season to go. You can then enjoy the benefit of a disciplined squad. Every once in a while, a captain needs to be stripped of their captaincy or a player needs to be removed from the team. If you go through a progressive discipline approach, you will know when that is. In my twenty eight years, somewhere around four of five players have left the team or were removed by me over the rules. The rest of the team will be blessed when that happens. If you yell more than once or twice, you will quickly gain the reputation for 'yelling all the time'.

My Take Away: Action Item(s):

CHAPTER NINETY-THREE

Being Unreasonable

The reasonable man adapts himself to the world; the unreasonable one persists in trying to adapt the world to himself. Therefore all progress depends on the unreasonable man.

~ George Bernard Shaw

The way people react to a situation or circumstance reveals a lot about their mindset. We learn a lot more about people when they act differently than conventional wisdom would dictate, then when they do. When something out of the ordinary happens, someone acts out of their perceived character, or there is adversity, the approach people take to understanding it reveals something about how they think. Sometimes people see a problem where there is none, prescribe treatment, and act on it quickly. It's much more common to react and act quickly than it is from a habit of actual mindful decision making. It's generally true that people tend to be negative and judgmental of things they don't understand. In fact, at many times, coaches habitually do that which is obvious to them. For example, if someone is not paying attention to my instruction, then the obvious solution would be for me to repeat my instruction. After that, if there is still little response, the next obvious response that most would default to would be to try and repeat the instruction in a different way, maybe using different words. Some coaches may raise or lower the volume of their voice or ask a question like, 'Did you hear me?' or 'Do you understand my instruction?' There are definitely obvious responses to any and all situations and there are definite reactions to how a person handled such a response. Many times, the above solutions work perfectly. When these obvious solutions are not getting the proper response, the team or individuals are traveling down the wrong path and a radical change needs to take place, then it's time to do that which is not obvious.

Avoid Over Reacting, Use WAIT

Have you ever read or heard something that someone did in response to a situation and have an immediate reaction of judgement, 'Wow, that was not good - they should have responded better to that situation.' Or 'There was a much better way to handle that.' Exactly! This is what I describe as an obvious conclusion. Later, when you found out much more about the background of what exactly happened, then it can change your mind about how that person dealt with that issue.

There is a story about a man on a train and when he entered the train, he saw three boys who were very poorly behaved. They were playing on the train, bumping into people, climbing all over the train car. The immediate response of the man was that something needed to be done. He looked for the parents, and seeing the only the father, he said, 'Aren't you going to do something about the behavior of your children.' The father just shrugged and responded, 'I'm sorry, their mother just died and they don't know how to act. Frankly, I am at my wit's end at what we are going to do next.' Suddenly, a moment of judgement becomes one of empathy when you gain more information about what has transpired.

Now armed with some perspective, it's a good time to W.A.I.T. That is short for Why Am I Talking? You should be able to answer that question especially before addressing a problem with your athletes. It's far better to ask questions before getting angry. Find out, 'what is going on here?' The answer might surprise you. If the why I am talking is for myself, then I might ask myself how can I turn it around, making it for them? I know that as a new coach, I was motivated as much for myself and to look good in front of others as I was for the success of my team. My emotions were partly or mostly motivated by an increase or loss of esteem. Nowadays as a grizzled veteran, I have slowly refined my selfish impulses to direct every possible moment toward the athletes. It's a tricky thing, and I still have pangs of wishing for more things to go my way, but in the end, it's really all about the athletes.

Our Values, Our Cultural Influences and Biases Guide Us

We do these things as coaches, we have behaviors that we accept and don't accept based on how, where, and when we grew up as a person, the influences around us will certainly affect the way we make these obvious conclusions. What if we were to take a breath, step back, and attempt to understand the situation and the response/solution to the situation in a transcendent way? This is what I mean, to see or discern beyond or above the range of normal or merely physical human experience. We are all limited by our experiences, how and why we respond to what happens around us, or what we read or hear. That is my dilemma: I'm limited by my experience. If I have a wide array of experiences, my response to any situation is more broad in perspective. I may tend to see the bigger picture of who the person is, what motivates them in the matter, their intentions as a person towards others, and their attitudes towards life in general. I will link the context of what happened to the context of the persona of the individual. I can understand in a better way the 'why' because I understand the 'who' in a deeper way and trust that person to always look to do the right thing at the right moment. Judgement is withheld for a time to investigate the deeper purpose of the action(s) in lieu of having a knee-jerk reaction that condemns instead of understands. This is transcending the obvious, the idea of seeing a higher level, a clearer perspective of all the variables that may have played a vital role in the decision-making process of reaction.

My Take Away:

CHAPTER NINETY-FOUR

Big Picture Blow Up

When we see something as beneficial, we want it more when we're angry. So, when used right, constructive anger can make you feel strong and powerful and help push you on to get what you want.

~ Jeremy Dean, Ph.D

When we get too close to a situation, it's easy to lose perspective on the bigger picture. We can change this by stepping back, or stepping up, getting a new perspective of how to respond to any conflict we face before reacting ourselves. Do I need to take a moment before I react? Usually, the answer is yes, because taking a moment to stop, find a centered place and think can protect us from an impulsive move that could end up being a major mistake.

So now let's consider some situations that at first flush, may seem problematic, but when taken into perspective, more can be known about the person and what motivates them.

Most chapters in this book originated as blog posts, and no sooner did I publish an article on discipline, then the next day I had a major discipline issue with my team. At the moment, I rationally chose to be angry. Rational anger is not an oxymoron. After thinking about it, I took an old racquet and in 10 seconds, I smashed it twice on the ground, kicked it toward the fence, picked it up, whacked it against fence post, and yelled at the girls "I AM TRYING TO BUILD A TEAM HERE, WE ARE TRYING TO BUILD A PROGRAM HERE!!!" All of this in reaction to the leadership of the time showing an extremely laissez-faire attitude about girls who were skipping practice. Their attitude was that neither a team, a coach, nor captains should infringe on player's personal liberty for the sake of creating something bigger. If we stop there, it would be easy to make a rush to judgement. Some of you will be completely on my side, others will judge my seemingly violent action as repulsive.

You Might Both Be Wrong

I then shared a picture of the shattered frame and told the story on a Facebook post. That touched off a storm of controversy, which ranged from concerned friends wondering about my mental health, polite questions, expressions of disagreement with my method, quite a bit of positive support including 'Mr. Tennis Parent's Bible', Frank Giampaolo, and one person who held my action up to judgement and ridicule. So, hmmm, which whack job insane person would then stop and write about it? That's the ultimate, right? I would have to be insane to allow people to scrutinize this behavior. Perhaps, but I opened it up for people to learn from it. How often does this type of behavior happen for the wrong reasons, and is highlighted in the press in a negative light, while there can be similar situations in which that reaction is exactly what players need at that time.

That team really responded by stepping up all the way, and began a recruitment process that showed how my behavior showed them exactly how much I cared, that I would sacrifice a racquet to the cause. In the years since that reaction two of the girls on that team stated that the passion they saw that day helped them to internalize more determination in their academics to the point that they were accepted by schools that they formerly would have never dream of attending.

In the next few chapters I am going to give a short history of times I went berserk, (while in complete control of my actions), on a tennis court with my players. Whenever you talk to top coaches, they will all agree that the capacity for doing the work lies inside the player; if they want it, they will do it. The occasional expression of passion by the coach can light a fire for players, but, it doesn't always work. Ultimately, it's the motivational underpinnings in the player that you are trying to reach, anything else is secondary. When you learn about parenting, you find out that whether or not that you use corporal punishment, that it's imperative to discuss the meaning of it afterward with your children. Kids need to know that what you did comes from love, caring, and setting boundaries. Our rule as parents was, 'If it can get you seriously injured or killed, then it's worth a spanking to keep you alive.' Yelling is the only spanking you can give your team, and you don't want to do it often. So, now I will go year by year into the times I can remember having a good blow up.

My Take Away: Action Item(s):

CHAPTER NINETY-FIVE

The 90's

*It may sound like an odd thing to say, but angry people have
something in common with happy people.
That's because both tend to be more optimistic.*

~ Jeremy Dean, Ph.D

Defending Standards and People

1995: Marek was a talented player and had been #1 on the team for
two years. It was my first year coaching the team and we had a hot
shot freshman who took over the #1 spot. Marek sulked. His effort in
practice diminished. The #3 player saw an opportunity, challenged,
and won the #2 spot. Marek dropped to #3. His behavior worsened. I
tried to be nice, encourage him, repeatedly. One day he was hitting
balls over the fence in a place where we cannot easily retrieve them. He
and his friend, who also seemed to choke in a lot of matches, were
laughing. I stopped them. I yelled at Marek for about a full minute (or
it seemed that long) maybe about one or two feet away from his face. I
let him know that he is talented, could play college tennis if he chose to
do so, but that this behavior was not going to continue. When tears
came to his eyes, I stopped. Then I quietly said, 'The reason I did this is
that I care, a lot. I care about you, I care about your tennis, and I care
about this team, etc.'

Within a week his father showed up for a match, and I saw how
extremely critical he was toward Marek, and it all made sense. So
while Marek was playing poorly, I helped encouraged him taking a
much more low key friendly tone, even joking around with him to take
the pressure away from his father's presence. The next year, he was
the only player to go undefeated when we won our first championship
in 26 years. He went on to play college tennis and became a much
sought after teammate as a 5.0 level USTA player. There were other
minor episodes with Marek, and he struggled for a short while. Later
he not only regained his #2 spot, but he finished his high school career
winning 21 of his last 22 matches.

Knocking Down Presumptions

1996: Twenty-seven out of thirty-six players showed up to the first day of practice without having their physical exam paperwork ready to turn in to me. I had repeatedly had warned them in meetings leading up to the first day of practice, 'It's your ticket to get in...', along with email reminders. I had my clipboard, and a piece of paper to check off who had paperwork and who did not, I grew more and more frustrated at NOT checking the box on my paperwork that said 'yes', I decided to stop, throw the pen down hard enough for it to break. I then let the boys know that practice is cancelled, 'but your team captain may run an optional practice for you, which I recommend that you attend. It's not mandatory, but I highly recommend that you attend.' I went into my equipment storage area, threw a few items around, and peeked outside. The captain was working those players very hard. That year, we won our first title in 26 years and snapped another local school's 19-year streak of winning league. To some degree, the tone that was set on the very first day of practice contributed to that championship.

Why did the players come without their paperwork you might ask? The year before I had been hired very late, and did not assume coaching duties until the Friday before the season was to start, so necessarily I was lax about collecting physical forms, the school administration said they would look the other way that time, and these players assumed that it would continue. They found out different, and every day I would follow up with them urging them to get this work done ASAP.

Don't Take The Bait

1998: My #1 player and captain on a girl's team were slackers; they would miss practice with lame excuses and not give 100% effort. I talked to both of them about setting an example for the rest of the team, and they never acknowledged their own importance in helping set the tone. That team was demoralized when the players they looked up to, were not good role models. Nothing changed. Eventually, we had a very heated meeting where I outlined exactly what I expected. I wish I had done it earlier. The level of frustration that I expressed, having previously been fairly patient created some empathy toward me from the girls who really wanted to do well. They felt bad for me.

Still nothing changed and yet, I did not become angry again, but I did notice that if someone did something that was against team rules, these young athletes would look at me with eyes that asked, 'are you going to get angry again?.' They were baiting me and I was not taking the bait. After some discussions with some of the juniors and other underclassmen, we all decided that the following year, we would be more committed. While that team did not go on to become champions, we had a much more satisfying season, exceeding expectations for a team that had lost it's top three players, and four other varsity doubles players. The next year, that team maxed out their performance, by making a strong commitment to the team.

My Take Away: Action Item(s):

CHAPTER NINETY-SIX
The 2000's

**The expression of anger, if justifiable and aimed at finding
a solution rather than just venting, can actually benefit
and strengthen relationships.**

~ Jeremy Dean, Ph.D

2006: I wasn't 'angry', I was disappointed. In one of the most manipulative ploys that I have ever pulled, the culture of a our team dramatically changed for the better. What I didn't know when I started the season is that the team had not won a league match in six years. The losing streak was in the sixties. Twenty-four girls came out for tennis because they were excited about having a new coach. After the first two days of practice, only fifteen girls were left. By the end of the second week, we had only eleven players. They didn't want to run or get sweaty. Occasionally, a girl would skip practice with an academic reason and when she returned, I would explain that practice is mandatory and that there are 22.5 other hours in the day to get the school work done.

One day, more than half the team was missing. When practiced started I asked, 'Captain, where is my team?' 'Chem lab, coach'. I headed over to the Chem Lab. I got there just as the girls were leaving and were presumably NOT headed to practice. 'Ladies, what does this do to our relationship? We have a player/coach relationship that I care about, and when you don't even talk to me, then it really suffers. I am trying to run a practice for you, and I don't even know where you are.' As you might be aware, 'relationship' is the kryponite word for teenagers, it repels boys and attracts girls. I said all of this in the best sensitive voice I could muster. When they were all near tears, I stopped and from then on, no one missed practice the rest of the year. That group went on to break it's 71 match losing streak, and were later featured on local high school sports news. The two captains and I were in 'featured team of the week', for the entire greater San Francisco Bay Area, including the Oakland and San Jose metropolitan areas. I tell this story because I probably could have yelled at them, but I am capable of using a full range of emotion. Yelling at these girls would have chased most of them away.

Disrespect for Opponents

2008: I took on a new team that was underachieving. They won the league every year, simply because they had a strong pipeline of talent, but almost every year they would lose in the first round of the playoffs.

We had an early season match against the last place team. Our school had a transportation problem, and while all the schools were not more than a 20 minute apart, the players were responsible for getting themselves to matches, this particular school was less than 10 minutes drive. Because it was so close, of course the teenage mind suggests to them that they can leave at the last minute and still get there before the match starts. Some of my players came well after the time when a good warmup would be possible. Among the players that arrived on time few of them failed to put in a good warmup to prepare to perform well.

What ensued was ridiculous. I had warned them that I wanted to see the best effort in every match regardless of opponent, but since we were just getting to know each other, they did not know how serious I was. Two players came so late that it necessitated a lineup change in doubles. My team played poorly, they spent way too long in winning the match. It could have been mercifully over in 45 minutes or less and then everyone could go home and do homework. The match lasted well over two hours. I was extremely disappointed with their effort level. I can understand a little bit of lost focus against a team that you expect to beat easily, but not a lack of trying.

After the matches, I would normally release players as soon as the varsity match has ended, but I didn't do that on that day. At the end, I had the players sit with the setting sun behind me, so they had to squint to see me. Normally when addressing my teams, I face the sun so that they don't have to squint. I didn't yell, but I did express the extreme disappointment I felt. They needed to know without any equivocation that performing that poorly at any time is not the recipe for winning sectional playoff matches. We then proceeded to do 5 spider run drills with the other team watching. Doing 5 of those is fairly grueling, and when you do, you will remember that you did them for a while. The lesson was taken well, and we did not have a repeat of the same kind of poor effort playing down to the opposition.

Later that year, we entered sectional playoffs as a #9 seed. We easily beat a favored #8 seeded team on the road for the right to play the #1 seed at a prestigious club in Marin County, CA. Some of our players played out of their minds and we narrowly beat them 4-3 because three of their players were so good we had absolutely no chance against them. It was our full team effort that made that happen.

My Take Away: Action Item(s):

CHAPTER NINETY-SEVEN

Big Picture Blow Up Full Story

Used right, anger can be a handy tool,
but use with caution as people find anger
the most difficult of all the emotions to control.

~ Jeremy Dean, Ph.D

Calculated Passion

2016: My team captain informed me that a player on the team was going to skip our match because 'It's the first day of school and she doesn't want to miss her 6th period class on day one.' Our team was short on players and we needed everyone to play. I thought about it for a few seconds. 'Captain, what do you think? Is that ok? Also, you, number one player, is that ok?' Both nodded tacitly. Captain nodded because she didn't yet have the courage to say no to the notion of skipping a match. Number One player nodded because everyone has the right to self-determination. I thought for another few seconds. Internally, I asked myself, 'Do I want to destroy this 5 year old feeding racquet in my hand in front of the girls? Yes, I do, and I must be careful not to hurt anyone, and we will stop practice at this point to talk about this issue.' So I smashed it down hard twice, kicked it to the fence, picked it up, and whacked it against the fence post. Then I yelled at the girls. 'I am trying to build a team here! WE are trying to build a team here. It's NOT ok to miss...' I went on for almost a full minute. I had our team captain run the rest of the warmup so I could think, and presumably cool down in their eyes, even though I was completely in control of myself. One player was arriving late to practice and saw his all happen, and she still came, so that says something about her bravery, or maybe that she trusts me.

A team that needed 10 players to be official, had only 6 that were close to being confirmed on a roster, with three or four attending on rotating basis, it was a serious concern for one player not to come. I told Captain Karla, 'It's time for you to step up as a leader, and if you become a great leader on this team, I will write you the best recommendation letter you ever get, to go to the college of your dreams.' Within 48 hours Karla had recruited six more players to join the team, we played a match with 9 players, by the end of the next week we had 12 players on the team. That's worth raising a racquet. Without going into too much detail, there were some cultural reasons why exhibiting that much passion communicated caring beyond simple logical reasoning about what is best. A mix of fellow coaches and professionals have taken supportive, questioning and strongly opposing stances on my behavior. I stand behind it, because I was 100% motivated by what was best for them as an education about what it takes to succeed in life.

My Take Away: Action Item(s):

CHAPTER NINETY-EIGHT

It's NOT All in Our Control

Spanning the Globe to bring you the constant variety of sport, the thrill of victory and the agony of defeat, the human drama of athletic competition, this is...

~ ABC's Wide World of Sports

We are certainly never ever alone when it comes to adversity. Every coach has had to deal with players who go off the rails. The reason we find stories of players who overcome adversity to succeed so enchanting, is because we know many who don't overcome to the same degree. Human nature dictates that because of free will, there will always be a small percentage of the people we meet who simply will not cooperate with the program. They choose non-compliance, or they have a fixed mindset that says, 'This is just who I am.' No amount of discussion, explaining, listening, or any other type of intervention will ever work with these people, as they are not open to the kind of growth and change that will help them become a lifelong learner. While it's always worth trying until the bitter end, sometimes we are going to face the challenge of having players, or even coaches who are not working for us, and may even be working against us.

Attitudes and Teachability

One such player seemed to complain about everything. He would blame his doubles partner for losses and had very negative body language on court, especially when his partner missed a shot. Between the two, they had enough talent to win at their position. Many times, they could come very close to winning, but almost always they played down to the level of the opponent or lower, coming out on the losing end. After matches, when asked to analyze what had happened, they would pretend to be positive with each other, finding positives in each other's performance, but never the areas of improvement that would be needed to succeed the next time. When I would point out the negativity going on during the match with lots of bad body language and critical comments when mistake were made, these two shifted into pure denial. It was either 'It didn't happen', or 'We were just kidding around', neither of which were true. I could not pin them down, and for a period of time, both of them were very elusive.

In terms of techniques and strategies, both players had weaknesses in their technique and in decision making. The one player would go for very big shots at the wrong times, making many needless errors, as though he felt he could make the other team explode and would win automatically if he made one of his 'bomb' shots. The other player had many odd little 'trick shots', and felt like he could make up new ways to hit shots from time to time, also contributing needless errors. Opponents were not fooled often, but just enough to motivate this trickster to continue. When these concepts were brought to their attention , they would intellectually accept that they needed to practice better decision-making and technique, but when the matches were on, they simply returned to what had made them unsuccessful. It seemed that they were more concerned with exercising free will, than they were with learning how to win a match.

The Downtrodden and the Coddled

One of these players had parents who were constantly critical of him and I got the sense that he had become immune to any kind of kindness because he had been brow-beaten so much. He waited for extreme criticism before really trying to perform. I made a conscious decision not to play that game. The other young man had a mother that would advocate for him, and so he let his mother speak for him. Later, she came to me to discuss her son's experience on the team and that he felt I was not coaching him enough, that I had my favorites and he was not one of them. I told her to have her son come to talk to me on this. I gave him a few days and he did not. At the end of the season, we had other problems from this boy, that were indicative of not being a team player. At various times, I would structure practice specifically to work on the weaknesses of that particular doubles team since they were the weakest position in our lineup, and never once was there a return on the investment of time into that team. Additionally, the overall negative attitudes brought by these two had an effect on the teams and players playing on either side of them, it was an infectious disease of attitude. Their general attitudes also affected the general team feeling and numerous players voiced their frustration at the lack of work put in by this team to improve themselves. As a team, we had our worst finish in the standings during my six years at the helm. Looking back, I may have worked to excise my team of these two for the overall health of the team and program.

Hidden Agendas

At another school, I had team captains that had a hidden agenda. No matter how much we talked about it, they never really seemed to understand how we could work together to make the team a better experience for everyone. It was my first year at the school, and there had always been a splintered, clique-based division on this team. These two captains not only were determined to keep that in place, but were happy to enforce this negative social structure of the team. Those not in the clique would need to suffer. When I expressed that I am more of a process-oriented coach and that I am looking for the improvement of performance, they latched onto the phrase, 'I don't care as much if you win or lose, as long as you are improving'. These captains completely missed the point about going all out to compete to win. After they lost a winnable match, I expressed that it was within their reach, but they parroted back 'Coach, you don't care if we lose!'. Their closed mindset did not allow for any level of argument. This became our team's 'truth', because those two did not want to pursue excellence or success, they simply wanted to be rulers of the team with a little fiefdom. Nothing now could now defeat that in the minds of their closest friends, it was our team's truth, because the captains were hellbent on perpetuating it.

I pulled the two aside to clarify, they simply nodded and smiled, and nothing was really done to clear up the agenda. Soon thereafter one of these captains threatened a player from another school with physical harm, I then removed her as a captain. But not without significant questioning from my athletic director who seemed to have the attitude that I had not done all I could to bring them into the fold. The athletic director then also pulled her aside to get her story on the matter. Clearly, the athletic director at this exclusive private school was not 100% supportive of me, his new coach. After a few incidents where these two also treated our number one player with extreme disrespect, I knew that the graduation of these captains would create an opportunity to reform the culture of the team. It didn't happen. After the season, the school offered my job in a 'want ad', while I was still holding the position. I saw that, resigned immediately, writing a full page letter to the head of school about the incredibly poor culture of respect at their school. If you are a coach in this type of situation, it's going to be hard for you to stand for character development.

Not Everything is Inside Our Control

These things are completely outside of our control as coaches. People have the free will to run their school that way, as principal, athletic director or coach. Parents can raise their children to be elite snobs, or passive-aggressive twerps. We can only do the best we can in the situation, working for good outcomes. Sometimes, we need to find a different situation, and a better fit for a place to establish an athlete centered program.

My Take Away: Action Item(s):

CHAPTER NINETY-NINE

Communication With Players and Parents

If everyone is thinking the same, then somebody isn't thinking.

~ George S. Patton

You can save yourself a lot of time and energy, by creating content that can be used over and over again. Refining your message into it's most concise and palatable form can be an amazing resource. Putting some energy into making excellent content in the form of flyers, videos, podcasts, or even publishing eBooks or print books to get your program information across to parents and players. You can even assign homework to parents and players to study your materials.

Parent Information Night

High School coaches generally are required to have a parent information night. The amount of preparation you give to that evening and depth and breadth you give can help you build your program, and solve problems moving forward.

Questions can be asked and answered. Presumably you can solve so many of the pervasive problems that coaches have with parents and vice versa. We know in the real world that people can be tone deaf to the words of a coach proactively taking issues head on, as they selectively listen with filtered ears to hear what fits their inner agenda. Anything outside their agenda becomes white noise, so I am not promising you that you will immediately get through to those people. But you can get a lot of the parents who don't know you yet on your side. Even the naturally skeptical can be convinced and developing this mandate for your coaching philosophy can help you if and when a political battles ensues over control of the team. It's amazing to me though how many parents go to a night like that, but don't take anything from it, and when their child is doing something that is against the team rules, they seem to have no memory of the meeting. But, that's partly why you have the meeting so that you can point back to it.

Your Inner Work For Coaching Expressed In One Meeting

This is where all your inner work will be a strong attraction to your program. You can express the pillars of your coaching philosophy, giving the why and wherefore of each one. Parents and players can then ask follow ups for clarity. Even so, it's naive to think that silence equals consent, and that people are all in if they don't immediately push back on your program. The proof is in the pudding as they say, and you will know how much buy in you have on the program as soon as you get to work. One trick, that seems to work quite well especially with players, and maybe with parents, is to ask them what they think are strong pillars of coaching philosophy, and then when they name the same principles, then you can affirm them by showing them that it is a part of the program. You can also redirect or refine the thoughts of those who propose something that's a little off, or diametrically opposed. Those people then make themselves known to you and the rest of the parents. Treat them with kid gloves. But this will show where you need to win the battle for hearts and minds. Consider how you would like to be treated if you expressed a dissenting view of the program. Be sure to give the utmost of respect, as outward expression of dissenting views is to be welcomed as you have seen in previous chapters.

If a parent or player is acting in a way that counters what you are teaching, then it's time to have a very serious discussion about that. I have had to give a gag order to players who spout the opposite of what I am teaching. Players or parents who are divisive may be among the most destructive forces in your program, and redeeming them, bringing them to the light is one of the most powerful life lessons you can provide. In an existential framework, sometimes showing them the door is the only realistic action. They then may be forced to deal with the outcome of their decisions. Existentialism is based largely on the idea that life is either guided by fate, or choice. I prescribe to the choice part of the philosophy, and that we start in a certain place, but where we end up is the product of our choices. For this reason, teaching great decision making is critical to our future. **The decisions and actions we take in our present, become our past, and form our future. We only do those things in the present moment, so being fully present and mindful about these things is foundational.**

Ever Present Standards

Developing 'absolutely present' content, gives you and everyone associated with the program a touchstone, a compass, a True North to guide them. If their compass is pointing in a different direction, or they won't approach the touchstone, then perhaps their path does not include being a part of that program. A great example of this was Karla who decided that because she could not match the passion and dedication necessary to really play the sport and lead the team, that she would direct her energy into her academics and she now attends one the very best public universities in the U.S. She cited my passionate response to a lack of commitment as something that spurred her on to that achievement. Another example came this year when I had a meeting with my athletic director, a player and parent. When we outlined the various ways that the player was not adhering to program standards, it turned out that the parent had never read or signed the athletic handbook agreement. At that point we knew that this player did not really belong in the program, because there was a serious lack of cooperation with the overall athletic program at the school. Once you have your standards established, the work becomes moving toward them moment by moment.

CHAPTER ONE HUNDRED

Interventions

**The influence of each human being on others
in this life is a kind of immortality.**

~ John Quicey Adams, Sixth President of the United States

One popular theme that runs through heroic coach movies is the coach how intervenes in the lives of players.

I once thought I smelled alcohol on the breath of my players, I was about 99% certain of it. So, I told him the story about Don Nelson addressing Chris Mullin's alcoholism. I left it at that. The player shifted into a strong stance of denial. I did not pursue it. At that time he was at least 30 pounds overweight, but because he had a very strong frame, he was able to carry it. In subsequent years, he thanked me for that moment, and now in his adult life he is an extremely fit person. He thanked me for caring enough to say something, but also for not backing him into a corner. He knew I accepted him, faults and all.

Look for those moments.

My Take Away: Action Item(s):

CHAPTER ONE HUNDRED ONE
Boosting Morale After Adversity

If we don't fight for what we 'stand for' with our
passionate words and honest actions,
do we really 'stand' for anything?

~ Tiffany Madison

2015: While working at an inner city school on cracked courts with a team that previously had a very permissive coach, we faced a significant adversity. Three of our varsity players were deemed ineligible, and immediately the team went into the tank, players began to quit on the inside, like a light switch had been turned off, most players were half heartedly going through drills. I needed the effort level to go way up, to get to the huddle, move to a drill, and execute a drill with 100% effort. The kids were bummed out, depressed, hopeless. That lasted about 10 or 15 minutes before I energized them with some anger, 'Noooo! We are not going to quit, every moment on this earth matters…' I think I might have cussed again, but I can't remember everything I said, but it was measured to the moment and it did not last long. This all happened with less than two weeks left in the season. We had some talent, but the players had been very undisciplined for a long time. So, they forced themselves to get through that practice, but the magic happened the next day.

The next day, I showed them the TED Talk by Carol Dweck on 'The Power of Yet'. The main subject of that talk is about having a growth mentality, and always believing you can improve. Suddenly the kids were energized, players began to improve a lot! We were in last place and lost a heartbreaking match playing poorly against our rival, the second to last place team. But now, we had something. Players competed hard, learned to make one more shot, gave their best on everything. In our final match of the season, against the first place team of the second division (our league was split into two divisions according to ability), we were about 5 points from pulling the upset, mostly because the other coach made some lineup changes that were a tad overconfident and she did not know how much we had improved in two weeks. We came very close to a win over the first place team, even after having lost convincingly to the second to last place team. While we did not come out on top, it was still one of the most dramatic improvements I have seen in any team I have ever coached. In the league tournament, our players went 4-0 in first round matches, which had to be the best the team had ever done, with my number two player going to the semi-finals and giving the #1 seed all he could handle. And we also gained two wins over that first-place team's players. We left that season on a major high! Ultimately, more than anything we want to see our players improve.

CHAPTER ONE HUNDRED TWO
When Athletes Succeed or Fail

Winning isn't everything--but wanting to win is.

~ Vince Lombardi

Success or failure are found in how you define them. We help guide athletes to create their own strategy for assigning success or failure. When they succeed, they may want to quietly celebrate alone, go crazy in a crowd, have the coach close at hand, or way over there. In general coaches tend not to get caught up in the frenzy of a major championship in the same way that players do. When players fail, mainly we need to know how we will support them during that time. There is a wide range of responses that athletes desire from coach after a loss from 100 yards of space to being in very close proximity immediately and sharing comforting words.

New Found Success

One of the very first issues a newly successful athlete faces is overconfidence. In 30 years I have yet to see a time where I could warn my players, or somehow guard them against being over confident. Not every player will struggle with that, most instead struggle with a lack of confidence. My experience has been that players will go into a competition over-confident after having succeeded at a much higher level for the first time. In the very next competition they will not give the require effort, feel a pressure to win that is not being placed on them by anyone on the outside, have a lack of concentration, make poor decisions, or all of the above. Perhaps we can identify this in the middle of competition and renew their respect for their opposition, get them to focus on the process, but if the train of their mind is completely off the rails, then our intervention may have to wait until after the crash. In my first season with any team, there is a common theme that would be an incident where a few players or the team as a whole would experience this overconfidence. The good news is that you can use it as a watershed 'never again' moment. What I underline with them is that being overconfident is disrespectful and every opponent deserves their respect.

Celebrate, Have Closure, Move On

Finding the right balance of supporting and appreciating a success, then moving forward into a challenge to go to the next incremental improvement is tricky business. Success or failure, each is stressful, and when players begin to succeed at a higher level, they may need a time to cope with their new level. On the other side players who have gone past their comfort zone may shrink back to a level of performance with which they are more familiar. Players naturally reach plateaus. Placing some closure on a success or failure can bring about a sense of 'that's over, now we move on to the next thing'. Aiding them to become more comfortable at this new level is huge! Acknowledging a plateau as a natural coping mechanism for our minds, allows us to get used to a new level. Experts in torture know that if you create an atmosphere of constant and unpredictable change, the human mind breaks down pretty quickly. It would be a very bad mistake to load more pressure and expectations on the player at this time.

The Future Is Unwritten

Players who struggle with a fear of responsibility can be triggered by statements like, 'Now you should do that all the time', or 'I told you that you could perform like that if you only fulfilled your potential'. I can relate to this as I was often chided about my unused talent, and that I could do anything I put my mind to, but that I was a shiftless lazy daydreamer who didn't often use their tools. The key that works with me, and with some of these players who fear responsibility is simply to ask if they enjoyed the experience of going all out, and if they want more of that. The answer comes in what they do. I can also follow up with, 'I guess you didn't enjoy that last experience enough to keep it going?' My case is common and I teach the parents of players I coach to empower their children, instead of trying to command them, or be the reason for their success. It's far more subtle to find mental strategies that allow players to grow into their own success. Young athletes will find their way, they have their own choices to make. They will run into fear, and need to learn to understand and mitigate their chief fears if they are to amount to anything. If we think we can make them fearless, it doesn't take long for us to reflect on our own fears to realize that it's not realistic for us to try to accomplish that.

My Take Away: Action Item(s):

CHAPTER ONE HUNDRED THREE

When It's Time to Let Go

**Two standing back to back can fight off a crowd,
and a three cord strand is not easily broken.**

~ Hebrew Proverb

Freeing up our players with the realization that they don't belong to us, is one of the most healthy and attractive things you can do as a coach. There was a time that I was jealous and possessive of my players. I wished for them to think that I was the most important coach in their game, and that I was complete enough to do it all in their athletic career. That turns out to have been a very maladaptive mindset. Of course, we want to feel important, but developing a trusting enough and collaborative space with players and their parents means we can be kept apprised of their decisions. Nowadays, I do my best to find out what other coaches are doing, and when appropriate to communicate with them. Both as a high school coach reaching out to a private coach to see how much we can work together and in the other direction. Part of what motivates the writing of this book is that I have mostly been disappointed by the level of collaboration to be found with other coaches. When it does happen, its a watershed for the player and parents as well. Everyone seems to grow together, and the player's outcomes seem to be enhanced. Mostly I see walls and borders between coaches, as if 'this is my space, stay out!' is the message.

I urge you to be the one who opens the door on your side, and knocks on the door of the other side. Especially in the U.S., we have this Lone Ranger attitude, one of staunch individualism where people try to project to their world that they don't need any help. I need help, lots of help, and it took way too long for me to accept it, but when I did, my own fortunes began to change.

CHAPTER ONE HUNDRED FOUR
Adversity And Growth

Adversity to a fixed mindset athlete typically means something very different than to a growth mindset athlete. The reality is that adversities push these growth mindset individuals through their imagined "walls" and upwards towards a higher level of competitive skills. This is emotional aptitude in sports.

~ Styrling Strother, Transforming The Practice Court

How many times do players most often lose in sports? At least three times.

"Players lose on the court or field, they lose with their coach, and they lose with their parent on the way home, or at the dining room table." ~ Vic Braden (paraphrase)

How do coaches help players to discover the value in adversity and turn that loss into a win?

Empathy
Goals
Lessons
Strategy
Mindset
Determination
Big Moments

The Situation

In our team's state championship match, the overall score was locked at 4-4, with one match left to decide the championship. One of our freshmen, Camryn was down 6-1, 5-0 and she then rallied back in the second set to win 7-5. The third set was very close finishing in a tiebreaker. Camryn lost the match in the third set tiebreaker. It was heartbreaking, but I felt so much pride in my heart for the way she battled. She gave her full effort, and yet she came up on the short side in the final score.

Engagement and Response

I walked out on the court and through the group of players and parents of the opposing team to reach her. As a put my arm around her shoulder I told Camryn that she had shown great strength in fighting back to the very end. I was proud of her! She smiled and said, "Thanks Coach."

After a Time of Reflection

Following the trophy presentation, the rest of our team began to make their way off the court, Camryn came up to me and said, "Coach, I'll never lose a match like that again - I know what I need to do and how I need to play from now on." I asked her what did she mean? She said, "Coach, my personality is to go for it and I'm going to continue my training to do just that, go for it. I know that's who I am!"

Concrete Example of a Shift

After that season, Camryn moved to South Carolina, but has come back to visit me about once a month to continue her training with me as her main coach. Largely due to that loss in the State Championship, Camryn and I were able to discover together what she really meant that day when she realized she wants to "go for it" and how that manifests on the court in her practice and match play.

Knowing Who She Wants to Be

She determined that she is an all-court player, looking for opportunities to attack and finish the point at the net. Powerful first serves followed by a '+1 Forehand' to the opponent's weaker side. She has made great strides, rising in the rankings now to making it into the top twenty in South Carolina. Top college programs from around the country are taking notice of her as a junior in high school. I'm so proud of her discovery and she has found how to win even when the scoreboard doesn't look hopeful.

My Take Away: Action Item(s):

CHAPTER ONE HUNDRED FIVE
'Cancer' Recovery

Imagine intentionally leaving one of your All-American athletes home when trying to win the national championship. This is exactly what Arizona Softball coach Mike Candrea did when he discovered that his talented yet turbulent All-American pitcher broke a major team rule the night before heading to the Women's College World Series. Sure Coach Candrea's move may have gambled away his team's chances by going to the Series with only one pitcher and having to play 4 or 5 games against the nation's toughest teams. Yet, he knew that if he overlooked her transgression and brought her along, the distraction and descension it would have caused would have divided and destroyed his team from the inside. So, using the "Addition by Subtraction" principle, he decided to leave his All-American pitcher home. The Wildcats came together as a team, went to battle with one pitcher over 4 games including a 14-inning game against arch-rival UCLA, and won the national championship.

~ Jeff Jansen, Jansen Sports Leadership Center

The team I was coaching had a legitimate shot at a league title, but we were slight underdogs to another team, as they had a bit more experience and depth on their team, especially in doubles. Even so, we trained hard, but we had two players who held themselves separate from the rest of the team.

The Cancers

Our team chemistry was lacking. After losing the first matchup with the first-place team at home, suddenly our #2 player did not show up to practice the next day. He came to one more practice, then quit the team. After it was discovered that he and the other player had plotted out what would happen if he left, assuming that the other player would take the #2 players place in the league tournament, he would also quit the team when I did not name him to that tournament team.

At that point, we were 9-1 and before the two of them left, we still had a chance of tying for a league championship.

Cancer Surgery

After those two left the team, I had to scramble to make changes to the lineup. We faced some teams directly below us in the standings and three 4-3 losses later, we finished 12-4 and tied for third place. The most amazing thing about this is that almost immediately after those two where gone, the whole team became happier. Practices were more fun and I even had more fun.

Bitter Disappointment

However, in one particular match, one of my young doubles teams that had often given away matches where they held leads, lost again. This time, it was to a team well behind us in the standings and they really took it hard. I can remember Noli head down on the bleachers sobbing. I had never seen this level of caring about the outcome, he and his partner Manuel were two of the happiest players I have ever met, win or lose. They could lose a tough match and be seen laughing and smiling minutes later. Not this time.

Engagement

So I approached Noli, and said, "It looks like you are taking this pretty hard. Are you ok?" He shook his head 'no'. So we talked for a bit. I sat next to him and put my hand on his back for a moment to reassure him, but did not keep it there long. I let him know that for the first time, he seemed to really care about the outcome and that's a good thing. Also, the other guys quitting was not really such a bad thing because they were negative anyway. He agreed.

The Response

Flash forward to the next year, my new team captain showed incredible leadership to get the former #2 player to come back with a very strong contract in place for his behavior. The young team that came in battle-tested was much deeper than the previous year's team, but we had graduated our #1 and some heavy hitters. Our team had one player with a 100 mph serve, and only one player over 5'8". I picked us to finish fourth. But a strange thing happened, in all the close matches our players showed a strength and determination that was born from the disappointment of close losses the previous year. Strangely enough, we played in six matches that were decided 4-3, and we won four of them. The first-place team from the year before found a way to lose to the third-place team and the fifth-place team. I believe they may have been overconfident. But this whole story revolves around one banner match.

The Magical Outcome

In one of the matches that would finish 4-3, Noli and Manuel were up to their normal trick of winning the first set, losing a tight second set, and getting their doors blown off in the third set. They were down 5-0 in the third. This would now be the pivotal match. With a note of resignation, I turned to my assistant and said, 'This will be over soon.' A couple minutes later there was a changeover and it was 5-2. 'This will be over soon, give it 5 more minutes' Then there was another changeover and now it was 5-4. I called the players over for a casual chat. 'Hey guys, what's going on here?' with a strange glee Noli said, 'Oh, coach, we are winning!' 'OK, what are you doing?' 'We are lobbing them a lot. 'OK, carry on!'. In truly a miracle match, they came all the way back to win 7-5 with the other team looking almost completely hopeless in the final three games. I knew I better not get too involved in the match from a place of coaching, because Noli and Manuel had found a way to win. In what to me is also a bigger miracle, that one win protected a tie for a league championship. One of only two in a 44-year span at that school.

My Take Away: Action Item(s):

PART NINE

FINAL THOUGHTS

Now this is not the end.
It is not even the beginning of the end.
But it is, perhaps, the end of the beginning.

~ Sir Winston Churchill

CHAPTER ONE HUNDRED SIX
Motivation Intrinsic Extrinsic

I want you to motivate my child.

~ Misguided Parent

One of the most important observations we can make in our athletes is in the understanding of what motivates them. You can throw different things out there to see what they respond to. From the days of the carrot and the stick, we have now come to the intrinsic and the extrinsic motivators. People are drawn to success, or repelled by it. There are those who also move toward death or avoid it. People may hate to lose, more than they love to win. These compulsions, attractions and repulsions give an opportunity for an existential examination of the choices people make. Existentialism is really about how much of what our lives are controlled by choice, and how much by fate. Certainly our path, our fate meets us at different times, but how do we respond? Soren Kierkegaard the father of modern existentialism, and an early psychologist/philosopher posited that from where we start, it's our choices in life that make us more or less intimate with God, ourselves and others. It's not my place in this work to force a discussion of religion, but we all have our spiritual side, and whether you choose to be a humanist, Christian, Hindu, Muslim, Buddhist or any other belief system is completely up to you. As if you needed my permission! I will say, don't ignore spirit, and I strongly encourage people to seek spiritually, I do believe the answers will find you. Back to Kierkagaard, he also shared that peoples choices make them more intimate or more distant from themselves and others. I can relate in various points of my life to times when my choices made me more distant from my true self, in kind I was also making choices that made me more distant from those I claimed to love, and away from my God.

All of my very best athletes have had a rock solid ethic, a belief system in something that they understood. They have all had that something that is their bedrock foundation that gives them reasons to proceed. Doing your own work there, also helps you to encourage this in your players.

The Choice Is Yours, The Choice Is Theirs

I'm unique in my coaching, in that I don't often try to motivate my players. Instead, I help them delve into their own motivation. I want to know that they want, then I get to work in helping them get what they want. Intrinsically, our inner satisfaction from being closer to where we want to be has the potential to align us with much more peace and contentment in our lives. Sadly, many of us live in a way that moves us away or out of reach of what we want. If you don't like your results, change what you are doing.

Extrinsically the desire to be recognized, or gain tangible benefits is not a bad thing, although many times the self-critic within us may put that down as materialistic, vain, or some other negative there is value in winning things. Of Course, when we focus too much on having stuff, trophies, wins, then we can easily lose sight of the intrinsic motivators. We can lose the joy of play very quickly. If we start our lives more extrinsically motivated, and move toward becoming more intrinsically so, I believe that is a good thing.

I don't give out many little prizes to young kids. When I have in the past with offers like 'Do this, get that', invariably it triggers the response 'What do I get?' for more requests than is appropriate. So I save these little gifts for big moments thus creating a much higher intrinsic value.

The key chain charm. I have a few simple trinkets that remind me of great times where being faithful to the task, and believing really showed the result of faith. Amazing minor miracles happened. People build altars as a way of honor and remembrance, so it's an outward symbol to remember an inward experience.

At the end of the day, when players and parents can get to a place where in the inner satisfaction of performing well, or taking lessons from whatever outcomes come along in their sporting world, they begin to realize the satisfaction of doing well, like in the very first quote in this book by John Wooden. Understanding that we all have our path to walk, and whatever is in front of us is that which we need to cope with, there is no way really to avoid it. We can learn to relish the challenges along with the triumphs, the thrill of victory and the agony of defeat.

My Take Away: Action Item(s):

CHAPTER ONE HUNDRED SEVEN
The Challenging Conclusion

A quitter never wins-and-a winner never quits.

~ Napoleon Hill

Conclusion

My goal for this book is to give you every possible thing to think about, that I could write. If you take this and come away with three to five action items, that you can work for a period of time, then you have something manageable in your grasp. I would feel overwhelmed if my feet were held to the fire to work on everything in this book at once, so I hope you don't feel that way.

Major In The Majors

Ultimately, I hope that I have helped you to shape your brand, your coaching philosophy, honing your own personal way of coaching. From there, you can come from a greater place of authenticity. Then to address your athletes to become their own authentic best selves can be an amazing thing. Knowing the border of where you end and the player begins is an important part of developing a great player/coach relationship. As was discussed in the chapter on ego boundaries, finding best fit and helping mold players into a place of being a great part of the team, or eschewing them altogether can be a make or break decision for a season, a career, a life.

The Challenge

I charge you with the solemn responsibility of being a positive influence on every athlete, coach, parent and organization with which you come into contact. Think globally, act locally! You might just influence someone to come to the light and avoid many dark outcomes as we discussed with the Larry Nassar's and Aaron Hernandez's of this world. Be true to who you are standing strong on ethics and principles.

Sharpen Your Principles

You will be empowered to use key principles in coaching and applying who you are and why you do things to the situation in front of you. Along the way, the rough edges get smoothed over. We as coaches learn to plan our way and move in a definite direction, sometimes in the simplest old-fashioned ways. This is not a glamorous book filled with tricks and tips. No, we don't need an app for everything! Once we know the definite plan, then it can empower our will to say 'no' to the wrong things that distract from the plan. Having a mission and objectives takes this pursuit up a full notch in terms of focus.

Be On Target With All You Do

From there, we have a basis by which to really listen, once we have established unbreakable parameters, we can operate within those. We also then make the big decisions first about our major objectives, the smaller ones will have to fit in somewhere. One of our largest objectives over the years can be to remold the team culture, and this does not often happen completely inside of one season. Of course, when doing all of the above, there will be some pushback from players and coaches. When the pushback is well-informed, then it's worth a listen; when it's not, then it can be a teachable moment. Ultimately, within the parameters of the finite structure of what our coaching philosophy allows, it's best practice to be as athlete-centered as possible. Of course, that does not mean being subject to player's whims. Looking at learning, adversity, challenges, and every other skill to be gained through the athletes eyes is the entire purpose behind this work. Join us in the pursuit of excellence in this way. We welcome you, and ask that you welcome others.

Go, Coach Them Up!

Best wishes,

Bill

CHAPTER ONE HUNDRED EIGHT
Presidential Speech

It is not the critic who counts; not the man who points out how the strong man stumbles, or where the doer of deeds could have done them better. The credit belongs to the man who is actually in the arena, whose face is marred by dust and sweat and blood; who strives valiantly; who errs, and comes short again and again, because there is no effort without error and shortcoming; but who does actually strive to do the deeds; who knows the great enthusiasms, the great devotions; who spends himself in a worthy cause; who at the best knows in the end the triumph of high achievement, and who at the worst, if he fails, at least fails while daring greatly, so that his place shall never be with those cold and timid souls who know neither victory nor defeat. Shame on the man of cultivated taste who permits refinement to develop into a fastidiousness that unfits him for doing the rough work of a workaday world. Among the free peoples who govern themselves there is but a small field of usefulness open for the men of cloistered life who shrink from contact with their fellows. Still less room is there for those who deride or slight what is done by those who actually bear the brunt of the day; nor yet for those others who always profess that they would like to take action, if only the conditions of life were not what they actually are. The man who does nothing cuts the same sordid figure in the pages of history, whether he be cynic, or fop, or voluptuary. There is little use for the being whose tepid soul knows nothing of the great and generous emotion, of the high pride, the stern belief, the lofty enthusiasm, of the men who quell the storm and ride the thunder. Well for these men if they succeed; well also, though not so well, if they fail, given only that they have nobly ventured, and have put forth all their heart and strength. It is war-worn Hotspur, spent with hard fighting, he of the many errors and the valiant end, over whose memory we love to linger, not over the memory of the young lord who "but for the vile guns would have been a soldier.

~ Theodore Roosevelt